RETIREMENT ON THE LINE

Shop floor in the late afternoon. Photo by Caitrin Lynch.

RETIREMENT ON THE LINE

Age, Work, and Value in an
American Factory

Caitrin Lynch

ILR PRESS

AN IMPRINT OF

CORNELL UNIVERSITY PRESS   ITHACA AND LONDON

First published 2012 by Cornell University Press
First printing, Cornell Paperbacks, 2012

Printed in the United States of America

Library of Congress Cataloging-in-Publication Data

Lynch, Caitrin.
    Retirement on the line : age, work, and value in an American factory / Caitrin Lynch.
        p. cm.
    Includes bibliographical references and index.
    ISBN 978-0-8014-5026-6 (cloth : alk. paper) —
    ISBN 978-0-8014-7778-2 (pbk. : alk. paper)
    1. Older people—Employment—Massachusetts—Needham.   2. Retirement—Massachusetts—Needham.   3. Vita Needle Company—Employees.
4. Manufacturing industries—Massachusetts—Needham—Employees.   I. Title.
    HD6281.M3L96   2012
    331.3'9887283209744—dc23   2011042186

Cornell University Press strives to use environmentally responsible suppliers and materials to the fullest extent possible in the publishing of its books. Such materials include vegetable-based, low-VOC inks and acid-free papers that are recycled, totally chlorine-free, or partly composed of nonwood fibers. For further information, visit our website at www.cornellpress.cornell.edu.

Cloth printing   10 9 8 7 6 5 4 3 2 1
Paperback printing   10 9 8 7 6 5 4 3 2 1

To my family (Nick, Cormac, Nicola) and to the Vita family

Contents

Cast of Characters

Listed here (in alphabetical order by first name) are names, ages (in 2008, unless otherwise noted), and personal details for most people who appear more than once in the book. Except for those indicated with an asterisk, the names are pseudonyms, and identifying details are slightly altered.

Abigail White, 83: Bookkeeper at Vita; mother and grandmother.

Allen Lewis, 84: Worked for seventy years as a machinist; longtime Vita employee; left Vita at 84 for health reasons; widower.

Arthur Johnson, 72: Retired at 65 from job as a corporate accountant and started at Vita two months later; lives with wife and adult son.

Ben Freeman, 29: Compares older coworkers to his grandparents; jokes around with David Rivers about his "stupid old guy" music.

Brad Hill, 36: Supervisor; immediate boss is Michael La Rosa.

Carl Wilson, 79: Retired tool designer; lives with wife; grandfather of six; first employee to arrive at Vita each morning.

Charles Young, 72: Retired high-tech sales manager with a master's degree in business; never married; father was a factory worker; refers to Vita as a "men's club" and a "refuge for old people."

Dan Jones, 44: Supervisor; immediate boss is Michael La Rosa.

David Rivers, 90: World War II navy veteran, served in the Pacific; joined Vita Needle in his sixties.

Donald Stephens, 75: Uses cane outside work; lost sense of purpose when wife passed away; lives in public housing; looking for a second job to cover basic expenses.

Ed Mitchell, 81: Retired middle-school English teacher; at Vita since age 74 to earn money needed because of "poor real-estate investments."

Esther Martin, 85: Considers work "therapy" after husband passed away; works in packaging.

Flo Cronin, 82: Held part-time jobs as a secretary after children graduated from high school; considered the "den mother" for her efforts to do nice things for workers in need; known as a good "taper."

*Fred Hartman, 56: Vita Needle fourth-generation president.

*Frederick Hartman II, 26: Son of Fred Hartman (fifth generation); director of marketing and engineering.

Gertrude Baker, 90: Former employee often referred to in stories for sleeping on the job.

Grace King, 94: At Vita since age 77 in order to "be busy"; urges coworkers to get to work when break ends.

Grant Harvey, 68: Former automobile assembly-line worker; reflects on meaning of work; questions social ideal of idle retirement.

Jeffrey Barfield, 74: Retired engineer; always tries to be more efficient and improve system when working.

Jerry Reilly, 73: Retired unionized factory worker; considers Vita owner to be doing a "good service" by employing older adults.

Jim Downey, 74: Retired architect; at Vita for nine years after thirty-year architecture career; is a father and grandfather; married forty-five years; considers Vita work like "vacation."

Larry Clifford, 77: Fended off 60 Minutes with story about being an ex-convict; jokes around with coworkers.

*Mason Hartman: Passed away at 81 in 2007; third-generation owner of Vita before his son, Fred, took over.

*Michael (Mike) La Rosa, 50: Production manager.

Pete Russell, 80: Likes to be productive and "make money for Fred"; revels in the freedom of work at this stage in life and clocks out if he does not feel like working.

Ron Crowley, 64: Retired schoolteacher; learned of Vita by watching the 60 Minutes story; believes retirement is a time for redefinition; unsure of future plans.

*Rosa Finnegan, 99 (in 2011): Retired waitress; widowed and lives in Needham; joined Vita at 85; the eldest worker and focus of much of the media coverage.

Ruth Kinney, 82: Longtime employee (came to Vita in her sixties); does multiple jobs (such as sandblasting, flaring, packing); has dinner out with coworkers on Friday nights.

Sam Stewart, 74: Jokes around about work dynamics, such as about what it takes to make money for Fred; dedicated to woodworking hobby; took college course from anthropologist Margaret Mead and is reflective on position of older adults in society.

Sophia Lenti, 78: Had recent knee surgery; decorates and domesticates work space.

Steve Zanes, 19: Contrasts comfortable coworker interaction with awkward interaction with grandparents in nursing home, where he was "in their territory."

RETIREMENT ON THE LINE

Weighing batches of needles. Photo by Caitrin Lynch.

INTRODUCTION

Making Needles, Making Lives

Legs kicking and fully awake at 3:15 in the morning, 79-year-old Carl Wilson figures he might as well go to work. Five mornings a week, Carl, who suffers from sleep apnea and restless leg syndrome, leaves the house well before dawn without waking his wife and sets off for Vita Needle, where he arrives in less than ten minutes and parks his car on the street out front. The parking meters do not need to be fed at 3:30 a.m., and he will make sure to move his car to a nearby parking lot before 8:00 a.m. A retired tool designer whose father was a local policeman, Carl has lived in this town for most of his life. Carl used to spend his early mornings at the Dunkin' Donuts socializing with his friends, who were mostly municipal workers—postal workers, police, firefighters, teachers. Carl says the police all recognize his car and know what he is doing, so his lone vehicle in front of the factory will not raise suspicion on the otherwise empty street.[1]

Carl finds his Vita Needle key on the same keychain where he keeps those for his car and house, lets himself in, punches in on the time clock, and gets to work shipping needles. Shortly after he arrives, 83-year-old bookkeeper Abigail White arrives to sort through paperwork from the previous afternoon (she would have left work by 1:00 p.m. at the latest). Abigail works in the office and Carl on the main shop floor. Carl tells me he likes the two hours of work he does before anyone else arrives to join him in the shop; he can get a lot done when there are no distractions. But he also likes it when he has company—people with whom he can "shoot the breeze." Coworkers start to arrive around 5:00 a.m., and by 6:00 there are a handful of people—long before any supervisors or managers arrive.

The right-hand row of time cards is for those who have punched in, and soon there will be ten or so cards in the "in" column.

By 7:00 a.m. the shop is busy. Within a few hours it will be full of all the sounds of a typical day at a needle factory. The loud hum of air compressors will be punctuated by the banging sound of needles being staked or stamped, and interrupted at times by the ear-splitting noises of saws or sandblasters or the more deeply resonant bursts from grinders, drills, and wire brushes. Whenever someone shows up, he or she will clock in, sometimes leave a snack at the counter (sweets go over best), and then stop to visit those already in the shop for a short conversation and update since they last saw each other. How was your grandson's violin concert? That pea soup was delicious! Did you see Ortiz sock it out of the park? How is the arthritis? I will be leaving early today to have that mole looked at.

Throughout the day the noise of the compressors, saws, sandblasters, and staking continues, stopping only at 10:00 for the coffee break and at noon for lunch. The most persistent sound, which becomes an ambient noise that you start to not even notice, is the pounding sound of the cannulas (needle shafts) as they are "staked"—that is, attached to their hubs (bases). Pch-chew. Pch-chew. A solid bang, followed by the release of air from the staker. Over and over again. This repetitive and consistent rhythm is occasionally interrupted by the loud, grinding sound of a chop saw biting through tubes of stainless steel, producing a grating noise reminiscent of fingernails scraping on a chalkboard (but longer and much louder). The machine called the "popcorn popper" makes the continuous bursting noises that earned it the nickname. But underneath the constant noise, it is, in a funny sort of way, tranquil here.

Conversations occur, not all work-related, and there are occasional sounds of laughter. Often someone is humming, and if Ed Mitchell is around, he is most likely singing. Ed assumes he is doing it quietly to himself, but the noise of the machine he often works makes him project his voice to hear himself, and he does not know that others in the shop catch every word. He is on a machine in the corner that flares open the tips of short tubes, a machine famous among the workers for making the operator feel as if the machine is working the operator rather than vice versa (picture Charlie Chaplin in the film *Modern Times*).

I remember in particular one sultry summer Friday afternoon when there were only five of us left on the shop floor. Ed was off in the corner, on his machine, singing lines from "Old Man River": "You an' me, we sweat an' strain; Body all achin' and wracked with pain; Tote that barge! Lift that bale!" Seventy-six-year-old Maurice Kempton and I were staking needles (affixing shafts to bases) and we had been discussing whether this was a song from *Porgy and Bess* or *Show Boat* (it's the latter). After some time Ed got up for a break, came over to me, and sang, "Tote that barge! Lift that bale!" When I asked him why he was singing that song, he said, "Because this is like you are stacking the hay and loading the bales." This coming from an 81-year-old man who joined Vita Needle when he was 74, and the last time he had worked a factory job—the last time he had even used a time card—was back in high school, from which he had graduated in 1944.[2]

After a long career as a middle school English teacher, Ed is spending his conventional retirement years far from retired. When he is not at Vita Needle, you might find him at the cash register at the Walgreens pharmacy in the next town over. He also enjoys his time with his wife of forty-eight years (when she is not working, as a grocery store cashier) and with his children and grandchildren when they come to town. Ed is working in his eighties because of (as he candidly puts it) "poor real estate investments in the 1980s." He states plainly that he is here for the money, but he also notes that he likes the interactions with his coworkers. But there are some aspects he does not care for, such as those that make him feel that he is merely "stacking the hay and loading the bales." His master's degree in education certainly did not lead him to anticipate doing unskilled manual labor well after he ended his teaching career.

The motivations for and experiences of working in retirement are varied and contradictory. This book explores what work means for people in the United States who are of conventional retirement age. To examine issues of aging, work, meaning, and purpose, I focus on Vita Needle Company, a family-owned factory that produces stainless steel needles in the Boston suburb of Needham. As of this writing, in May 2011, the median age of the roughly forty production floor employees is 74 and the eldest is Rosa Finnegan, a 99-year-old former waitress who joined the factory when she was 85.[3]

As a cultural anthropologist, I immersed myself in life at Vita Needle for nearly five years (more intensively in some years than in others) in order to learn what, on top of a paycheck, Vita Needle provides its employees. The story I tell is based on interviews but also on my own work on the shop floor. The distinctive research method of cultural anthropology is "participant observation": we immerse ourselves in the societies we study in order to understand experiences and meaning-making from an insider's perspective. Sometimes we study our own societies, sometimes societies quite foreign to us, but even when we study our own, we remain outsiders and can never fully access an insider viewpoint. Though as anthropologists we can get quite close, and we use research methods and narrative techniques to bring out the insider perspectives, our stories always reflect our own priorities and perspectives that come from our personal biographies and professional positions.[4] I was drawn into Vita Needle and became part of the story itself, and so these pages include my personal reflections on the complexity of a research design that required my own immersion in order to explore lives and dreams and situate them within the context of a broader analysis. It is my hope that readers will discover as much about their own views on aging and retirement as they do about people at Vita Needle.[5]

Vita Needle Company

Vita Needle is a family-owned company; the fourth generation is currently represented in the position of president, and members of the fifth generation occupy positions in management, marketing and sales, and engineering. It has been operating since 1932, first in the third-floor home attic, then a few years later in a building in the center of Needham, and then by roughly 1939 in its current spot a few doors down from there. The shop floor is a former dance hall that still contains a doorway with a peephole for entry inspection during Prohibition, and above the doorway into the production area is a posted "Public Hall License" (expiration date July 1, 1929) authorizing its use as a public hall and signed by the Massachusetts Commissioner of Public Safety. Vita Needle's forty or so production floor employees are from varied work backgrounds—retired engineers, schoolteachers, realtors, waitresses, and lifelong factory workers. At Vita Needle, these diverse workers design, construct, inspect, pack, and ship hollow needles in an assortment of diameters, lengths, and sharpness levels; the needles serve in a multitude of applications that include dispensing glue, inflating basketballs, and performing brain surgery.

A sign to the side of Vita's front entryway advertises job openings for "light machine operators/assembly." Boasting that there is "no suggested retirement age" and that it has "never had a layoff," it notes the prevalence of "senior citizens" and the flexible work schedule. With only a few exceptions, all Vita employees are white and nonimmigrants, and most are from Needham itself. There are many more men than women, though in its earlier history the gender ratio was inverted—during the Second World War rows of young women sat side by side making hypodermic needles for the Red Cross. Today the very same worktables used for the war effort are occupied by mostly older workers, though there are a few high school and college students (especially during the summer), and there are several people in their thirties, forties, and fifties. (Vita Needle actually has employees in every age decade from their teens through their nineties—talk about intergenerational contact!) This book is primarily a study of the retirement experiences of the men at Vita Needle and how these experiences match up with their own and society's ideals for men of retirement age.

These workers exemplify a range of personalities and backgrounds and a diversity of reasons for working. Even those who come out of financial need also seek social engagement and purpose. The production workers are all part-time (up to thirty-four hours), and none receive medical or retirement benefits—the employer banks on the employees' eligibility for receipt of Medicare and Social Security.[6] The pay rate generally starts at roughly nine dollars per hour, which is above the state's minimum wage of eight dollars per hour (in 2011). Workers typically set their own hours, and some are like Carl, who arrives for a seven-hour shift at 3:30 a.m.; others might start at a more conventional 9:00 a.m. and clock out by 2:00, and yet others show up for a four-hour shift at 3:00 p.m. Upstairs from the production floor is the sales office, where the eight or so employees are full-time salaried workers in their twenties through fifties, more characteristic of the age of office workers elsewhere in the United States.

For some of Vita Needle's older workers, the paycheck is mad money (a term some workers actually use). It may give them the chance to buy nice gifts for grandchildren or splurge on Brooks Brothers clothing. One man turns over his entire paycheck to his grandchildren. We will meet people like 74-year-old Jim Downey, who sweats through his factory work—with little time for idle chatter—before he clocks out to swim at a private pool club. Some people may be like Jim, who retired from a career job for which he collects a pension, lives with his wife in the same home they bought forty-five years ago and which has long since been paid for, and has adult children who have moved out but visit on holidays with grandchildren. Others may be of conventional retirement age but not technically retired because they lost their last job through a layoff. For some of these workers, the Vita paycheck goes to everyday expenses, including rent and heat, and perhaps helps to support an unemployed adult son who has moved in and is back to expecting meals on the table; these people survive paycheck to paycheck. One widower, Robert Benedict, supports three live-in young-adult grandchildren on his own. Yet others may have never stopped working. Allen Lewis had worked as a machinist for seventy years when he finally stopped working at Vita at age 84 because he was having trouble seeing the needles he was supposed to be sharpening—and a magnifying visor did not help. Rosa Finnegan took a short hiatus after a long waitressing career before she found work at Vita. The vast majority of the women at Vita are widowed or divorced, now living alone, sometimes in the same house in which they had raised their families.

How did Vita end up with this older workforce and what does it do to retain it? Vita Needle has received international attention for its elder-employment policy. Fred Hartman, the fourth-generation owner and president, has said in numerous media interviews that in the mid-1990s he began to notice that his long-standing employees who had grown old and stayed on were superior employees with a strong work ethic, reliability, discipline, and vast experience on which they could draw. He also realized that the only people willing to work part-time were older adults, and so he began to target hiring older workers. In 1997 Fred (as he is known to everyone in the factory, including his own children) issued a press release announcing Vita's sixty-fifth anniversary and noting its employment of older workers. The press release led to national and international media coverage, which continues at the time of my writing in mid-2011. The summer of 2008—the summer I was working there—saw a burst of media interest, this time mostly from Europe. In a three-month period, Vita was visited by journalists from France, Germany, and Italy—for a documentary film, television news, and slick magazine coverage in two leading German magazines.[7]

Fred is attuned to the age-related social, health, and economic needs of his workforce, and the company accommodates this workforce in various ways. For example, managers work closely with shop workers to make an ideal flexible schedule that might accommodate grandchild care, medical appointments, volunteer work, and the early rising that is common among older adults (starting work at 3:30 a.m. is convenient for Carl, whose restless leg syndrome is a condition more common and severe among older people). Vita Needle's is a surprisingly flexible production system, in part because workers are trained on multiple jobs (someone is usually able to step in for a coworker who is absent or who clocks out early) but also because of the nature and size of its orders and the store of backup inventory. Managers communicate with families of their employees if there are health concerns such as memory lapses or narcolepsy. They have also been known to curtail a worker's hours at the end of the year at the worker's request if he or she is approaching the federally mandated "earnings limit"—a limit to how much money a person below full retirement age can earn before the amount of his or her Social Security benefit will be reduced.[8]

In media interviews, Fred explains that he employs older workers as a social good—to counter adverse health impacts of isolated old age. Yet he and observers invariably also note the success of this business model, with Fred leveraging his employment policy as an ethical business practice (for instance, the Vita website refers to the company's commitment to "quality and socially responsible business").[9] Fred knows that this employment model is a selling point, and he has told me that his older workforce appears to help attract customers. He describes how customers choose Vita Needle over competitors because Vita Needle's story shows that it occupies the "moral high ground."

Fred claims that Vita Needle has become increasingly profitable since it first began employing older workers. Media coverage invariably notes this point. For instance, the German business magazine *Brand Eins* noted, "Sales have increased by 20 percent a year to about 10 million dollars, not in spite of, but because of, the advanced age of the employees."[10] Media coverage only very rarely mentions that Fred's elder-employment policy is structurally in dialogue with government support for older adults in the form of Medicare and Social Security. As the same German article notes, these employees were a windfall for the employers:

> Not only was the quality of their work first-rate, they had fun on the job and they were motivated. They also exhibited a loyalty the employers had not known in younger workers. Sure, some of the seniors were drawn to the meager wages as a way to improve their retirements. But their main motivation in taking the positions was in almost every case the need to feel useful again and to get away from the monotony and loneliness of retirement. They saw the work not as any kind of burden, but as a great opportunity. For their part, the Hartmans had only to pay a minimum wage. They even saved on the employer's contribution to retirement and healthcare benefits because the elderly already had claims to those benefits through their earlier wage-earning years.[11]

With low wages and no employer-provided health care and pension benefits for the part-time production workers, Vita Needle devised a profitable business model. In an economic context in which some U.S. employers have shifted operations abroad to reduce labor costs related to health care and pensions (often locating outsourcing operations in countries where governments bear the costs of those benefits), other employers have stayed in the United States but concentrated on employing part-time workers to whom they are not legally obligated to provide these benefits.[12] In Vita's case, the costs of these benefits are borne by the government in the form of the continual provision of welfare benefits to older adults through Social Security and Medicare, a guarantee that is not ensured as of this writing in May 2011, when both programs appear subject to radical revision.

The Vita Needle case offers us a window onto competing moral values in American society and often-unarticulated cultural assumptions. Economic decisions, policies, and conditions emerge from and also create cultural values (think of policies on child-care tax credits and the embedded assumptions about what makes for good parenting). The Vita Needle example raises ethical and cultural questions such as, Is employing older workers a social good? Is it exploitative? Should people be spending their golden years at a factory, in a rocking chair, on a golf course, or elsewhere? What is best for older adults themselves and for the society? What is appropriate, possible, and valuable for older adults? In what ways is it socially responsible to employ old people? The Vita Needle example also raises important larger questions about where we are headed: Why are there not more places where older adults can engage in meaningful work? Why is this internationally heralded example (which even appears in business school textbooks)[13] one of *factory* work—work that is unskilled, low-paid, and not particularly respected in American society? Is that the best we can do for older workers?

Vita Needle seems to raise a complex set of responses in those who hear about it, and many observers either have strong responses or do not know quite what to make of it. In October 2010, National Public Radio's *Morning Edition* aired a feature about the company that focused on two workers in their nineties. The NPR website reveals complex listener responses. We see obvious approval in posted comments: "My warmest admiration goes out to these gentle souls and the company that sees their worth." But we also see anxiety about the role of "greedy geezers" in perpetuating unemployment among younger people, reflected in this sarcastic comment: "Let's make retirees work hard and [keep] young people out of job[s]. New American dream."[14] When I mention Vita Needle to friends and colleagues, I am met with questions that reveal attempts to reconcile cultural expectations and assumptions about age with the idea of people in their seventies, eighties, and nineties doing manual labor in a dusty, noisy, crowded factory: Are the workers being exploited? Do old people have the vision and dexterity for factory work? Are they working because they need the money? Do they like working there?

In the chapters that follow, I address these and the many other questions that are raised when demographic, economic, and social changes lead us to reassess what retirement, work, and growing older mean. While we may at first glance think it cannot possibly be positive to be 99 and working in a factory, Rosa and her colleagues challenge us to think through this assumption more carefully. Of course, there are examples of disputes, complaints, anxieties, ambivalences, problems, and misunderstandings within the Vita Needle experience—and we will read about these in this book. The Vita Needle case challenges us to consider critically questions in aging research and policy studies about what constitutes a successful or positive aging experience. Since the 1990s there has been an emphasis in the United States on social engagement and physical activity for positive aging experiences—symbolized in the rebranding of retirement communities as "active adult living" or "active lifestyle" communities.[15] What makes for successful aging? How do we define success? Can factory work possibly fit into that definition? What contribution does Vita make to its own workers' positive aging experiences?[16]

Work and Retirement

There is more to work than the paycheck. Work can enable social engagement, provide a sense of contribution, and offer a respite from domestic troubles. In

American society, paid work is integral to one's sense of self-worth and value, and nonworking adults struggle to develop a sense of value that counters the cultural and economic norm. How does one respond to the common question "What do you do?" if you are a stay-at-home mom (perceived by many as nonworking), unemployed, or a retiree? One sign of how Americans measure themselves by work is that retirees often ask each other, "What did you do in real life?" The subjects of this book are older adults—past typical retirement age. They live at a confluence of contradictory social and economic values.

On one hand, many have long looked forward to and planned for a life stage called retirement, a phase of life in which one is no longer ruled by clocks, schedules, and bosses. This is especially true for the many people with alienating, demeaning, difficult, or unpleasant jobs that simply have not provided meaning for them—though even here, work can be an important aspect of identity, a point vividly made by the journalist Studs Terkel in his book *Working* and in the Broadway musical based on it.[17] This retirement phase is idealized in American society in many ways, often through romanticized images of golfing, traveling, fishing, knitting, and relaxing in recliner chairs. (Have a look at the retirement greeting cards at your local pharmacy for relevant cultural images: fishing poles, torn-up or empty "to do" lists, numberless clocks.) The dominant U.S. norm is that as we age, we transition from a period of labor productivity to a period of nonproductivity, beginning in our sixties.

On the other hand, many American older adults want to be engaged in work well past traditional retirement age. If during the lengthy period of labor productivity, our value is measured by our ability to earn income, how do we measure our value when we are nonproductive? Many people want to remain busy and engaged throughout their lives, and they want to be recognized for the contributions they make. Retirement thus is a complicated ideal for people across social classes—not only because of the cultural connotations and experiences that accompany it but also because of the economic position in which retirees find themselves.[18]

Retirement has long been unattainable without middle-class financial security, but with that security eroding (stock portfolios and real estate decreasing in value, pensions disappearing, health-care costs rising), retirement is increasingly unattainable for the middle classes as well.[19] The global financial crisis that began in roughly December 2007 has adversely affected many older adults in the United States and elsewhere. In publications including the *New York Times,* the *Economist,* and the *AARP Bulletin,* stories abound about older Americans who have had to delay or come out of retirement. Some parents have interrupted retirement plans to support unemployed adult children, and there are reports that traditional teenager summer jobs have been filled by older adults.[20] Even those in the upper middle class have been affected as many private retirement portfolios lost as much as 25 percent of their value during the financial crisis.[21]

Some companies have been targeting older adults since at least a decade before the crisis. The retailer CVS offers a "snowbird" program in which older adults may work summers up north and winters down south.[22] The AARP national conventions include a job fair where numerous employers recruit older workers— Home Depot, Walgreens, and Walmart, to name a few.[23] In the first decade of the twenty-first century, politicians, policymakers, and employers scrambled to create employment programs for older workers. In 2006, the National Governors Association (NGA) Policy Academy (a policy arm of the association) developed a multiyear program to assist states in promoting civic engagement among older adults by providing more avenues for volunteering and employment. The program's impetus is summarized in a 2008 NGA report: "The percentage of the U.S. population that is 65 years of age and older is expected to increase by nearly 60 percent during the next four decades. This demographic shift will have important implications for state action, including helping to ensure older adults remain healthy and active as they age."[24]

Even if retirement is financially feasible, it is no longer desirable for an increasing number of older adult in the United States. As a *New York Times* journalist explained in a 2008 article entitled "Whatever You Do, Call It Work," "It is better now in retirement to be a consultant, an independent contractor, an owner of a business, a dedicated volunteer, a portfolio manager, a pro bono worker or any variety of self-employment, as long as it is perceived as work."[25] There are a range of reasons for this desire to do something that is perceived as work, and my own interviews and discussions with workers from Vita Needle, Office Depot, CVS, and elsewhere reveal the diversity and complexity of people's motivations to work in typical retirement years.

Older workers seek from work a paycheck but also a sense of belonging and friendship, as well the experience of productivity, purpose, and usefulness. Grace King, at 94, says she was "going crazy" in retirement: "Nothing to do all day long, and it drove me crazy. I wanted to be busy." So Grace ended up at Vita Needle, starting a new job when she was 77. Grace and her peers subscribe to a "busy ethic" in their retirement years. This is a term used by sociologist David Ekerdt to describe a concept that has arisen in response to the leisure-filled stage of life called retirement. In a society that values productivity and a work ethic, retirement is "morally managed and legitimated on a day-to-day basis in part by an ethic that esteems leisure that is earnest, occupied, and filled with activity—a 'busy ethic.'"[26] For the Vita Needle employees, the key to successful aging is not a busy *retired* life, a life of "busy leisure." Rather, it is a busy *working* life where one contributes to the economy and participates in an interdependent production process with peers. Earning money is important to these people—they are explicit that their sense of purpose and meaning comes in large part from the paycheck they earn. This is distinct from people who find purpose in volunteering. The sense of meaningful and collective contribution is reflected in Vita Needle workers' common deployment of the phrase "making money for Fred," the business owner. As I discuss in chapter 1, this is a phrase usually used positively (as they highlight the value of their labor), though sometimes critically (as they question who profits the most). Vita Needle employees, even those collecting pensions from career jobs, do not consider themselves retired; indeed, some openly scoff at the concept—and frequently at the concept of golfing as a middle-class retirement ideal in the United States. As one man explained, he prefers to do something "practical and productive."

Although journalists and policymakers from around the world have looked at Vita Needle as a model of elder employment, I make no claims for the replicability of this particular model. I know this is a small, quirky factory that happens to work well for the employer who seeks to employ older workers and for some older workers who seek meaning, purpose, productivity, and a paycheck in their retirement years. A number of factors contribute to the success of this "eldersourcing"[27] model, including the nature of the product, the location of the business in a suburb in a high-technology region of the country (particularly with a number of start-up medical device companies), the personalities of the employers, the goals of and dynamics among the employees, and the relatively high percentage of older adults living in the area.[28]

Even though there are a number of aspects that make Vita Needle seem unique, there are lessons we can take from this example: lessons about what some Americans—and white American men in particular—seek in their retirement years; lessons about how older adults seek and create meaning in the world around them; lessons about the role of work in the creation of meaning, purpose, and life; and lessons about the need for government support of older adults (pensions and universal health care) to facilitate models such as this. My exploration of the specifics of this factory and its workers can be extended to a larger social and economic context. Sure, the Vita Needle case is unique, but I can situate its uniqueness in the forces that constitute it—forces that are not unique but that are deeply situated in American society and in its valuation of busy-ness, of mattering, and of work as an important route to meaning.[29]

Finally, I do assert that this book can offer key insights in light of the anticipated near-term increase in labor force participation by older workers in the United States. As a 2009 study noted, "According to one government estimate, 93% of the growth in the U.S. labor force from 2006 to 2016 will be among workers ages 55 and older."[30] The forerunners in these demographic and social shifts are the Vita Needle workers who have vibrant work lives well into their seventies, eighties, and nineties.

The Cultural Construction of Aging

"Are you old?" This is a question I have asked in many interviews. First replying "No" or "Well, I am old, but," often the respondent goes on to explain that there are some ways in which he or she is old (bodily decline often comes up) and some ways in which he or she is not (active lifestyles and outlooks are mentioned). In their at-times convoluted responses, we can see people trying to reconcile cultural expectations about a life stage with their own experiences. We can see how they are trying to live their lives in the face of this concept of old that carries with it numerous and mostly negative connotations, expectations, and images. A case in point: the anthropologist Jay Sokolovsky's edited collection *The Cultural Context of Aging* contains an evocative short discussion about "the dirty words for old age," which includes analysis of how Americans of different ages feel about words such as "geriatric," "geezer," "gramps," "codger," and "matron."[31]

In their responses to the question "Are you old?" we can also see how age is simultaneously important and unimportant, significant and insignificant, for this group. As the anthropologist Caroline Oliver has shown for her work among English retirees in Spain, for these older adults who live active lifestyles, a "paradox of aging" is that age does and does not matter. In the Spanish retirement communities where Oliver did fieldwork, the residents' lives defy old age stereotypes, and yet there is a constant underlying attention to age: peer-to-peer health monitoring and discussion, illness, death, and a discourse about its being "time to move on" (i.e., go to assisted living).[32] Among the Vita Needle workers, too, the workers are both old and not old at the same time. As the anthropologist Sharon Kaufman notes, we must remember that just because people may look old (and may identify as old for Medicare, Social Security, and cheap movie tickets), we cannot assume they experience themselves as old—or that old is an ever-present category for them. My Vita Needle respondents show us that, as Kaufman explains, we cannot assume that the political and bureaucratic identity of old age (where one may embrace the category of "old" in order to receive benefits or assert solidarity) is the essence of a person's individual identity.[33]

Of course, one might think that working at a place famous for employing old people makes Vita Needle's employees especially conscious of being old. They articulate a complex sense of what it means to be old. Indeed, despite the media coverage (and the journalists who seem to be interested in talking only to the gray-haired workers) some consider Vita Needle a place where they and their coworkers are not old, where they ward off death, or where they drink from a fountain of youth. In these comments we can see how people work to reconfigure what old means in American society. Vita Needle's older workers are people who, despite their individual differences, are grouped by American society as old. They are members of a group for whom perception matters greatly in daily life. When they drive their cars, walk through the grocery store, or wait at a doctor's office, they are judged by others to be members of a category with which they may not self-identify. People interact with them by reference to cultural assumptions about what being old means. And these older workers make sense of their own individual aspirations, choices, and experiences in light of U.S. cultural norms for what being old should mean.

In the following interview exchange between me and 84-year-old Allen Lewis, Allen eloquently described the cultural construction of aging when he explained that the people he works with are not old because old is a way of thinking and acting that is not found at Vita Needle. In other words, rather than being determined by a particular number of chronological years, to Allen, old age is characterized by feeble bodies and particular attitudes and ways of being. His articulation of old age is entirely negative:

> *Caitrin:* So, do you ever spend time at the senior center?
> *Allen:* I've walked through there a couple of times to vote or something, but I wouldn't go near that place.
> *Caitrin:* Why not?
> *Allen:* It might catch.
> *Caitrin:* It might catch? What does that mean?
> *Allen:* Old age.... I can still remember walking down the street...and all of a sudden I said, "The hell it is, it's learned. Old age is something you learn." It's like a toy. Your little girl with her doll carriage and the dolls and she's learning.... You're around old people...and you learn, this is how you get. [But] you don't have to get like that. So that's one reason I wouldn't want to work with a bunch of people like you find at the senior center....
> *Caitrin:* But you do work with old people.
> *Allen:* These aren't, they're not the same. Go up to the senior center, you'll find out the difference.

Allen then described the people at the senior center "walking and shuffling along" and sitting in chairs for hours, and he reiterated that being old is "all in your mind." Then he added, "If you start to think you're old, you're ancient, you're feeble, you can't move.... You've probably said it to your children more than once: 'Act your age.' But all of a sudden you're 70. 'Act your age.'"

For emphasis, Allen repeats "Act your age"—a common expression replete with cultural assumptions. Allen perceptively notes that this expression has different meanings for a 5-year-old and a 70-year-old, and his commentary questions what it means as one ages. Why do we need to act our age? What if we don't? Can we safely defy the cultural expectation? Allen would say we can, and we must if we are to authentically live our lives. Anthropologist Mary Catherine Bateson also mentions this same phrase in her book *Composing a Further Life* when she notes that in the process of aging, "Physiological changes are accompanied by social changes as one suddenly encounters a new set of attitudes and expectations and must grow into new roles." As she says, "There was a time when our parents said to us, 'Act your age.' Now, shockingly, our children may begin to say it."[34] Both Bateson and Vita Needle's Allen Lewis point out the social pressures to live up to cultural expectations for age-appropriate behavior, and Allen is emphatic in his desire to chart his own path.

In Allen's words we hear a man trying to reconcile cultural expectations about aging with his own experience. He and his coworkers are grappling with what it means to grow old. Being old is certainly important to them (and we will see this especially in chapter 2), but they do not want to be entirely defined by stereotypes of old age. Their dilemmas show us how aging is "culturally constructed." That is, we do not act merely in response to a given social world. Rather, as people in society, we make sense of and create the world around us. When anthropologists refer to society as culturally constructed, they mean that social, economic, and political phenomena are created and made sense of through a cultural lens that also carries with it norms and expectations about what is right and possible.

The book is an extended examination of how age is culturally constructed in the United States. We make sense of bodily change and difference—we attribute meaning to the physical body and we continually reproduce our worlds through interpretation and attribution of value. Age is like race and gender in this way. Much of what we think about the categories of age, race, and gender is based on bodily attributes, but our understanding of these categories is not entirely grounded in biology. In terms of gender, our numerous assumptions about women's and men's differing abilities, proclivities, and interests do not all correspond to actual physical differences between men and women (think here of the pervasive and erroneous assumption that girls are not good at math). The ways in which we culturally construct age are not entirely grounded in the physical, and yet, in the United States, physical change and decline are important to our interpretations and experiences of aging; we try to extend life and conquer aging, which we consider a disease. In India, by contrast, one is old when one's children marry, even if one would not be considered old by U.S. standards.[35]

Although mine is a study of norms and expectations about aging among white nonimmigrant Americans, the global media coverage of Vita Needle and the responses to it show that the Vita story appears to resonate across a variety of cultural differences—though my discussion in chapter 4 of how the story plays out in France shows how we interpret experiences in our own socioeconomic context.

Though we culturally construct age, gender, and race, age is different from the other two cultural categories in one important way. With the exception of those who die early, everyone (regardless of gender or race) enters a period called "old." Our lives are replete with negotiations about where that crossover point is and what it means. Whereas in the United States we seem to have normative agreement about what, biologically, constitutes racial and sexual difference, we do not agree about where to draw the line for old.

Grappling with these same notions of the cultural construction of aging in American society, gerontologist Robert Butler coined the term "ageism" in the late 1960s. He wrote,

> Ageism can be seen as a process of systematic stereotyping of and discrimination against people because they are old, just as racism and sexism accomplish this with skin color and gender. Old people are categorized as senile, rigid in thought and manner, old-fashioned in morality and skills.... Ageism allows the younger generations to see old people as different from themselves; thus they subtly cease to identify with their elders as human beings.[36]

I find it unsettling to realize that this concept was coined around the year of my birth, in 1967, and yet it appears to describe today's attitudes toward older adults. But I hope that by focusing on the experiences and meanings of retirement, this book will contribute to a reevaluation of this long-ignored life stage. I seek to take up Butler's own identification of retirement as a key node of cultural meaning-making in regard to aging and ageism. As he wrote in 1969,

> Age-ism reflects a deep seated uneasiness on the part of the young and middle-aged—a personal revulsion to and distaste for growing old, disease, disability; and fear of powerlessness, "uselessness," and death. Cultural attitudes in our society reinforce these feelings. We have chosen mandatory retirement from the work force and thus removed the elderly from the mainstream of life.[37]

Not long after these words appeared, the anthropologist Ruth Landes also wrote insightfully about retirement. In 1971 she argued that since the 1930s, "retirement" has been "a term covering the limbo in which Age was to be deposited,"[38] and that the "calcification" in retirement is a harmful result of negative stereotypes of old age as "waste." Landes wrote about the importance of having a sense of *duty* in life, *throughout life*—and for the afterlife—when she described the philosopher George Santayana's end of life in an Italian nunnery:

> A nunnery is a complex, highly disciplined community, with duties in this world and duties anticipating the next. The nunneries contrast serenely with the monstrous anarchy of our principal cities, not only for their internal order but for the psychic or spiritual dimension they create that bridges life and death. To them the aged are ongoing members of the community.[39]

Landes clearly lauded this nunnery example for the perpetual sense of community, purpose, and duty—not the ideas of anarchy, calcification, waste, and decrepitude that characterize societal attitudes toward the aged. For Landes, the nunnery provided a model for overcoming our negative cultural attitudes toward aging (how to get out of "our cultural trap").[40]

Landes and Butler both were right to pinpoint idle retirement as a problem, and the question of how to find purpose in one's retirement years is central to this book and of great concern today among policymakers and scholars worldwide. Today there are important vocal movements for healthy and positive aging— entire communities are built around preventing the calcification of the potentials of older people. And yet we still have a cultural ideal of retirement as an idle time characterized by rocking chairs and fishing poles. Could we perhaps think of Vita Needle as akin to the Italian nunnery? Is it a sense of duty, purpose, and belonging that brings people back there, even in their late nineties? What would Landes and Butler see in the Vita Needle example? What do we see in it? Is it a way to fight against negative ageist attitudes, and if so, how? These are questions we will return to throughout the book.

In the United States, cultural assumptions abound that characterize youth as a time of activity and vitality and old age as a time of decline, decrepitude, and death. But will the increasing prevalence of older workers counter those stale images, expectations, and stereotypes? When we see a white-haired person at the Walgreens cash register, will we continue to roll our eyes in anticipation of how slow we think she will be? Sociologist David Ekerdt has asked if the increasing presence of older workers in American society may change cultural attitudes toward aging. He cautions that he would not want to deny retirement to those who need to retire because of mental or physical disability or the need to care for others. Many people *need* to retire as soon as possible, and many others deeply *want* to retire, having merely tolerated long-term jobs for the sake of supporting a family. In retirement many people want to pursue other paths, perhaps just as productive as the paid jobs they have been in. Ekerdt (and this is echoed by others who work in the area of older workers and public policy) argues that he envisions an "opening up" of the possibilities for older adults—not a "narrowing down" to the single option of "Work until you die!"[41]

At a September 2010 forum for the Massachusetts Healthy Aging initiative, a communications professional named John Beilenson spoke to the audience of health-care workers and policymakers about the critical need for a "new frame" and a "communication strategy" that will change how people in Massachusetts think about older adults. Calling this a quick "Framing 101" course, he explained that frames are "thought organizers" that influence how the audience understands an issue, and that they are stronger than facts (which people do not even hear). He used the example of the concept of an "aging tsunami" to show the adverse effects of some current popular frames about aging. The use of an evocative term such as "tsunami"—never a positive image—shows us that the popular discourse is that the country (and the world) is heading toward decline because of the forthcoming overpowering and unmanageable wave of older adults. By contrast, Beilenson provided the example of a communications frame he created, entitled "Put Life Back in Your Life," the tag line for a chronic-pain management program for older adults.

Speaking to this group of professionals crafting the early years of the state's new aging program, Beilenson encouraged the audience to generate a new frame for aging in Massachusetts by considering what actual healthy older adults look like and what they do, using diverse and nonstereotypical images and examples.[42] We can situate this presentation in a history of attempts at "rebranding" aging to be a positive experience—a history that goes back in the United States at least to Butler's first articulations of the concept of ageism and includes a May 2011 launch of a self-designated movement called Rebranding Aging by the International Council on Active Aging ("ground-breaking movement aimed at shifting society's perceptions of aging and countering aging stereotypes").[43]

As Sokolovsky points out in *The Cultural Context of Aging*, especially since the 1990s there have been various attempts to rebrand aging in the United States. He mentions the creation of new vocabularies with terms such as "saging" and "eldering" rather than "aging" and notes the numerous efforts to emphasize successful, active, and productive aging (and the notion of the "well-derly" rather than "ill-derly").[44] Civic Ventures, the think tank that aims to help baby boomers find meaningful work, uses a number of catchphrases obviously aimed at this kind of rebranding: for example, they focus on "stage, not age" (what life stage people are at, not what age they are) and they argue that "60 is the new 60" (in other words, rather than thinking of 60 as a new way of living an earlier life stage, we need to think of it as a vital age on its own terms).

Cultural and Workplace Immersion

From spring 2006 to spring 2011 I conducted in-depth ethnographic research on Vita Needle that involved interviews and participant observation. The source of my description and analysis in this book included the anthropological methods of participant observation from my summer working on the Vita Needle production floor—making, inspecting, and packing needles. My methods also included examination of particular people and situations based on long-term friendships as well as semistructured interviews (more than 80 total, including with focus groups) with Vita Needle owners, managers, employees, and family members; other local people over 60 years old engaged in paid, unpaid, or no work; geriatricians and elder-care service professionals; and European journalists covering Vita Needle. To provide the wider context for understanding Vita Needle, I also analyzed cultural material (such as retirement magazines, senior citizen newsletters, and popular books on aging) and attended events at senior centers and retirement communities.

During my summer of work at Vita Needle, one would have found me packaging needles alongside Esther Martin, being trained by Rosa to work alongside her, or huddled in a corner working the foot pedal on the machine that flares the ends of six-inch-long tubes and made Ed think of stacking hay and loading bales. I would work a shift, sometimes sneaking into the bathroom to take notes, but always composing field notes on a digital voice recorder the moment I stepped onto the sidewalk outside to head home—trying to retain as much as possible before my immediate memory faded. I would joke with Vita Needle workers that Vita Needle was my Samoa, a reference to the famous fieldwork location of Margaret Mead, the well-known American cultural anthropologist whose work reached scholarly and nonscholarly audiences in the middle of the twentieth century. Mead was known to many of Vita Needle's workers, especially the one who had taken an anthropology course from her in the 1950s.

Back when I first visited Vita Needle, if someone had told me that this factory made hollow needles, I probably would have drawn a blank. What are hollow needles? For injections or for drawing blood? For inflating basketballs? My guesses might have ended there. With a little more time, I might have thought about glue dispensers and tire inflation systems, and of course hypodermic needles for injecting insulin or antibiotics. But I certainly would not have come up with the following applications, all real examples of products I have worked on or heard about while working at Vita: picking up soil samples on Mars, squeezing anesthesia into the artery during open heart surgery, tagging live salmon with computer chips to study their movement, and embalming corpses. Each different usage evokes discussion on the shop floor, and the embalmer's needles were no exception. One day, 94-year-old Grace and I were eating at our worktable; we had pushed aside needles, cardboard, cellophane wrappers, and boxes to make room for our home-packed lunches. With a grin, Grace said to me, "Yesterday I did embalmer's needles. Eight-inch, six-inch, and four-inch. The eight-inch made me shudder. Good thing you're dead when they use those!" This from a woman who told me that during a recent hospital stay she had been temporarily disoriented when she awoke one morning and could smell roses (which I had given her the previous day) on the bedside table. "I thought I must be dead and was smelling the roses in the funeral home."

If there was a time when my inventory of uses for hollow needles would have been thin, there was also a time when I would not have been able to say what a cannula is on a needle. Or a hub. (The cannula is the tube; the hub is the base.) Second-pointing? Probably not. I might have been able to guess what a burr is, but it is unlikely I would have known what it means to refer to a tube's ID and OD (the internal and outer diameter). I definitely did not know about Gertrude Baker, who was a master at sleeping while appearing to be working. I never would have guessed that there was a diversion called the Dee Dee Game—a game I now know I will never win. And I would not have known that the small wooden boxes used to transport parts throughout the factory were made in a home woodshop in the 1960s by Walter Gustowski, the husband of Alice, a Vita worker back then whom I now know from her photo in the hallway. I might not even have noticed the intricate tongue-and-groove joints of these boxes—no nails in Walter's workmanship.

The world of Vita Needle products, process, and people was new to me in the spring of 2006 when I first started this project in earnest. But I was welcomed into this world by many—the Hartman family that owns this business, the manager and supervisors, the salespeople, and especially the workers on the production floor. Ed, Rosa, Esther, Carl, and others let me into their lives to teach me what they know and believe, what gets them up in the morning, and what keeps them coming back to Vita Needle. Some of these people even began to look out for me, to be an extra set of eyes and ears for what they thought I might want to know. Once a worker left a voicemail in my office alerting me to the fact that a French film crew was in town and that he had given them my business card. Another time, I got a call from Allen with the phone number of a visiting German filmmaker. In both these cases, these Vita employees knew that I would want to talk to the European journalists. These workers had become aware of the significance of their lives and work for the journalists and me, and they had begun to turn a critical and reflective eye on what they were up to. It was as if I had my own cadre of research assistants on the factory floor, and to those people I am forever grateful.

The fact that I was allowed to work there was wonderful, both because of what this enabled me to learn and because of my own relationship to work. Frankly, I love work, especially manual work that delivers an immediate sense of accomplishment: mowing a lawn, cleaning a really dirty house, organizing a messy office. What I probably liked best about delivering newspapers in high school was the obvious productivity. I would set out at 5:30 a.m. with a bag full of newspapers, and the load would gradually lighten; by the time I returned home, newspaper ink smudged on my face and an empty bag swinging at my side, it was clear that my job was done. I enjoyed working at Vita Needle: there was always something to do, and I could see my work move to the next step in the production process and ultimately out the door with the FedEx deliveryman. But I also enjoyed working there because I knew I was furthering my understanding—already developed over a two-year period of offsite interviews and occasional workplace visits—of everyday workplace dynamics, the ways in which people try to live out their dreams for community and productivity at work, and how management and employees reconcile their joint social and economic goals. Insights arose from experiencing many things I had heard about in interviews and many things that had never come up. For instance, I had conversations during breaks about the effect of deteriorating eyesight (from cataracts or macular degeneration) on quality control; I heard jokes and complaints about the sweltering ninety-four-degree factory temperature; I saw great concern about a coworker's unexpected absence; and I got to feel what it was like to finish inspecting a batch of three hundred needles only to be given three hundred more!

Making Needles, Making Lives

This book is divided into two parts, both introduced with vignettes from my fieldwork that show my own role in the Vita Needle story. Part 1, "Up the Stairs," brings us inside the factory to focus on the ways in which the work process, the production, the relationships, and the daily interactions enable people to feel alive, productive, and useful—to matter in the world. We see how a sense of productivity (chapter 1) and a feeling of family and community (chapter 2) lead what some observers might consider "exploitation" to operate as freedom and flexibility for the workers (chapter 3). Part 2, "In the Press," brings Vita Needle into the world and focuses on the company in the national and international media. We see how journalists and audiences interpret Vita Needle (chapter 4) and then how the workers themselves make sense of all the attention they get from media and from the visiting anthropologist (chapter 5). Vita means "life" in Latin, and indeed it is life (and life with meaning) that is created at Vita up the stairs (part 1) but also in the press (part 2) through the sense of mattering that is generated by media attention and the ability to engage or not with the attention. At Vita Needle, not only needles but also lives are made on the shop floor.

In the pages that follow, I analyze cultural assumptions we all bring to bear on aging and work. Many scholars of aging and work tend to be in sociology, public policy, economics, and medicine, and they often use quantitative measures to analyze opportunities and quantifiable standard-of-living outcomes. But missing from these analyses can be the real people, their experiences, and their motivations. What do employers want and why? And how about the employees? What are the hopes of and possibilities for individuals after traditional retirement age? This book's deep ethnographic focus on a single workplace allows for an analysis of the more humanistic side of this issue; I focus on values and meanings and on the insights we gain by understanding struggles and victories of particular people. A fundamental premise of this book is that anthropologists who specialize in the world of work have a critical role to play during the current financial crisis—we can lend our analytical insights to understanding the histories, experiences, and possible futures of people worldwide as they make sense of and respond to dramatically changing socioeconomic landscapes. I hope this book will contribute to the body of academic and policy research on how the United States and other societies will support (both economically and socially) an aging population in future years; the mechanisms needed for and benefits of raising the age of retirement; and how to keep older adults engaged in meaningful activity. I especially hope it will contribute to scholarship that exposes or probes cultural assumptions about the meaning of the life course; how to make late life meaningful; and how to find, create, and maintain value in late life.

Part I

UP THE STAIRS

From the outside, Vita Needle looks out of place—but only if you happen to notice it. It is located on a main road in the center of Needham, an affluent Boston suburb where the median income and home price are well above the state average.[1] This is the town's central retail shopping area, just a half block away from the town hall and town common. The block includes a bank, sporting goods and music stores, a travel agency, restaurants, clothing shops, and hair salons. A faded wooden sign, black letters on a white background, sits above the recessed door and reads Vita Needle Co.; the generic orange-and-black Help Wanted sign is the most noticeable doorway feature. I never would have noticed Vita Needle if, shortly after moving to town, I had not walked directly into someone who was exiting the doorway. I pardoned myself, looked up to see where the person had come from, and saw the words "Vita Needle." Because I was in the midst of writing a book about Sri Lankan garment factory workers that fall of 2005, I thought about sewing needles and became nosy (or, more charitably, curious). "What's this place?" I asked the man whom I had nearly knocked down. He told me that it was a needle factory and that I should stop in sometime. I distinctly remember that this 40-something-year-old man (I have not been able to figure out who he was) said to me, "I am definitely one of the youngest people working in there."

Some weeks following that fateful collision, I looked up Vita Needle on the Internet and learned that it did not make sewing needles. But I did stop in to take a look. With a long-standing interest in industrial production and globalization—plus a newer interest in aging that had been piqued by exchanging book chapter drafts with the anthropologist Sarah Lamb, who specializes in aging in India—I needed to see Vita Needle for myself.

On a late September morning, when walking downtown with my two-year-old daughter, I spontaneously decided to go into Vita Needle. I knocked on the recessed door, waited awkwardly without reply, then timidly opened the door and walked up the stairs;

ever-inquisitive Nicola wondered aloud where we were going and why. The door opened onto an ascending stairway. Lining the stairwell walls were glass-framed newspaper articles about Vita Needle and handwritten letters by people from around the world congratulating the company's owner on his forward-thinking employment model, requesting jobs, and sending greetings to the employees. Little did I know that to Vita Needle's workers and managers, and to journalists and media consumers, these very stairs were a symbol of the world Vita Needle represented—a world where stairs were not an obstacle for aging bodies but a sign of vitality, productivity, and belonging.

On the landing, Nicola and I were welcomed by Jim Downey, a Vita Needle production worker who happened to be walking by. After escorting me to the office to introduce me to the factory owner (who gave me an informational folder about the company), Jim took me for a quick look inside the production area. I remember noticing not much more than gray hair and noise and the smell of something—was it oil? I was struck by the sense of busyness and bustle.

Today I know what that busyness and bustle really entails; I am able to identify the noise as coming from air compressors, table saws, and steel grinders; and I now know the names, personalities, and many of the stories behind the workers with the common hair color. I also now know that hair color is not the only commonality among the employees—most are white, nonimmigrant males, and most are retired from jobs they had for a long time (schoolteachers, engineers, lab technicians, postal workers, waitresses). But I also know that diverse histories and motivations have brought these people to Vita Needle.

When I first typed these words in summer 2008, I had been favoring my left pinkie, blistered from my most recent shift on the factory floor two days earlier. After one hour of gluing together two stainless steel parts (dip piece one into acetone, drip glue onto it, join to piece two, screw pieces together, place in a box), my latex gloves tore as a result of the chafing motion to reveal a blister caused by the repetitive pressure. Jim happened to be grinding needles at the workbench near me, so I walked over, proudly showed him my finger and said, "My first Vita Needle blister," to which he routinely remarked, "There are Band-Aids under the time clock." Undeterred by his unimpressed response, I joked that this must be a meaningful sign, to which he said, "Some days I get a cut five minutes after getting here," and he returned to grinding needles to a sharp point. It was ninety-three degrees in the factory, and we were all sweating; whenever we had the chance we would stop to drink water. With a few more hours left before he normally clocked out, Jim did not have time to chitchat. He still had needles to assemble or grind; others to inspect, straighten, and pack; as well as tubes to cut to specified lengths, and yet others to bend. Eventually he would grab his time card, punch out, and go home to get his wife for an after-work swim at their private pool club. But right now he had work to do, for this, his retirement job.

Jim is a 74-year-old retired architect. He has worked at Vita Needle for nine years, since shortly after he retired from thirty years at a Boston architecture firm. A busy man, involved in many volunteer activities, civic organizations, and social groups, committed to his family, and a frequent traveler, Jim came to Vita Needle for "meaningful interaction." He works five hours a day, five days per week. Whereas Jim heard about Vita Needle from a friend, others heard about it from doctors, who recommended they work there because of the importance of staying active for healthy aging. Indeed, it is common for Vita Needle workers to note that "this job keeps me going." One 74-year-old told me that he considers Vita Needle a "fountain of youth" and that after six months of working there his memory tests with his geriatrician had improved dramatically.

If they did not hear of Vita Needle from friends, doctors, or neighbors, workers may have heard about it when there was a spate of print and broadcast media coverage in the late 1990s and early 2000s. There was an Associated Press newswire article reprinted throughout the country, lengthy features in the *New York Times* and *Boston Globe*, segments on the national television news programs *60 Minutes* and *The Today Show*, and even a feature in the *National Examiner* tabloid titled "Nobody is Ever Fired from...America's Best Workplace!" The media interest extended to Europe, with print and television coverage and two documentary films. Ron Crowley, a retired schoolteacher who now works in Vita Needle's shipping department, learned about the company when he and his wife saw the *60 Minutes* episode, a few years before he retired. As he explained in an interview, "On a Sunday night we had tuned into *60 Minutes* and we didn't see the introduction, the first fifteen seconds, twenty seconds, or whatever, but they were talking about a company in Needham that hired the elderly. And so we both kind of joked, 'Oh, there's the retirement job.'"

Jim, the retired architect, enjoys the work at Vita Needle and finds that it satisfies his desire for meaningful activity in retirement. To Jim, Vita Needle feels like a good deal—he gets what he wants from the job and gets a paycheck on top of that. The paycheck is more critical for some Vita Needle workers than others. With Social Security income and private pensions, some report that they do not need the money for day-to-day survival;[2] one man described his paycheck as his wife's mad money. As with Jim, Vita Needle feels like a good deal to Charles Young, a 72-year-old retired high-tech sales manager who is unmarried and needs the money to cover everyday expenses. Charles does not want to rely on his retirement savings just yet. He predicts that he will need to stop working someday because of deteriorating health, but until then he will work rather than live off savings. Charles needs his paycheck, plus his Social Security income, to survive—to pay for the daily expenses that increase over the years: food and property taxes, home heating oil, gasoline, and medicine. Charles is not there just for the paycheck, however; he also values Vita Needle because it provides him with something to do. The alternative is not promising: "There is only so much television you can watch." As Charles commented to me one day when I was coiling tubes at a table near him, "I think of this as a men's club. You come in, get some exercise, talk, do something, and get paid." A nearby coworker retorted, "You don't get paid at a men's club," to which Charles quickly replied, smiling at me and jabbing his calipers in the air for emphasis, "It's *better* than a men's club!"

This "men's club," however, is not just for men. A handful of the production workers are women, and their stories provide an interesting and important lens for examining women's experience of aging. Across the factory from Charles, you would likely find Vita Needle's eldest worker, 99-year-old Rosa Finnegan, working the machine that is affectionately nicknamed "The Rosamatic" because of her skill at operating it. She would be imprinting numbers onto stainless steel needle hubs with this machine. Rosa came to the factory at age 85—leaving a Cape Cod retirement that she found lonely. During summer 2008 Rosa trained me on one of her jobs, which involved assembling devices for inserting glue under linoleum; we would attach four-inch-long needles to plastic dispensers with rubber bands, and we would fill boxes with three hundred dispensers. I was counting to three hundred by twos, and Rosa laughed and told me I should count by fours: 4, 8, 12, 16, 20, 24... she rattled off more quickly than I could follow. Three years later, Vita Needle workers still joke that I had been unable to keep up with Rosa!

Media coverage of Vita Needle invariably refers to the stairs; a 2008 German magazine article was even entitled "Stairs of the Willing."[3] The stairs, which came up in many of my interviews, are a complex symbol for Vita Needle's workers. They invoke issues such as the stigma of being old in the United States and the consequent feelings of invisibility and loneliness, for they lead to a place free of stigma and isolation. The stairs also raise health concerns, for one cannot get up the nineteen steps (everyone knows the number!) with a walker or an impeded gait, and climbing them means making it to a place where one can be productive, alive, and vital. In my five years of research, I have met and in some cases interviewed a number of older workers elsewhere in town (bagging groceries, serving coffee, working cash registers) who tell me they would like to work at Vita Needle but that they cannot climb the stairs. The stairs do sometimes keep away even Vita Needle's own workers, such as when one woman missed two months of work because she was using a walker while recovering from an injury. Another woman, Sophia, at age 78 and just out of knee surgery, had to take one stair at a time and rest at each step. I have heard stories of employees nearly falling down or tripping up the stairs, definitely missing a step. A German documentary film ends with a poignant depiction of a man whose back is humped (perhaps as a result of osteoporosis) helping a woman with a cane down the stairs. Both the man and the woman walk cautiously, arm in arm, as if supporting each other.

The Vita Needle workers who climb those stairs challenge many of our expectations and assumptions about aging, work, and retirement. While the stairs are an obstacle and barrier for some people, for Vita Needle's older workers, they are in many ways a symbol of possibility. They are a metaphor for the lives that working at Vita Needle enables them to experience. Let's go on up.

PIGEONHOLED

By Jim Downey

Since there is no air-conditioning on the shop floor at Vita Needle, we occasionally have to open the door to the fire escape and its corresponding inside door to the shop in order to provide a breeze and ventilation. The shop floor gets up in excess of ninety degrees at times in the summer, and any air movement is appreciated.

A fake owl and its accompanying loudspeaker had been installed on the roof to prevent the town pigeon population from making Fred's building a preferred roost. Sometimes people on the street are startled by the sounds of an owl shredding a pigeon for a repast and by the pigeon's noisy but ineffective protest. However, we have seen a pigeon actually sitting atop the fake owl, unperturbed by the recorded cries of one of its fellows.

With all these extensive preparations, it was probably inevitable that a pigeon would fly through the open door and become entrapped in the Vita shop, as happened last week. There was an interruption to the flow of work, as several people followed the path of the bird through the many obstacles in the ceiling, including pipes, ducts, fans, wires, and the structures enclosing the old band stage. Salespeople from upstairs came down to ogle and offer suggestions. Supervisors notified Fred, who came out to look as well.

While the discussion continued about what to do, Fred decided to call Needham's animal control department, run by the town police, and they said they would send someone right away. As soon as the officer arrived, wearing a smile and carrying a long-handled fishnet, the scene quickly became one of set-piece entertainment, with everyone's riveted attention focused on the officer and his charge.

Having reconnoitered the entire scope of the ceiling, and having found no outlet at that level, the pigeon had meanwhile settled itself on a one-inch diameter tie-rod supporting the arched roof near its junction with the wall. Our animal control officer, sharply dressed in his dark blue uniform, with all its accoutrements on his ample belt, called for a stepladder and approached the pigeon. What happened next added to the fun and excitement of the event.

The pigeon, seeing the sweep of the net coming, simply launched itself upward and away and flew wildly around the ceiling again, doing an artful slalom through every pipe, duct, and wire. Eventually, the officer's persistence paid off, as he was able to corner the bird in the interior of the stage area, which is a cul-de-sac. Triumphant with his captive in the net, he went out on the fire escape, and spent a few minutes trying to free the bird and get it to fly off. This he did, and he pointed out to onlookers the pigeon's successful escape to the top of an adjoining building.

After a little escape from tedium, a successful afternoon at Vita continued, and the shop began to hum again with its usual rhythms.

Attaching needles to glue dispensers. Photo by Caitrin Lynch.

MAKING MONEY FOR FRED

Productivity, People, and Purpose

One day Arthur Johnson called me over to where he was grinding needles and said "There's an expression you need to know. 'Making money for Fred.'" For keen insight into his own situation and surroundings, I knew I could count on 72-year-old Arthur, who has been at Vita Needle since he retired at 65 from his job as a corporate accountant. I had already heard this expression from others, and although I did not fully understand it, I had begun to identify this as a key expression that symbolized how, for Vita workers, working there presented them with an opportunity to do productive work with and for others. Arthur had now confirmed that this was a term I needed to understand. Today I better appreciate the ways in which this expression encapsulates the significance of productivity, collectivity, and value that is so key to what keeps Vita workers coming back day after day, well into their nineties. The phrase links together instances and incidents of everyday factory life that seem unrelated—daily life concerning factory efficiency, productivity, and the dependence of one worker on another in a multiperson assembly process.

There are several connected pieces that underlie the significance of this expression. There is a pervasive sense of cooperation at Vita Needle, of working together in an integrated fashion and toward a collective goal. We see this in worker descriptions of the relative value of their own work to the workplace, in their efforts to be more efficient on the job, and in their deliberations and observations about coworker productivity. For these older workers, many of whom consider this job their last chance to earn pay for work, there are myriad ways in which the social and economic value of their labor is visible daily in practices, discussions, and conflicts. It is through labor that these workers feel affirmed and valued, connected and needed, and this feeling is confirmed in daily interactions such as compliments from a coworker or a supervisor and in less intimate moments such as receiving monthly paychecks and participating in the annual profit-sharing bonus.

The Fred in this expression is Fred Hartman, Vita Needle's president and fourth-generation owner. Allow me to paint a picture of Fred's persona at the factory. He is often out on the shop floor, visiting Rosa, Esther, Jim, Charles, or any of the workers to ask after them, their health, their grandchildren, or the job they are working at that moment. He likes to peek at the needles under production, ask about the process, and check in about how things are going. Aged 56 in 2008, Fred is young enough to be the child of many of the employees. His own father, Mason, who passed away at age 81 in 2007, had originally hired some of the old-timers here, such as Esther, as well as Ruth Kinney and David Rivers, those who have the longest work record. Fred's children grew up coming in and out of the workplace, and many employees have told me nostalgic stories about the kids being present at work, even painting the bathrooms during a school vacation. There is a famous story, which I heard from several people, about some workers asking Fred's young son, then in elementary school (now their boss), to cajole his father to pay him more money for a job he was doing. Here is one version of the story:

> Frederick, his son, he used to work there when he was a little kid and they had these cards they used to punch out for the needles and the punch never worked quite right and you had to poke the things out. And then you'd have a box about that big. And Fred was paying him a nickel a box. Well, I don't know, Freddie was maybe 9 years old then.... And a couple of us had a conversation, "You ought to go in and ask your father for a raise." He'd go in and say, "They said you ought to give me a raise." Fred came by later and said to us, "What the hell are you trying to do"?

This 9-year-old Freddie was none other than Frederick, who is now in his mid twenties and the second in command at the business. This is a story about connections across generations and between workers and the employer. It is also a story about the ever-present question of the true value of labor power, a topic usually broached only in humorous guise.

There is often visible affection between Fred and the workers. The German documentary film *Pensioners Inc.* includes a touching dialogue between Fred and Rosa. At the time, Fred was 55, and Rosa was 96. In this clip, Rosa is working on the same flaring machine that prompts Ed Mitchell to sing "Old Man River." This machine's operation is so repetitive that it is assigned on a rotating one-hour shift basis to prevent people from making errors as a result of boredom-induced inattention. Fred approaches Rosa, who keeps working but does slow down to talk:

> *Fred:* You're doing all right now, right?
> *Rosa:* Yes.
> *Fred:* Yes?
> *Rosa:* Yes.
> *Fred:* You sure?
> *Rosa:* Yes. (Rosa then giggles, smiles, and rubs her fingers affectionately under Fred's chin—a little tap—as a grandparent would to a grandchild; she then turns back to work.)
> *Fred:* This is your one hour, right?
> *Rosa:* Yes. They don't want us to do this for any more than an hour.
> *Fred:* I don't want you to do it more than an hour either because I don't want you to get tired.

This scene was filmed for a documentary, so we might wonder about the extent to which it was staged. But the care and affection demonstrated—Rosa's giggles and chin tap, Fred's words—are consistent with other interactions I have seen between Fred and Rosa. There is, for instance, considerable good will on Rosa's birthdays, when it is customary to serve cake and sing "Happy Birthday" at the morning coffee break. At one point on her ninety-eighth birthday, Rosa sat laughing perched on Fred's lap, while all sorts of suggestive jokes were made from the participants and observers alike. Of course, over a five-year period I did hear concern about some of Fred's policies and managerial practices (the lack of air-conditioning on the shop floor was a common complaint), and some skepticism about just how much money the shop workers were making for him. But the overall sense was a feeling of gratitude from the workers for being employed at an age when it is difficult, if not impossible, to find a job. As Rosa explained in the German documentary film, "It's a wonderful place to be when you get to be my age. Where could I go? I don't want to go to a nursing home yet. And I hope I never have to. But [pause], so, here, you learn, and you even learn new things. You know, still, I don't care whether I am old or not. I still learn new things here."

Employees generally consider Fred to be the one who gets the most financial profit from Vita's production, though many employees fully understand that this is a family business with shareholders and a formal method for determining where profits are directed. Many appreciate Fred's personable demeanor and feel connected to him and his family. But many also know that Fred drives a high-end sedan with vanity license plates, lives in a nearby town even tonier than affluent Needham, and vacations at his summer home. As the spouse of one worker observed, "Financially it's wonderful for him with all that he has. There's nobody working there that has anything close to what he has." It does not take much for workers to piece together the fact that their hard work contributes to the company's financial gain—and Fred is the personification of the company for the workers. One former worker referred to the employee-owner dynamic as "feathering Fred's nest," an idiom that refers to people in power selfishly providing for themselves. Unhappy with the pay rate, this employee left after only a short time there and claimed to be reporting on what others had said—but my sense is that he may not have appreciated the complexity of the dynamic during his short stay there.

The expression "making money for Fred" is more nuanced than the concept of feathering a nest. Workers will use it among themselves on occasion, and it seems to evoke a smirk or a shrug. A definite sense of humor envelops the phrase, and I learned a lot about this phrase, and its subtlety, from Arthur. When he first told me I needed to know about this expression, I told him I had heard of it, but I asked what it meant. He explained that it was a sardonic concept, and he was careful to explain that by this he meant it was "skeptically humorous." This concept contains a positive evaluation of Fred's profit making: "If Fred makes money, we do too." There is a sense of doing something for someone—in this case, doing something for Fred. We might be tempted to think about making money for Fred as a gift from worker to employer. But this is not merely some kind of selfless giving, if ever there was such a thing; the French sociologist Marcel Mauss helped us realize long ago that every gift is exchanged in a social context of expectation and reciprocity.[1] As Arthur points out, "Nobody is altruistic in this venture at Vita—we give something, and we get something back." Indeed, the concept is subtler than a simplistic gift metaphor implies; there is also an underlying sense of sarcasm, because Fred presumably makes more money than do any employees (as any business owner would). Arthur told me the phrase first came from Allen, a long-time Vita Needle employee. "I think Allen is enough of a realist to recognize that if Fred makes money on what we provide in the way of labor and skills, then we benefit also. But Allen knows from experience that it's not a one-for-one deal, and hence the nature of his humor."

It is in part being self-described worker bees (for Fred's queen bee) that motivates the company's employees to work. In the following story from an interview with 74-year-old Sam Stewart, a retired engineer, we get a flavor for the humor, the context, and (more profoundly) the underlying critique of labor relations that pervades the shop floor. The term "bench work" that Sam uses refers to repetitive machine work done at a workbench, where one assembles hundreds of needles at a time. Before I had ever done bench work, I remember being incredulous that anyone could fall asleep while doing it, a claim I heard about 90-year-old Gertrude on multiple occasions. But when I eventually did the work, I soon found myself needing to shake my head, get up to walk around, hum quietly, or talk to my neighbor—anything to keep from dozing. Here is Sam's account:

> I'll tell you a funny story.... I was a little off the wall today. By that I mean, I was in a gregarious mood and... I say and do stupid things because I like to get people laughing. To me, that's a fun thing to do. And I'm doing my bench work and I think of different things, one of which is, I was conscious of the fact that the job I was doing, I picked up some pieces in this hand, and with two fingers, I took one [piece] out and put it on a thing and then I used my finger to push the thing down to make the hole. And I was doing that for two hours, so I went over to my friends Henry and Jack, and I said… "Fred came out to me a while ago and asked me to define my job so that in the future they could say to somebody, 'Well this is such-and-such a job.'" And I said [to Fred], "In my particular case right now, I'm doing a 'three-finger job.'" That's what I said to Henry and Jack. And they're going, "What the hell's he talking about now?" Well, I said, "It's very simple. I start with this hand and I pick up the material, so I'm going to call that my start-ing hand. Then that's for the things that I take with two fingers. I take this part out, put it into there and with this finger I push it and then put it into the case so it's finished." So I said, "My job, the description of my job is that it's a 'three-finger job.'" And I said, "Three-finger jobs are better than six-finger jobs because it gets the material done faster and Fred makes more money and it's more efficient." Well, now they think, "This guy didn't take his pills today!" So I said, "Well, now. Look at you. Show me how you do it." And they're doing bench work, and I said, "There's an example. You use three fingers to do that and you use your whole hand to do that. Too many fingers." So now I get them laughing, and I'm being stupid....
>
> So, Flo, who's a kidder, I went over to Flo and she wanted to know what they were laughing about. I said, "Flo," and I told her the same thing, "Fred told me to do this, and I'm doing a three-finger job over there, and it's good because it's faster. Fred makes more money," and I went through the whole thing. Now she says, "Well, what do you mean by that?" and I said, "Well, show me what you're doing now." So she did, and I said, "See, now look here." I said, "You're using three fingers to stop the envelope from moving." I said, "You could use the side of the box, and you'd use two fingers to do this. And then you put it down and you'd use two more fingers." I said, and I was counting, so I said, "This would be considered an eighteen-finger job." So she goes, "What are you talk-ing about?" So I couldn't help but laugh, you know.... See. So when she caught on that I was being stupid as usual she laughed. But I said, you

know, "This could be really happening, Flo. Because if you do too many things, it's like doing nothing. The work doesn't get done, doesn't get out, and Fred doesn't make any money." I put it all on Fred.

When Sam told me this story, we were both laughing. The interview transcript contains multiple notes indicating that "Caitrin laughs" or "Sam laughs." But this is much more than simply a funny story. It is a funny story that reveals the friendships and connections among coworkers, all in their sixties, seventies, and eighties (his coworkers realize he is being "stupid as usual," that this is not a one-off humorous incident). It is a funny story that indicates an understanding of the relationship between an employee's productivity and a company's profit. It demonstrates that although these workers are certainly at times having fun while working, they are aware that they are all working toward the collective goal of making money for Fred. After all, Sam's closing lesson was "Because if you do too many things, it's like doing nothing. The work doesn't get done, doesn't get out, and Fred doesn't make any money."

When Sam began this story, he said he thought a lot of different things while doing bench work. It was in this meditative work process that he thought up this scenario about the correlation between using fewer fingers and increasing efficiency. This idea led him to entertain his nearby friends, get up and move over to another friend, laugh—all techniques one employs to be able to get through the workday. Noteworthy is that he actually stopped his work altogether to regale his coworkers. Not very efficient. Eventually Sam would have gotten back to his bench, to restart his three-fingered needle assembly.

Sam's three-fingered job story was just one of many daily examples of the pervasive talk of, and private challenges about, how to be more efficient to better advance the collective goal of "making money for Fred." This term, it should now be evident, is in some sense a code phrase. It is code for a cluster of ideas about productivity, efficiency, work process, and connection to a place and a mission. I certainly did not understand all this when I first heard it, but over the course of my research I began to unravel its significance.

These private challenges for efficiency are what I call "efficiency games," and there is no better way to describe them than by reintroducing Carl, who arrives at work well before the sun rises and lets himself in with his own key.

Efficiency Games

For some Vita workers I would sometimes wonder, "Does he ever stop talking?" or "Is he snacking again?" But then there was Carl. Carl was always working, very rarely chitchatting, and he was almost always silent (though I once saw him approach Betty Goode, an 83-year-old coworker who was sharpening the points of a seemingly endless batch of needles and affectionately inquire with a low voice, "How you holding up old lady?"). I would wonder what he must be thinking about when he ground needles, when he cut tubes, or when, as on my first day, he sat across from me doing bench work: setting pointed cannulas into their hubs, over and over again, hundreds in one sitting. Right then, he was wearing an Optivisor (high-tech magnifying glasses) and was hunched over on a stool, forearms set on his custom-made blocks of wood that were covered with terry cloth. Carl's eyes were focused on the tiny cannulas and hubs, and one hand was feeding them onto a crimping machine while the other picked the joined assembly out with tweezers. (Now that I think about it, this was a four-fingered job!) Was Carl thinking about how tightly the machine crimped together the hub and cannula? About the paycheck he would get at the end of the week? About making money for Fred? About his wife's pacemaker? The Red Sox? His stiff hip that had started to make him limp? What does one think about while making needles?

Sure, I thought about my kids, my lunch, my grocery list, my next interview, and my field notes. But I also thought about the task I was working on. I found myself continually setting goals, creating challenges, and being my own efficiency expert. Is it quicker to move my left hand first and then my right? How soon do I have to pull my hand back before the infrared safety light shuts the machine down? Can I prep incoming needles with one hand while doing the operation with the other? Can I do 100 in the next thirty minutes? What about 250 in an hour? Can I fill up two boxes before lunch? Am I faster than the 94-year-old woman who just trained me? Some of what went on in my head was more contemplative, but it was still about my tasks. Am I good at this? Am I as good as the 81-year-old woman who normally does this but is out for cataract surgery? Should I stop to get water or will that make me look lazy? Would I be enjoying this as much if it were my real job?

It turns out that Carl also plays these efficiency games. One day, I spent three hours testing tiny needles to see if water and air would pass through them. My field notes tell it best:

> I was squirting water through the needles and then squirting air through them to make sure that the water could go through and the air could go through. So when Dan Jones [the supervisor] asked me to do this in the morning, he showed me: "First you pick up one needle, and you squirt water through, then you pick up the air compressor hose and squirt the air through." I asked him if I should do the water and the air for one needle, or if I should do the water for a batch, and then the air for a batch.

Dan said that I should do water and air for one needle because the needle was already in my hand, so you might as well do the water and, while you were still holding the needle, do the air. So I did that all morning, from 10:30 to 12:00. And then from 12:30 to a little after 1:00 I was doing that, but then I started to wonder if it would be quicker to test them in batches, all water and then all air. So I took off my watch and decided to time myself, to see how long it took me to do five needles with water and then those same five with air, and then how long it took me to do five by alternating between water and air. I was doing that, and I had just done the all-water batch, and Carl came over. I told Carl what I was doing. He said, "I do that sometimes, I don't tell anyone that is what I am doing, but I do that." And I asked, "Just to keep yourself entertained?" And he said "yes." And then I tried it out, and found out it did seem to be faster doing all water and then all air. Carl, who had left, came back over and said, "A long time ago, there were these time-and-motion studies. You have just done your own time-and-motion study."

Carl here invoked a concept that harks back to Frederick W. Taylor's 1911 treatise *The Principles of Scientific Management,* which was a prescriptive account of modern management principles.[2] Taylorism is also called "scientific management," referring to the "scientific" method for managing workers that Taylor developed out of a systematic study of work behavior. Time-and-motion studies emerged from his principles, as did forms of work regulation such as piecework, incentives, and bonuses. These principles were more pervasive in early-twentieth-century managerial practices but remain in various forms today. Time-and-motion studies, according to one description, "were characterized by the use of a stopwatch to time a worker's sequence of motions, with the goal of determining the one best way to perform a job."[3] So when Carl referred to my doing a time-and-motion study, he situated us both in one aspect of the history of industrial labor in the United States—how an employer can optimize the labor-to-cost ratio.

I should pause here to scold myself for asking Carl such a leading question when I wanted to know why he timed himself: "Just to keep yourself entertained?" Of course, it would have been better for me to simply inquire "Why?" But in light of what else I know about Carl and his coworkers, I can speculate about why he would do his own efficiency study. It was in the process of setting and achieving goals throughout the day that we were able to enjoy the work but also get the work done in an efficient manner. I am struck that Carl and I were both enacting these time-and-motion studies. Others would tell me they also tried to find the most efficient method, set challenges for themselves, and tried to beat their personal best. We each developed our own system for how to best get the job done.

These efficiency games on the Vita shop floor are similar to the games that assembly-line and machine-shop workers use in settings in a variety of times and places. The anthropologist Garry Chick tells of contests among Pennsylvania machine-shop workers to see who can make the most aesthetically pleasing parts (criteria include smooth, intricate, interesting) and in the least amount of time. And he describes a case of betting among workers in an Illinois Kraft Velveeta cheese factory to see who could go the longest without making a mistake as they packed cheese into boxes. The stakes: the loser would buy the winner a fifth of Wild Turkey bourbon.[4] In both these cases, as well as in many (though not all) of the Vita cases, "play" on the job is in the aid of productivity. The opposite approach—tactics of resistance and subversion—has been documented in other studies of factory work, perhaps most famously in the 1987 book by the anthropologist Aihwa Ong entitled *Spirits of Resistance and Capitalist Discipline* about Malaysian electronics factory workers.[5]

At Vita Needle there were many times when Dan Jones, the supervisor, would teach me how to do something, and then eventually I would develop my own system or observe a coworker doing it slightly differently and start to emulate the coworker. Jim Downey explained to me that sometimes the shop worker comes up with his or her own technique even after a supervisor explains how to do something: "We on the shop floor notice things that they do not, or pick up on whether or not a procedure is successful in eliminating a perceived problem or defect, from having worked on several hundred or thousand devices." Here and elsewhere Jim was eloquent about the creativity and personal contribution that can go into the job, and Carl's self-imposed time-and-motion study was one of numerous examples of bringing creativity and experience to the work process.

Jeffrey Barfield, a 74-year-old retired engineer, told me that regardless of the operation he is doing at Vita Needle, he is always trying to do two different things: "One is to make myself more efficient, and the other is to see if I can improve the system for others." Note that his goals are both oriented outward. He wants to be more efficient so he can produce more good work in less time (good for Fred) and he wants to make the system better for his coworkers. He commented that the supervisors are always "open to ideas" from the workers, and I heard this from others as well. There is a definite sense of being part of a team here, where employees can contribute ideas and help each other out. (The favored metaphor is more often one of family, which I will discuss in chapter 2.) Jeffrey's most recent attempt at such process improvements had visible impact. He had been assigned to a job where he would thread six needles onto cardboard cards to prepare them for packing and then shipping. "I realized that if the person doing the staking lines up all the needles in the same way, I could thread the needles much more quickly." Realizing this, he walked over to his friends who were staking and asked them to line up the needles all in the same direction. He told me that now things are going much more quickly for his task: as he describes it, whereas previously those who were lacing the cards could not keep up with the stakers (who affix tubes to bases), now the card lacers are waiting for more needles to come to them. (Of course, this raises the obvious question: are the stakers now grumbling that their process has been made more complex?)

From these few examples we see Carl, Jim, Jeffrey, and me all endeavoring to beat our personal best. In so doing, we would make ourselves feel good, entertained, alert, and, perhaps even in a state of "flow," to use the concept famously advanced by the psychologist Mihaly Csikszentmihalyi. Csikszentmihalyi describes "flow" as a state of happiness that is achieved when one is "completely involved in an activity for its own sake."[6] Of course, when we were beating our personal best we would also do a better job for the company. Thus, on one hand efficiency games provide a personal or psychological benefit—an inward-oriented benefit. But on the other hand, they also provide a definite sense of outward-oriented benefit, though even this comes full circle: good for my coworkers, good for the company, good for Fred (who will then make more money, some of which ultimately comes back to me in the form of the annual bonus).

These efficiency games raise questions that get to the heart of the experiences of working in one's stereotypical golden years in a dusty, noisy, crowded, and stale-smelling factory. In whose interest is it for the workers to be more efficient, to produce a better needle, to save excess material? Who profits, and at whose expense? These are critical questions to understand because the most common query I have gotten from outsiders over the years I have been doing this research has been about exploitation: Are the old people there being exploited?

Although I will discuss the question of exploitation more extensively in chapter 3, it is essential here as it illuminates what workers get out of making money for Fred. When I once mentioned to Jim that people often ask me if the Vita Needle employees are being exploited, he replied, "That is an interesting question. I don't mind being exploited. I know that I could get paid a lot more for things I do. I am not in it for that. This is work I like to do." Jim is one of several workers who are candid with me that they do not need the Vita Needle paycheck for day-to-day survival. "I could go volunteer, I could go work in a hospital or something like that. But why would I leave here, where I have people here that I like. Why would I start over again?" He went on to tell me that what he really likes at Vita Needle is the sense of cooperation and support among the workers. He explained to me that there are little things that may not seem that important to an outsider but that make a big difference to the workers.

He gave me the following example. Recently Charles had come up with a method to do something that worked really well, so Jim told him, "That's great. You did a great job on that." He says that Ruth has said to him, after he squares needles,

"You do this well, and I like to get the squaring after you've done it, because then it makes my job [of sandblasting] easier." Jim added, "We're supportive, we support each other. There are a lot of things that we do that the boss doesn't even know how to do. We are all just part of it together. Even outside of the boss relationship."

Of course, we should acknowledge that Jim, who doesn't mind being exploited (or, at least, who reimagines what "exploitation" means in light of his experiences) is able to say this from his relatively privileged socioeconomic position. Yet I would not therefore dismiss the significance of his sentiments. In a follow-up letter a few days after this discussion, Jim wrote to me, and referred to my speculative use of the term "win-win" (which I had heard from one of Jim's coworkers) to describe what workers and employer get out of the wage bargain at play at Vita Needle. "How do you define what is 'exploitative'? If both Fred and his employees agree on a working arrangement, for a huge variety of reasons that Mary Parker Follett would applaud, how does that register as being exploitative? I agree that it's a 'win-win' situation. We not only both win, we enjoy it, even if we complain about some details."

Jim's reference here to Mary Parker Follett is insightful, and it is striking that both Jim and Carl invoked well-known management theory in discussions with me (a clear remnant of their pre-Vita job histories). Follett was an early-twentieth-century sociologist of management who published important work on industrial relations and is often described in contrast to Taylor. She is known especially for her understanding of the ways in which people work together in reciprocal re-lationships, those that form outside the normal hierarchical organization of the workplace. As one management scholar describes her:

> She recognized that in dealing with personnel the human and technical problems could never be completely separated and that an organization's standards must be allowed much more elasticity than Taylor's system had allowed.... Furthermore, Follett...recognized that a worker was a complex person so that even at work one could still be a father, a mother, a citizen, a religious believer, an artisan, and a businessperson. Thus, one should not be dealt with solely as an employee but as a whole person with other interests, abilities, and persuasions. Unlike Taylor, who had focused on management's need to control the individual worker, Follett perceived the ability of groups of workers to control themselves.[7]

Follett conceived of the workplace as so much more than simply a labor market-place; her work highlights the many ways in which workers live out their hopes and dreams in the workplace. When Jim describes Vita Needle and what the workers get out of it, and when he invokes Follett, he is describing a complicated balance of so-cial and economic value. The workers' sense of value comes through being needed and useful, which is such a strong contrast to American cultural expectations that old people are useless and should be put out to pasture. Their sense of value comes from selling their labor, even if at low cost, because, as Rosa says, "Where could I go? I don't want to go to a nursing home yet." Their sense of value also comes from doing something for someone and with others. Jim referred here to liking the people he works with and relishing the sense of cooperation and support; he cited the value of being appreciated and recognized. People work hard and return day after day to Vita Needle not only so they can entertain themselves with stories, jokes, songs, and efficiency games. They also work hard in order to be recognized and feel valued.[8] These immediate everyday pleasures of work are augmented by a distant pleasure, the monthly paycheck, and especially the annual Christmas bonus.

Codependency in Space and Process

Among the employees, there are everyday interactions in the cramped, cluttered, and sometimes stiflingly hot work space and during steps of the work process that contribute to their sense of value and working toward a collective goal. In some ways, we could compare their sense of interconnection to the camaraderie that comes from sharing a tragic event or to the esprit de corps—the common spirit—of a military unit or sports team (analogies that may be fitting for this primarily male workforce, many of whom are war veterans and were on sports teams in their youth and are avid sports fans today).

Jim Downey's story, "Pigeonholed," which appears before this chapter, provides a good introduction to the atmosphere at Vita Needle. Jim wrote this for me so I could learn about an event that happened on a day I was absent. I love the perspective it provides on a typical workday at Vita Needle. Jim vividly describes the space of the factory (high ceilings, exposed pipes, former dance hall stage); the heat (a never-ending topic of discussion); the sense of small-town Needham (corroborated also by the fact that the chief of police stops by each year on Rosa's birthday to wish her well); the thirst for entertainment and diversions (which we know three-finger Sam often provides); and Fred's integral role in day-to-day matters (he is not a hands-off boss and will even take care of the pesky visiting pigeon).

Vita Needle is a factory in an old dance hall. The former stage is piled high with boxes of needles, tubes, and various stainless steel parts. Its overall production space is small (roughly three thousand square feet), and because nearly every work surface has something on it, sitting down to complete a new task often requires clearing off a space. Some employees spend the bulk of the day in a particular spot (even if they might do multiple jobs), and they may be a bit territorial about their workspace, feeling they need to defend it from encroachment by others. They might even have customized their space with family photos, calendars, plastic flowers, or their own special equipment (calipers, noise-blocking head-phones, safety glasses). One man has replaced the wooden countertop with a piece of marble from home (where his home workshop bench is also marble) "because I like a marble bench." Others also bring in specific items from home, such as the hot water heating pad one woman keeps on her lap; another woman has made a little shelf under her workbench, where she keeps tea bags and cookies. Then there is the "men's lunch corner," where the walls are adorned with racy pinup calendars from years past and posters and postcards of bikini-clad women.

On one of my first visits to Vita Needle, at the annual Christmas party, I met Sophia Lenti, who took me by the hand and told me to come with her. "This is my space, from here, to here." Sophia's space is about three feet of an eight-foot-long workbench, and it looked much neater than anything nearby. Sophia's two stools are adorned with removable handmade cushions, and the work surface is covered with flowered shelf paper. On the shelf above the table are a houseplant and a radio that is tuned in to easy-listening songs and news. Pinned to the shelf and dangling over her workspace, is a large Ziploc bag filled with a stuffed animal and memorabilia (including family photos and postcards); the bag prevents these items from getting soiled by dust and debris.

Women's spaces seem to be neater than men's, and one man described the women's space maintenance as "nest building." He continued, "Well, I mean, they have their work space—and you don't violate their work space. And they're spending, like, a half an hour at the end of the day just to clean the whole thing. They bustle very pointedly cleaning up their little thing." But he did say that some men also have their space. "Carl has marked off a ten-foot space on his counter, and he guards that as *his* space. Now, it's all company space, but I have to *ask* him if I can use it."

At least ten thermometers are situated throughout the shop space, and the ambient temperature may be one of the most frequent topics of daily conversation—especially on a hot summer day, when the absence of air-conditioning is evident. The temperature is a recurring source of conversation, jokes, complaint, and disagreement (too hot in the summer, too cold in the winter). I even heard that when Fred bought new windows to insulate against the cold in winter, they made it too hot, and so now the windows are always cracked open during the winter! I have heard the disagreements blamed on old age—Sam described this as "another problem with the old people." We were discussing this on a very hot July afternoon, in Sam's air-conditioned living room, and he said, "I mean, there's a woman right now, a day like this. If the door is open, the side door, she will complain about being chilly. So they close the door, and somebody else, another elderly person, will say, 'Gee it's stuffy in here.' So that's, you know, everybody's got a different thing going on. And I don't think young people would be bothered by much of that."

There are perhaps ten days a year when the shop floor heat reaches into the nineties, and, as Mike La Rosa, the production manager says, this happens only when there have been three or four straight days of intense heat so the shop does not get the chance to cool down at night. During those times, there is continual conversation about which thermometer is more accurate. Is it the little thermometer by Dan's desk, the tiny thermometer up on a metal pole by Esther's table, or the one by the computer in shipping? Donald Stephens will turn his head and look at Esther's thermometer and will say, "It's ninety-four degrees." But then someone else will look at the thermometer by the microwave, which Dan once designated as the "official" temperature reader, and say, "It's ninety-five over here." There is a refrigerator centrally located in the shop, where people keep their lunches and cold drinks. I heard that one particularly hot day Dan put the thermometer in the freezer because he was sick of people talking about the temperature. When I asked him why there are thermometers around to feed these discussions, he responded with a good-natured sense of defeat (he probably would have thrown his hands up in the air if he had not been holding boxes of cannulas and hubs): "Because they want to talk about how hot it is."

Indeed they do, and there is a palpable sense of bonding or community building that seems to result from the shared experience of sweating and complaining during the process of working. Jim's pigeon story describes a moment of diversion in an otherwise humdrum and sweaty day. Yet even on a day such as that, the workers are nevertheless building a sense of connection with each other in the process of making it through. The hotter it is, the more significant the experience and the resulting bonding among coworkers. And the bonding connects the shop workers and their supervisors because of the marked contrast between their position and the air-conditioned spaces occupied by Fred, his son, the secretary, and the sales staff. Community is built in the context of support and counterpoint.

Many on the shop floor refer to Fred's office as "the meat locker," and the jokes emanating from the temperature differential are widespread. I once heard one worker tell another, "You're not going to believe it. The air conditioning is off in the meat locker." One day David grabbed a flashlight, went into the office, and shone it on the ground and said, "Yep, looks good, just doing my inspection. Yep, yep, yep." He walked around the office, shining the light in there slowly, giving himself ample time to cool off. He finished up, said, "Yep, passes the inspection," and left. When he returned to the sultry shop, his coworkers laughed at his description of his jaunt, especially when he said Fred had come into the otherwise-empty office just when David was finishing his inspection.

In addition to providing an arena for discussion and jokes, the very hot summer days at times provide a tangible reward for workers: the supervisor Brad Hill told me that the workers obsessively look at the thermometers because they want to know if the threshold has yet been hit after which the managers will bring in ice cream or cold drinks for all (though he told me there is in fact no official temperature threshold for that occurrence). As one worker said to me, "It's waiting for the ice cream that gets me through those hot days."

The space at Vita Needle is cramped, a point frequently raised with me in discussions and interviews. Jim once described, for example, that often when one is carrying tubes, there are tables, stools, boxes, machines, or people in the way, and "you'd have to get close to somebody to work around them, to...get the stuff out of there. You're right in the middle of what they're doing." Tight spaces, bumping into others, brushing up against someone—all this can lead to conflict but also to intimacy and joking, depending on moods and personalities. David, a World War II navy veteran who served on submarines in the Pacific Ocean, drew an analogy between the tight spaces at Vita Needle and working on a sub: "We're on a submarine in a sense of our closeness and we just really have to walk or work around each other."

The submarine analogy is relevant to the work space but also the production process because people work on multiple jobs and are often taking over from someone else. David explained that on a sub there is an expression "hot-bunking," which refers to crew members' sharing bunks on a shift basis. Similarly, at Vita Needle, they are hot-bunking in that "we're substituting for each other on the job and somebody will do the fun part, the next person will jump in and take over." As David explains, this requires a lot of cooperation, and as on a boat, "you have to learn to get along or you don't stay on the boat."

The submarine analogy also draws attention to the heavily male atmosphere at Vita Needle, especially in some spaces such as the men's lunch corner with its pinups. The U.S. Navy's announcement in April 2010 that it would place women on submarines was met with resistance in the service because it was believed that this would interfere with the male bonding that many submariners saw as critical to the ship's successful operation. As one sailor commented, "The chief of the boat calls it a brotherhood of master mariners—not a brother and sisterhood.... If all of a sudden they put females on my submarine, things would change so drastically, I don't think we would be able to flow as well."[9] As I discuss further in chapter 2, at Vita Needle, men and women work closely together and enact expected (and what we may consider "traditional") gender roles: women as the nest builders and caretakers (one woman always buys greeting or sympathy cards for coworkers to sign) and men as those who help women with physically intensive tasks such as carrying heavy boxes and brushing snow off their cars.

From start to finish, producing needles may include the following steps: pulling tubes (removing tubes from storage racks), cutting tubes down to size, taping tubes or needles together so the next operations can be done on multiple pieces at once, squaring off the bunch so they are all the same length, and sandblasting or grinding. Needles then are sharpened to a first point and then, for some, to a second point. Some needles are then stamped with needle gauge size and customer name, staked and then quality-tested. The packing and shipping involves sometimes assembling multiple needles onto cardboard (a process called carding), then wrapping and packaging the cards, placing them in boxes, and shipping them out. Some orders will require bending of tubes or needles, flaring ends, gluing or assembling parts. Some jobs are quirky and quite repetitive, such as that which Donald does all day long: he places single, long stainless steel tubes of various diameters into plastic tubes and tops off the tubes with plastic caps. (With the exception of an hour break on the flaring machine off in the corner, Donald does nothing but fill tubes. He tells me that he has elected to stick to one operation rather than being trained on multiple jobs so he does not get confused.)

Other jobs involve receiving tubing that is shipped in, logging it, and putting it on the correct shelves. Two men are charged with designing and making prototypes and customizing machinery to produce those prototypes. The three men in shipping process outgoing deliveries and receive incoming parts. Jobs move in a "progressive bundle system," under which employees work on a batch of needles or tubes and then pass the batch on to coworkers at the next step in the operation. Vita Needle is known for producing small-batch jobs, and at any one moment numerous orders are being filled on the shop floor. Shop workers rotate in and out of jobs all day, so on one workday someone may do three or four different operations. But there are some people who specialize in certain operations, which they are known to be good at, such as Henry Leonard on staking, Flo Cronin on taping, and Jim Downey on squaring.

Jim introduced me to a concept he refers to as "codependency." "We are very codependent. And the quality of the work that somebody does on the front of a job really carries all the way through the job and each step is important. It could be screwed up anywhere along the line." He then described this codependency in an interview worth quoting at length. He started off by referring to a coworker who seems to spend a lot of time "in his own head" and not working. Jim said it makes him wonder, "Are you working?"

> *Jim:* And it's not admired when people don't chunk the work out. . . . And, in fact, I know it *is* admired when you do a good job because I used to get these comments back from Ruth after I'd square stuff. She said, "You do good work," and she . . . has the next step of sandblasting. If it's badly done she can tell right away.
> *Caitrin:* And she'd know whom it came from.
> *Jim:* And she felt very, you know, she took it all to heart, "I'm part of this workforce." And it's ownership of the management responsibilities at

a lower level, that's basically what it is. And a lot of people do that. Not, well, I wouldn't say "a lot." Some people do it.

Caitrin: What do you mean? So, meaning, you're keeping an eye out on how things are turning out?

Jim: Yeah, because I maintain that this is not independent the way Fred says it is. It really is not. It's a fiction. And anybody with any brains can figure that out.

Caitrin: What does Fred say?

Jim: Fred says anybody can come in and just jump in the job and do the next thing. Blah blah blah. That's not true simply because if you screw up the first part of it, everything from there on is going to suffer. And guys like Brad and Dan [supervisors] know better but, the thing is, that their assumption is "you do it to a certain extent," and they're, like, the whole principle of mass production. If you do it that way, you have replaceable parts. They [the new worker on the task] will march through the sequence and be fine if you do it within tolerance [within the required specifications from the buyer]....The problem is that even within tolerance you could screw it up....For example, if David doesn't cut them pretty much the same length, then it's tough for Flo to tape them right.

Jim then discusses various effects of good or poor tube cutting on the final product and how the quality of the cutting affects the ability to tape and then square the cannulas, and then whether or not the cannulas can fit into the hub correctly. And he ends by saying, "So these things are codependent....It's not independent at all. The theory is that it is, but the reality is different."

Jim argues that Fred believes if he puts someone into any job, that person can do a fine job, and the quality of the work is simply up to her or him—each person works an independent step in the production line. But Jim describes the reality otherwise. Interestingly, he uses the term "codependent," though in other interviews he used the term "interdependent" to describe the same phenomenon. When I first heard him use the term "codependency," I questioned it since the term typically has negative connotations of overreliance on a partner. But Jim considers the word in this context to be a positive term synonymous with interdependency. I asked him if this is a technical term or his own:

I've come up with it in an effort to try to explain. If you've done enough of the jobs as I have, you see where [your job] goes. You see how the problem here gets exacerbated here....If you don't straighten it out here. So you try to do the best job you can in the front end so the guy on the other end is not going to have a real difficult time. The people that don't care and are just sloppy, throw it at you, and you end up...you compensate for it by fixing it or throwing it out or something and then you may end up short in production because you've got to throw so much of it out.

In another interview, Jim described a time when a number of shop workers were trying to resolve a problem. The hubs were being drilled out incorrectly, which caused the cannulas to sit crookedly in the hubs. Jim said that he was trying to figure out how to address the problem when Grant Harvey came along, "took the bull by the horns," and figured out how to straighten out the machine. "This is what I call interdependence of different things throughout here. Here's two experienced people that understand each other. We're working together. The boss isn't telling us how to do this. We're working it out."

Jim refers several times to the difference between the managerial perspective and the workers' experiences and understandings. There is much that happens on the shop floor that is not known to managers, and there is a vast industrial relations literature on this topic of the hidden skills of "unskilled" workers. Perhaps the most famous work is the 1978 book by the sociologist Ken Kusterer, *Know-How on the Job*.[10] The hidden skills include inside knowledge of how to get something done, as we see in the various examples here and as I experienced myself. But they also include the ways in which workers serve as their own overseers of productivity by admiring, criticizing, and policing each other for their contributions to the workplace.

Productivity Policing

Back in 1911, Frederick Taylor wrote about the common understanding among workers, at its most extreme, that there was a danger for them in being efficient: more efficiency would mean less time on the job for hourly employees and thus ultimately less pay. As Taylor writes, workmen in almost every trade "ignorantly" believe "that it is against their best interests for each man to turn out each day as much work as possible."[11] Jim and Charles are two people whose past work experiences enable them to devise time-saving processes and tool customizations at Vita Needle. I learned in a joint interview that they both worry about whether or not the efficient methods they devise could ultimately lead to automating people out of a job. This was a prospect Charles worried about because he considered Vita Needle's "prime directive" to be "to hire old people." Jim disagreed with this characterization and said the prime directive was to make money. Charles then conceded:

> *Charles:* In general the prime directive is to make money and, in fact, I think if Fred had a choice of making money or hiring older people, I'm not quite sure. I'm not sure which one would weigh more. I think they're close because his father, I think, started the hiring of older

people, so I'm not sure.[12] And he doesn't want to sell the business, he said. He's mentioned it a couple of times. What would he do? I assume he wants to leave it to his kids, which is why they're there.

Caitrin: So it's striking to me that you say that you think that there is a social part about the hiring of older people.

Charles: Yes, there is.

Caitrin: You think that's actually truly important to the owner of the factory?

Charles: I think so. Yes.

Jim: He's been very forgiving about people. Like Gertrude, who preceded you [speaking to Caitrin]. She was the other lady in her nineties and Gertrude used to fall asleep. We worried about her because the machine would come down like that on her. She wasn't watching what was going on. There was a hundred pounds of pressure on the staker. And I mentioned that I was concerned about that.

Caitrin: You mentioned to whom?

Jim: To Dan and he said, "Well" [Jim mimics a shrug]. And then some other people when they came in, I won't mention their names because they're still there. They were not producing anything either. And, you know, that was an item of concern. And they [the supervisors] weren't worried about it. Basically this blends out in the sense that we all can help each other and the bonus at the end of the year is really everybody's effort. It's not just one person. But people in general, including David and others who spend a fair amount of time talking, admire or don't admire behavior, in terms of getting the job done. You know where Grace stands because she tells you. But other people are quieter about it, but they appreciate the fact that you're out there punching in [on the time clock]. And, yeah, the job is boring sometimes and tedious, but we do it. But along the way we get to interact with each other. We joke around. We lighten it up.

Charles: Actually lightening up is a thing that keeps you going. It's the thing that sort of allows you to maintain your sanity and that's really always been my impression. I used to do that at my other jobs. It's like the whole world is insane. Just let it go. Take it in your stride.

Jim: That's right, it doesn't matter that much anymore.

Here we see Charles and Jim trying to articulate what is the prime directive of their workplace and what their own roles are. We see them trying to understand the balance of social and economic value at Vita Needle. This exchange reveals their sensitivity to managerial perspectives; their own desire to work hard and see others do the same; their enjoyment of the workplace's relaxed, jocular interactions; and their sense of the role of work in their lives now that they are "retired" ("it doesn't matter that much *anymore*").

They also describe here what I call "productivity policing," when coworkers watch for and sometimes act on (enforcing, critiquing) what they perceive to be relative productivity or nonproductivity among coworkers. Ninety-four-year-old Grace is known for getting others to work, which is what Jim has in mind when he remarks that "you know where Grace stands." When Grace notices that the lunch break is taking too long, she will get up and turn on the air compressors and, in so doing, tell people to get back to work. In like vein, I would occasionally hear concern about coworker nonproductivity. At several times one worker confided in me (less like a tattletale and more like a concerned coworker) about those who were talking too much or eating too often. Regarding a coworker he once told me, "He is always feeding himself. How can he be working if he is always eating?"

One day when I was carding needles across the table from Esther, Carl stopped by and suggested to Esther that she "take a good look" at the needles that had come to her for packing from Grace, who had just clocked out. Carl said, "She was doing it faster than I could do it." I was struck by the fact that he was suggesting quietly to Esther that Grace might not have been able to stake the needles as well as she thought she had, and my definite sense was that this skepticism was related to the fact that Grace was 94 whereas Carl was only 79 and had had many more years of industrial work experience. But note that this was not an outright critique with harsh words—merely a gentle suggestion to take a good look. Another time I heard two men discussing a box of needles prepared by another man. Frank said, "Those are from Pat. You know, he just throws things in." And Lou said, "He always does." Then they both in unison said, "When he does something" and laughed faintly. This was in reference to a worker who I had noticed seemed to spend a considerable amount of time tidying his work space, snacking, talking, and relaxing on the fire escape.

When Jim approached Dan about Gertrude's falling asleep while staking, he was concerned about her safety, but there appeared to be an underlying curiosity about her relative nonproductivity. In his comment, safety and nonproductivity seemed to go together: "They were not producing anything *either*. And, you know, that was an item of concern." I found that when I would ask Dan about workers who fell asleep or were less productive than others because of health problems, these conversations always seemed to end up at the same point: a bit of a shrug and a smile from Dan. It was clear that he was performing a complicated balancing act between the two prime directives: providing jobs for old people and making money. This was definitely a managerial challenge for Dan, Brad, and Mike, and I will discuss this more in chapter 3.

But Dan was not the only one who had to perform this kind of balancing act. The shop workers also did on a daily basis, and it was not easy to do, as we can see with Jim's stated concern about Gertrude. I saw a stark example of this balancing act one morning when I was on the job. Shortly before the coffee break, I was inspecting needles, a task that Dan had assigned to me the previous afternoon. I looked up when I overheard 82-year-old Ruth and Dan speaking. Ruth, who had arrived at 6:00 in the morning, had been working on the flaring machine when Dan arrived for the day around 9:30. Dan quickly went over and told her to do something else because they had enough flared needles in stock. Ruth got up, moved to another spot, and began packing needles into boxes. But two hours later, I saw Ken Macaulay working on the same machine, and Ruth saw it too: she stopped by to say to me, "Why did Dan take me off but now Ken is doing that?" Ken never looked well when I knew him (swollen and blotched hands, pale complexion, awkward gait, withdrawn eyes, very thin), and he passed away about six months after this incident. A fellow employee once described him as someone who "moves at a speed that is imperceptible, but that's all right." I understood the last phrase as an indication that this was not a personal insult about Ken, but rather a concession that people work at different speeds and bring various contributions to the workplace and an acknowledgment that there are two prime directives at Vita Needle.

Seeing Ken on this machine just a few hours after Ruth had been kicked off, I wanted to ask Dan about the discrepancy, but I felt I should keep on my job. When eventually I had some damaged needles to show Dan, this gave me the chance to inquire: "Why did you put Ken on a job that you told Ruth was not needed?" Dan was silent, looked a bit uncomfortable, and then said, "That is all Ken can do. His abilities are less and less each month." I was struck that Ken was assigned to do work on an operation that was not needed. What kind of workplace was this where someone was retained even though he could not do the work? I was reminded of an interview I had with 94-year-old Grace, who described Gertrude, the famous sleeper: "She got so that she'd sleep all day long." Grace continued, "She'd have the needle in her hand and she'd fall asleep. She got so bad that we were afraid she'd fall off her chair and get hurt, you know? She'd walk with a cane, she could hardly walk. She really got very bad. But she, I'd say for a year that they practically, you know, just let her come and sit there and sleep."

It is noteworthy that Grace is keenly aware of managerial permissiveness—this is a workplace that allows one to come and sleep! She is not alone in having this awareness, and it certainly affects manager-worker dynamics, underlies the sense of gratitude workers have to Fred for employing them, and enables certain worker diversions such as Sam's three-finger-job joke. I expressed my surprise to Dan that Ken was still working at Vita given his obviously diminished abilities. He replied that he had had to "let people go" because of sleeping and health decline in the past, and that he might need to again. He had at another time told me how difficult he finds this conversation. He has had to phone adult children of an employee to say, "Your father should not be coming to work anymore."

This interaction made me recall my very first discussion with Mike, the production manager, back in 2006. Fred had asked Mike to give me a shop tour, and I vividly remember Mike's telling me that Vita Needle would shock an ergonomics or efficiency expert. This place is not designed for efficiency, he said. When a worker finishes one operation, she might need to walk all the way across the shop to give it to the next worker. Or someone may need to go to two different spots to get the equipment needed to inspect finished needles. So while this may not be the most efficient setup, Mike told me it is good for the Vita Needle workforce. He argued that it is good for the older workers to get up to stretch their legs, walk around, or visit with a friend when they are squeezing by someone as they zigzag from one side of the shop to the other to bring needles to the next production station or retrieve needed parts.

The Christmas Bonus

This crowded and inefficiently designed factory gets transformed once a year into the site of the annual Christmas party, which I have attended four times. At first I was inclined to call it a "holiday" party because of my socialization in a multicultural society, but I was more than once told by workers that it is not that. It is simply a Christmas party. "We don't need to be PC here," one worker explained, a quick dismissal of political correctness and an affirmation of the presumed old-fashioned homogeneity that makes Vita Needle so comfortable for many of those who work there. The party takes place in the production area. Needles, tubes, jigs, packaging, boxes, and dust are pushed aside to make room for an elaborate spread of sweets and savories, sodas, waters, and juices, enough for lunch and then some. Colored Christmas lights dangle from pipes that carry high-pressure air to pneumatic machines throughout the factory. The company covers the cost of the party, and workers joke that it is funded by the proceeds from selling rejected scrap parts that pile up in a box in the corner throughout the year: the more scraps in the box, the bigger the party!

The party begins at morning coffee break time; those who have clocked in stop work to celebrate the holiday—still on the clock. People who have the day off come by, as do spouses, children, and grandchildren (of the Hartman family, supervisors, sales staff, and production workers). Food and drink are consumed amid talking, joking, laughing, and reminiscing, and the celebration is punctuated by holiday hugs, kisses, and best wishes as well as the sound of snapping cameras. There are no formal announcements or speeches, though the informal main event is when

Dan makes his way around the room handing each production worker a wall calendar for the next year (carefully chosen to fit different personalities: flowers, dancing hula girls, sports) and an envelope that contains the annual bonus check.

In a straightforward business-model sense, if Fred makes money, the workers do too. But at Vita, under the Christmas bonus system, the more money Fred makes, the more the workers expect they will make too. From my very first Vita Needle interview through almost every subsequent interview, I would hear about the Christmas bonus, which the workers, supervisors, and Fred himself describe as "profit sharing." The Christmas bonus is best understood as a complicated nexus of productivity, profit, and value.

I heard from many workers about their surprise at the generous size of the bonus check, though the size seems to vary greatly: on one extreme I have heard it described as far bigger than the monthly paycheck. No workers appear to know precisely how the figure is calculated, and they do not seem to know the size of each other's bonuses (though they know the size varies by person). I often heard it described as being based on the size of one's contribution to the year's business. As Allen described it, "Well, they call it profit sharing I think now, but for whatever reason. Maybe it's some legal reason. Or just sounds better, I don't know. But it's probably…it's got to be a share of the profits. Fred decides what you're doing for the company and what you're worth." Another worker called it a "beautiful bonus." He said, "We get a really good bonus. It's like a profit sharing. And, you know, so it should be good this year because we've been *really* busy." Jim told me that the idea behind the bonus is that "We've done a good job on something and made a lot of money, we really worked hard to get it out, so then we all benefit. Which is good." One employee noted that in the white-collar job from which he retired, he had gotten an annual profit-sharing bonus: "It was nowhere near as generous as Fred's, percentage-wise."[13]

Of course the Vita workers receive a regular paycheck throughout the year; the amount varies greatly from person to person depending on the number of hours worked, the base pay rate, and whether or not they worked weekends on overtime pay. Most workers appear to start at above minimum wage, though some with relevant experience earn much more. But it is the Christmas bonus, not the monthly paycheck, that workers return to again and again when they discuss the cooperative, or codependent, work environment at Vita Needle. We heard Jim argue that if some workers are "getting the job done" and others are sleeping on the job, ultimately it "blends out" in the Christmas bonus, which reflects everyone's joint contribution. In fact, it appears to be the sense of joint contribution among all the workers that allows this system to work. Granted, Jim is a very hard worker, never sitting around waiting for something to do. As he described the bonus another time, "I try to do my part. They all benefit from what I do, that is the way I look at it. That bonus at the end of the year. I help create it." Note that here Jim puts himself as a central figure in the value of the bonus, and there is also a clear sense that the size of an individual's bonus is based on her or his contribution.

Something extremely interesting underlies this setup. In one way, the work effort blends out, and it is okay if one person is a little slow because of arthritis or fatigue, or if another one naps on the job. There is a sense that filling the orders is a joint effort at the shop; the shop in this sense is a community. But in another way, workers themselves are the first to expect hard work from everyone, and they are constantly policing each other's productivity. Jim noted that it is clear who is admired or not admired for getting the job done. In regard to those who are not admired, he said that some people are "just marking time and collecting pay, which really annoys me." Or, as he said another time, in reference to a 90-year-old coworker, "David doesn't admire when people come in and just sit on their can and don't do things, wait for somebody to bring them work. I'm not like that, I go out and... say, 'I need something to do.' Most people are like that. There are a few people that just don't have any motivation."

In an interview, Arthur connected his continual efforts to make himself do a better job (with his efficiency games) to the Christmas bonus profit-sharing model. He described what he thinks about while working:

> *Arthur:* I'm thinking "how can I make this better, how can I go faster?"... Dan has come over to comment on it at times: he said, "Arthur, you've already had your career. There's no reason for you to push yourself. You're competing against yourself." That was his comment on me.
>
> *Caitrin:* Really? Wow.
>
> *Arthur:* Yes. And he's right!
>
> *Caitrin:* So there's no reason? But you just said, "I'm trying to think, how can I make it better, how can I make it faster?" Is there no reason to make it better or faster?
>
> *Arthur:* Yeah! Because, at the end of the year, Fred has a bonus, and we all benefit from each other's contribution. So to that extent, people there, who've been there a long time, recognize that: that you're trying to, you know, make a little contribution—turn in a good product, quickly. And they [the management], they support that!

This is a rich exchange for several reasons. Arthur is struggling to reconcile his desire to work hard and to best himself with the fact that he does not need to do so. This is not his career. At other times he has told me that he does not even want a job back in the rat race, where, as a corporate accountant, he long felt the need to ascend a ladder, to advance in his job. But Arthur also likes that the workplace recognizes hard work. The monthly paycheck is one form of affirmation, but there are others too. Fred will call shop meetings to share information about sales figures, and he will enthusiastically thank workers when business is booming. On a one-to-one basis, Fred, as well as Mike, Dan, and Brad, is quick to compliment workers for good work, such as when Fred makes his rounds on the shop floor and visits people as they work. And we have already heard of compliments among workers for a job well done. The more distant form of affirmation is the annual Christmas bonus, which is always expected.

But what happens when the bonus does not meet expectations? I heard about one case, from many years before, in which a worker received a much smaller bonus than he was accustomed to. The person who told me the story said that for some reason this worker and Fred had gotten into a lot of small arguments all year. When the check came out, "He went storming in wanting to know why he didn't get as much. And he said, 'Don't I do the work?' And Fred says, 'Well, I don't just mark on the work.'" And I also heard concern after one recent year when sales figures were high and bonuses were low. After that year I heard some skeptical and critical comments about the bonus. For example, three-finger Sam told me that after that year of small bonuses, he developed a newfound concern about the addition of machines to the shop. Referring to Fred's purchase of a new machine, he said, "And he just bought this $100,000 machine so I kiddingly have been saying… 'Oh, see that machine? There goes our bonus.' I say it out loud, you know. And that's what's going to happen. But he's entitled to it. He's the boss…. As I tell people, 'Wait a minute. He can do whatever he wants with his money,' which is true." Here Sam was using humor to "kiddingly" criticize Fred for a capital expenditure that Sam predicted would come directly out of his future Christmas bonus, and yet Sam was obviously trying to empathize with Fred's position as boss and business owner. It's Fred's money. He can do what he wants with it. This sentiment is consistent with a pervasive feeling at the factory that the workers' own ability to work there and to get a bonus is entirely due to Fred's largesse. It is due to Fred's business acumen but also to his good will and social conscience that they have jobs in the first place. This is a very personal dynamic. They are not dealing with an anonymous and distant boss at the central office. They are making money for Fred, the very man who visits the shop floor, jokes around, checks on their work, brings his dog to the office, sends flowers when someone is ill. This is the same man who greeted the workers one after another in the receiving line for condolences at his own father's funeral.

Productivity, People, and Purpose in Retirement

Efficiency games, codependency, policing productivity, coworker affirmation: all these experiences combine to reveal the significance of the phrase "making money for Fred." They all have in common a sense of being productive and purposeful and in interaction with others in old age.

One might be surprised to think of assembly work as enabling creativity and a sense of purpose (claims that fly in the face of Marxian notions of the alienation of factory work), yet Carl, Jim, and their coworkers in some ways exemplify Csikszentmihalyi's arguments about how activities that are optimum for the participant can provide a state of flow. He explains that when one is in flow, "The ego falls away. Time flies. Every action, movement, and thought follows inevitably from the previous one, like playing jazz. Your whole being is involved, and you're using your skills to the utmost."[14] In his numerous writings on flow, Csikszentmihalyi argues that happiness emerges when one can achieve flow, and that in a state of flow, one experiences a sense of purpose, resolve, and harmony. When I think of Carl and many of his coworkers—dedicated, hardworking, and spending their retirement years in a factory—I think about people who have found a sense of purpose in the process of work.

Indeed, Csikszentmihalyi argues that work is an important place for people to achieve flow, and he emphasizes that the work does not need to be glamorous and high-status, like that of a surgeon. He mentions several times that even assembly-line workers, who have what are perhaps the most stereotypically boring and alienating of jobs, can achieve flow. He describes a Chicago factory worker named Rico, and if we think back to Carl's reference to time-and-motion studies, this description is strikingly similar to my own and Carl's experiences at Vita Needle:

> The task he has to perform on each unit that passes in front of his station should take forty-three seconds to perform—the same exact operation almost six hundred times in a working day. Most people would grow tired of such work very soon. But Rico has been at this job for over five years, and he still enjoys it. The reason is that he approaches his task in the same way an Olympic athlete approaches his event: How can I beat my record? Like the runner who trains for years to shave a few seconds off his best performance on the track, Rico has trained himself to better his time on the assembly line. With the painstaking care of a surgeon, he has worked out a private routine for how to use his tools, how to do his moves. After five years, his best average for a day has been twenty-eight seconds per unit. In part he tries to improve his performance to earn a bonus and the respect of his supervisors. But most often he does not even let on to others that he is ahead and lets his success pass unnoticed. It is enough to know that he can do it, because when he is working at top performance the experience is so enthralling that it is almost painful for him to slow down. "It's better than anything else," Rico says. "It's a whole lot better than watching TV."[15]

Csikszentmihalyi notes here that the financial rewards of high performance are not the simple end goal. There is a sense of satisfaction gained through experiencing top performance. When Carl mentions his time-and-motion studies, and when Jim describes the worker finding the best way to approach a task, we see these workers achieving happiness through work even though they are well past an age when they typically might have an opportunity to do so. They are challenged, rewarded, and feeling productive. And meanwhile, they tell me that they have seen retired peers and siblings struggle with the common retiree ailment of feeling bored and unfulfilled, as they lack that mooring and purpose that work can provide.

Rico's reference to television is similar to Charles's earlier remark: "There is only so much television you can watch," he said, listing the most obvious alternative he could think of—and an alternative that many in the United States know has adverse health effects. As Allen once said to me, alluding to the health effects of a sedentary lifestyle, "You look at these people who've retired, and I've got some of them in my family. They retired, they bought matching recliners and went down the cellar and . . . they've got the medical bills to prove it." Indeed, Csikszentmihalyi notes that it is more often during the process of work, rather than at leisure, that people experience flow.

This point about the surprising pleasures of work over leisure corroborates the growing understanding of how the transition to retirement can be more difficult than retirees expect. In recent years a small retirement-planning industry has emerged in the United States, offering seminars, for example, on how retirees can find meaningful hobbies and volunteer activities—even before they retire. I have yet to see such a seminar focus on the benefits for happy retirement that minimum-wage assembly-line labor can bring, and I hope it is evident that I do not suggest something as simple as that. There are a variety of reasons that Vita Needle works for its employees; this is not a solution that would fit all. But two key lessons we can learn from Vita are that having a sense of purpose in retirement is important and that it is critical for people to interact with others.

The organization Civic Ventures is spearheading the creation of opportunities in the United States for people to do meaningful work in their conventional retirement years. Mark Freedman, Civic Venture's CEO and founder, identifies a number of elements that older workers value. One he refers to with the phrase "people and purpose." As he says, older workers value "connections to others committed to similar goals, and a reason to get up in the morning."[16] Another element he identifies is that older workers want their work to have social impact. Freedman describes this as "work that is not only personally meaningful but that means something important in service to the wider community." Freedman's comments about the importance of people contact resonate with Csikszentmihalyi's insights that the happiness achieved in an optimal experience provides a sense of purpose, and such happiness is also often found in the company of others. As Csikszentmihalyi notes, "Everyone feels more alive when surrounded with other people."[17] He adds that being with others can help people focus their thoughts and not, for example, obsess over problems.[18] This point certainly reminds me of comments I would often hear from Vita employees about how working keeps them busy, and, as Charles once put it, "keeps my mind off my aches and pains."

I heard about the significance of people, purpose, and social impact when I interviewed Dr. Simon Weitzman, a Needham physician who is also the medical director at a local continuous-care retirement community. I had heard many times at Vita Needle that some workers were there on their doctor's recommendations, so I wanted to get a sense from Dr. Weitzman of what work provides to older workers—in addition to a paycheck. In response to a question about how work affects older workers' health, Dr. Weitzman said the following:

> I think that a lot of the older people we see here who are sharpest, are people who remain employed. And it's hard to separate whether you are employed because you're still sharp or vice versa. But definitely…the sharpest older people that we have [as patients] are working, are usually doing something and most of the time, [they are] doing something *for* someone. The interaction *with* other people or the work *intended for others* helps.

Dr. Weitzman here emphasized working *with* people and working *for* people. He also added that for older workers, "Work provides an umbrella. It provides a blanket. It provides love. It provides warmth. It provides everything that has nothing to do with money."

Vita Needle's workforce is definitely older than what would be found in your typical manufacturing facility, though, as we saw in the introduction, the workers may not necessarily consider themselves old. The employees bring to work considerable and varied past work experiences. Some have age-related health considerations that may lead to their inability to contribute as much as others or may necessitate flexible scheduling (such as Carl, who arrives to work at 3:30 am, wide awake due to his sleep apnea). Others may have health problems that necessitate specific work assignments, like Grace who suffers from macular degeneration but whose work relies more on her other senses. They have a work ethic they claim is connected to their age and generation and that they assert is absent among young people. And they seem to want to do something for someone. Yes, it seems surprising that the *someone* includes their boss (and not hospital patients, premature babies, illiterate adults—to name more obvious volunteer options), but this is one thing that makes Vita Needle so fascinating. Dr. Weitzman was careful to say that the work that provides an umbrella, a blanket, love, and warmth does not need to be *paid*. Volunteerism can also provide a sense of purpose, but earning a wage plays a critical role for workers at Vita Needle as they make sense of the value of their skills and time. These workers are making money for themselves. And, more important in some forms of accounting, they are making money for Fred.

Pizza Times

This evening, minutes after finishing this chapter, I went to the grocery store in Needham, where I ran into Pete Russell, a longtime Vita Needle employee. When I told him I had just finished writing a chapter called "Making Money for Fred," Pete responded instantly, "Oh, we like that."

> *Caitrin:* You have heard that expression?
>
> *Pete:* Yes, we use it a lot. I don't mind making money for Fred.
>
> *Caitrin:* Why not?
>
> *Pete:* Bonus! We get a bonus. [Laughs.] But not just that. It means we're succeeding. We're doing a good job. Just the other day Fred had a lunch for us, a big spread, pizza and everything. To celebrate the most profitable first quarter in the company's history.
>
> *Caitrin:* How did you feel about that?
>
> *Pete:* How did I feel? Indigestion. [Laughs.] Is that what you mean? [Laughs.] Naaaw. I felt good because *we* did that [i.e., we made it a profitable quarter]. And we were still on the clock. Got a longer lunch break. Thirty minutes. I liked that the most.

In that brief exchange, Pete—yet another Vita Needle employee who is always joking, always so much fun to meet up with—had affirmed my understanding of this phrase. Moments after this conversation, I drove to the center of town to get pizza for my kids in a restaurant directly across from Vita Needle. I pulled my car into a metered space in front of Vita Needle and looked up to see Fred, with his German shepherd, who sometimes accompanies him to work. Fred said, "Coming for the late shift?" I laughed and we chatted about my poor parking skills, pizza, the dog, and other mundane topics. When I walked away, I thought I heard the sounds of the fake owl atop the roof, the very one that Jim Downey described in "Pigeonholed."

Shop floor. Photo by Caitrin Lynch.

ANTIQUE MACHINERY AND ANTIQUE PEOPLE

The Vita Needle Family

The Dee Dee Game: only two players are needed, the setting is the shop floor, and the objective is to stump your opponent. One worker stops by the workstation of another, humming the tune of a popular song from an age long past, a song that just happened to pop into his or her head. The listener in turn is challenged to recall the song's title. The game's name comes from singing a song's melody (as in dee dee dah dah duh dum). I had heard about this game in interviews, and only three days into my work at Vita Needle I saw a round played. While Pete (age 80) was teaching me to coil tiny wire tubes with a custom-made jig, we were talking about how many children we each have, how many grandchildren he has, and where everyone lives now. Pete then mentioned a family tragedy, and when I expressed condolences, he said, "Aww, that was a long time ago," and then started to sing a song I did not know but whose lines I now cannot forget: "Into each life some rain must fall / But too much is falling in mine / Into each heart some tears must fall / But some day the sun will shine." Pete put down his work, walked over to Flo Cronin, and said, "Here's one." Flo paused from grouping needles into packets, cocked her ear and tapped her fingers, and hummed along hesitantly. It sounded familiar, but she could not quite place it until Pete began to sing, "Into each life some rain must fall," at which point Flo laughed and joined in, singing this 1944 top-of-the-charts hit sung by the Ink Spots and Ella Fitzgerald. "That's the first time I've seen him stump her," remarked Charles, who was working nearby. A few days later I saw Flo one-up Pete when she hummed to him "The Way You Look Tonight," first sung by Fred Astaire in 1936, known by many for Frank Sinatra's 1964 rendition, and performed by numerous artists before and after Sinatra.

The Dee Dee Game exemplifies something Esther once told me. I had heard stories and reflections from some employees implying that Vita Needle was an oasis in a society that looks down upon or ignores older adults or assumes they are "the living dead" (as one worker put it). I have often heard people say that old people are invisible in U.S. society (an experience similar to being black in the United States, which Ralph Ellison so famously described in his 1952 book *Invisible Man*).[1] Esther was eloquent on this experience of invisibility:

> You just feel like you're a fifth wheel when you're with a younger group.... They don't let you join in in anything.... You're just sitting on the outside, looking in. And I felt that almost the day after my husband died, that feeling. It's just depressing. I remember being over at my son's around Easter Day, and my husband died in February. I remember being over there for Easter, and I was joining in, but I felt like a fifth wheel. And when you're outside, you love to be with your family too, but somehow you become closer with those of your own age group.

In this comment, Esther slides between, on one hand, a notion of inside and outside her family and, on the other hand, a notion of inside and outside her workplace. Within her own family, she has the feeling of being outside (like a fifth wheel) the world of younger people. By contrast, when she is inside Vita Needle, among people close to her own age, she feels like an insider.

Moments earlier in that same interview I had asked Esther what she liked about work. Referring to Mason Hartman, the former company president (Fred's father), without hesitation Esther said, "The friendships. When I lost my husband, Mason said to me 'You come back to work, Esther, because it's therapy.' And it is. It truly is. It truly is." Esther next told me that a former coworker developed a severe illness after she stopped working at Vita Needle. When Esther then pronounced, "It is the beginning of the end when you stop working," I asked her why:

> Well, because it [work] gives you a reason to get up in the morning. And if you're hanging around the house all day, you know, it would be pretty boring. You can't be doing something every day. And we're all approximately the same age, so we can all talk about our aches and pains. Sing the old songs... talk about the old times. And, when I'm with my kids, half the time I don't know what they're talking about. And I look back and now I know what my father meant when he said, "I wish somebody my age were still alive."

So here is 85-year-old Esther, working at Vita Needle five days a week, reminiscing with friends about old times and comparing notes on aches and pains. Esther says here "we're all approximately the same age." Although we know that the ages of Vita's workers are diverse, Esther thinks of the other people who are old by conventional definitions. To Esther, Vita is marked by a sameness of aging experiences.

Esther prefers to work at Vita Needle rather than volunteering somewhere. She says she spent many years volunteering in her children's schools as a room mother, but she prefers the regular contact with coworkers that you get at Vita— personal relationships are central to her assessment of the value of Vita in her life. Esther had earlier mentioned that she uses her paycheck for "my gasoline, and my groceries, and my hairdo." I asked if it is the pay that makes the difference between this work and volunteer work. "I really don't think it's the pay, I mean ... [pause], we don't get paid that much. We're not going to make our fortunes. So um, I don't know what it is really [pause]. Well, it's almost like we're a family." Esther then paused again and asked me to turn off the voice recorder. I complied and then, although we were alone in her house, in a whispered voice she told me about some of her coworkers who felt estranged from their families and unwelcome at family get-togethers. It was when I turned my recorder back on that she described herself as feeling like a fifth wheel.

Esther was not at all alone in describing Vita Needle as everything the outside is not. Vita Needle is closeness, friends, being part of a community, being needed, being relevant, mattering. When Esther grasped for a word and eventually said "it's almost like we're a family," she was attempting to explain what Vita means to her. She had settled on the concept of family but then immediately contrasted this Vita family with her and her coworkers' outside-of-work families. For the sake of clarity I designate the outside families as "real" families, but I caution that with the term "real" I imply no value judgment. In Esther's comparison, those kin-based families came up short.

Like Esther, others confided with me about problems with family relationships, such as children's persistent worries about a parent's health and children wanting parents to stop driving or stop working. One man and his three brothers do not speak to each other because of a conflict over the inheritance when their parents died. Another man divulged that he was hurt when his great-grandson had a recent birthday party, in the next town over, and he was not invited. Others wish their out-of-state children would visit more often. Women are divorced. Men and women are widowed. I heard that one former worker had been vocal in her anger at her deceased husband for dying first and thereby putting her in the situation she is in: lonely and in financial need.

Even in the face of painful family relationships, Esther and her coworkers frequently use the term "family" to describe Vita Needle. This "imagined" family is the one that seems to match their ideal of what the concept of family *should* mean, and here they invoke an idea with a complex and changing history in the United States.[2] When the workers refer to Vita as family, they are attempting to create and preserve an archetypical desired family that they long for even outside work. In so doing, they fight against the sense of marginality, loneliness, and uselessness that they often feel as older adults outside work. They settle on the word "family" because this is a term readily available to describe relationships of closeness—even if in practice families are often estranged, competitive, and full of misunderstandings and argument. When we hear Esther describe the pain of outside-of-work families, we see her making sense of how Vita Needle may be more like a family than her real one. Although it may seem counterintuitive, in some ways it is the sense of alienation in their family situations that sets Vita's older workers up for finding meaning and intimacy in work.[3]

Esther brings her own experiences with family into conversation with her idealized image of family, an ideal that has a deep hold in American society, where popular culture is replete with notions of an idyllic family symbolized in the phrases "Home sweet home" and "Blood is thicker than water," as well as in practices such as the family dinner and family reunions.[4] But we also see that Esther is up against American society's imperfect vocabulary to describe family. There is no single term for what Esther describes. When Vita's workers use the term "family," they employ a ready kinship analogy, yet they describe something that this kinship term does not always capture: friendship, intimacy, connection, sameness, and belonging. Although anthropologists conventionally use the term "kinship" to describe people's relatedness by blood or marriage, the term has come under scrutiny because it fails to capture forms of relatedness not covered by conventional understandings of blood and marriage—the most obvious examples being adoption and homosexual families. Anthropologist John Borneman advocates replacing the term "kinship" with the phrase "caring and being cared for," because it allows us to examine the "processes of voluntary affiliation" among people, the many forms of deep relationships of care and reciprocity that do not fit into a normative notion of kinship.[5]

To the workers, being part of Vita Needle's family means the chance to care for others and to have that care reciprocated. Core meanings of family at Vita also include the chance to belong, to be with multiple generations, and to work toward a common purpose. For Vita's workers, the notion of family takes an unusual and marvelous turn; theirs is a new kind of family, similar to families described by the anthropologist Kath Weston. Her work on gay and lesbian families shows how they challenge us to see that the meaning of kinship is culturally constructed (like age, race, and gender) in distinctive ways in different social settings.[6] In keeping with what Borneman has suggested, these workers have chosen to be here, among peers and coworkers who are friends, who make them feel alive, and who provide them with a sense of purpose and belonging. This sense of vitality, belonging, and care is produced in daily interactions on the shop floor; in some cases, the interactions may have nothing to do directly with the work process, but they give that process meaning. Management in various ways condones much of this. Pete, for example, knew it would be okay to put down his work to play the Dee Dee Game. Does Vita Needle management intentionally create a family environment on the shop floor to cultivate worker loyalty, a managerial technique familiar to us in the history of capitalist labor-management relationships? Let's take a closer look.

Family Business and the Idealized Family

Vita's Jerry Reilly, a 73-year-old former Raytheon unionized factory worker, once spoke with me about the Hartman family, who owns Vita Needle:

> They're like the last of a breed of, of, well, Yankee entrepreneurship. I think of Abraham and his family going across the [desert]. Because he had his family but he also had his slaves and his servants. But you [the slaves and servants] were part of the household.... A small business entrepreneur is really struggling today to stay alive. Same as the family farmer. But they are vital to the health of the nation. And sure, they should get paid more [than their employees]. They own the machines. They made the investment.... They own the building and they own the machines, they own the capital.... So, a family-owned business: a person gets rich, fine. But he's doing a good service and he's working and he's creating value for the community, he's creating value for the marketplace. But the other thing about it is... corporations don't care about the environment, they don't care about the future. They don't care about my grandchildren. But a guy like Fred [does], because it's already a fourth-generation family, a fourth-generation business.[7] And it's a nice enough business. In all probability, his kids and grandchildren will probably want to take over it. And... that's good, but the thing is that when he's thinking of the future, when he's making a business decision or an investment decision or spending decision, he's thinking about his grandchildren. And if he's concerned about the world that his grandchildren are going to grow up in, my grandchild is going to grow up in that same world.

Jerry highlights assumptions about the meanings we attach to family, and he depicts Fred as a father figure like the biblical Abraham, providing a service by employing people. And Fred's beneficent reach as a father figure is not just over

Jerry, Grant, Rosa, Flo, and other workers—it also extends to Jerry's own grand-children. As Jerry imagines it, Fred's concern for his own grandchildren will ben-efit Jerry's grandchild. Jerry ends on a multigenerational family note when he explains that Fred has the welfare of Jerry's own grandchildren in mind when he makes business decisions. Important to Jerry is the fact that Fred's is a *family* business. In his analysis, unlike absentee-owner stockholders, a family business owner takes risks and makes decisions for the greater good. Here Jerry even la-bels Fred's employment policy as a "good service"; another time he called it a "public service."

The concept of family provides a framework for Jerry and other workers to describe the sense of comfort and sanctuary that Vita Needle enables, and it is an imagined, idealized (homogeneous and happy) family that they have in mind. The family business model provides the basic structure for the family metaphor, for it provides a ready example of multiple generations, emotional involvement, and work toward a common purpose. As Arthur said, "When it's a small firm that's family owned like this, you identify with the owners, you identify with the family." And as Jim once noted to me, "The three generations of family involve-ment have set an atmosphere that goes further than it initially appears. Both Carl and I were very attached to Mason [Fred's father], and working alongside the children of employees and management cements the bond we felt." The Hartman family's presence permeates the workplace: there are several Hartmans around on a daily basis; the factory shut down for a morning in 2007 for employees to attend Mason Hartman's funeral; the longtime workers have seen Fred's children sweep floors and paint bathrooms; Fred's and Frederick's dogs (Ivan and Milo) both sometimes come to work, the latter a giant Newfoundland who drools on the office floor; photos of deceased past-president family members are on the walls in the hallway. The Vita Needle photo album, which is located in the hallway for anyone to thumb through, includes Christmas party photos of Fred's kids as babies and growing up, and it also includes photos of family members of workers and managers who have attended these parties.

The meanings of family at Vita are deeply embedded in U.S. notions of family, which are complex, changing, and contested—and yet these workers appear to agree on a certain image of family as harmonious and integrated.[8] Vita's workers have invested in a certain memory of a bygone age in America where things were simpler; their own sense of identity comes from their sense of participation in a traditional, Protestant ethic-imbued, American life.[9] The vast majority of Vita workers are men. Born in the 1920s and 1930s, Jerry, Jim, Pete, and most of their coworkers are white Christian men who profited from the post-World War II eco-nomic prosperity in the United States. Most are at least high school graduates— some the first in their family to have graduated from high school—and some have master's degrees. They worked hard to live the stereotypical American dream: they married, supported children who went on to get college degrees, saved money, and owned their own homes. Much of this was financially feasible because of federal financial policies such as housing loans established after World War II. They all now draw incomes from Social Security and support from Medicare, policies adopted in the United States in the 1935 Social Security Act and, in the case of Medicare, with the Social Security Amendments of 1965. And many also draw income from private pensions and investments.[10]

When these men, and the many fewer women with whom they work, refer to Vita Needle as a family, it is a specific kind of family they imagine. This is not a racially diverse multicultural family, but a hard-working white Christian family steeped in traditions of thrift and hard work. *The Adventures of Ozzie and Harriet,* the 1950s television program that has come to symbolize an idealized vision of American family, would be significant to many Vita workers. They were at least teenagers if not adults during the heyday of the 1950s American family fable that sociologist Judith Stacey (*In the Name of the Family*) and historian Stephanie Coontz (*The Way We Never Were*) describe in their work.[11] Likewise, the historian John Gillis meticulously demonstrates the relatively recent vintage of romantic concepts of family values that we assume have deep histories.[12] These scholars have demonstrated the mythical status of the widespread image of the 1950s' happily married heterosexual couple with breadwinning father, stay-at-home-mom, and children on a straight path to success. So although even the 1950s picture is much muddier than this fable implies, the Vita workers came of age at that time, and their own memories are often couched in its idealized images.[13]

Family Features at Vita Needle

In Vita Needle, the workers seem to find much of what an idealized family connotes to them: support, interdependence, common purpose, comfort, resilience, and honest, open, shared memories and experiences. Workers commonly invoke the concepts of interdependence (Jim's codependence) and common purpose in the production process. Coworkers help each other out: they fix someone else's crooked needles, pick things up off the floor, carry boxes, find missing parts. Coworkers, managers, and owners have a strong perception of mutual obligation to each other and address each other on a first-name basis, a linguistic gesture of equality and common purpose. There are also shared memories and experiences rooted in shared backgrounds and age. As Allen once said, referring to management, "They're reasonable, we're reasonable."

TABLE 1. Positive meanings of family at Vita Needle

FAMILY FEATURE	POSITIVE CONNOTATION
Mixed gender	Harmonious integration of women's and men's presumed natural inclinations toward caregiving (women) and provisioning (men)
Father figure	Taking care of and providing for family
Mother figure	Hominess, nurturing, cleaning
Multigenerational relationships	Learn from and teach each other; older folk stay on top of things because youth are around; young learn from old
Emotional bonds	Love and support, receiving and giving care

Notions of family are deployed in daily life as an expression of the close ties that connect people at Vita Needle, creating a kind of intimacy, the sense of sameness and connection (due to shared experiences and a shared stage in life). Table 1 is a schematization of the varieties of positive meanings of family at Vita Needle. While each of these family features can have its negative aspects (even mixed gender, for those who seek camaraderie in same-sex environments like men's or women's clubs), at Vita Needle it is generally the positive that is emphasized when workers invoke the family metaphor for their workplace. Vita employees' idealization of the concept of family minimizes or neutralizes any of the negative connotations that can be evoked by the features above.

Mixed Gender

At Vita Needle, men and women reproduce long-established gender roles and identities in the workplace.[14] Men are in the overwhelming majority at Vita Needle, and the majority of them have retired from some other job (the few exceptions either have been lifelong factory workers or did not retire but were laid off). They find Vita Needle a sociable place where they can also get paid. Arthur contrasted working at Vita Needle with the option of volunteering someplace, such as at the nearby hospital: "I want to be part of something that people care about and, it's not as if you wouldn't care about your work in the hospital, and you wouldn't form associations there, too. It's just that it's a different deal and maybe it's the number of men that are there [at Vita]. I like the ladies, too, that's not a problem. It adds a different flavor to it." Arthur then recalled his career job in an office and the men he knew there. "We had a lot of relationships with people. It was nice." He pointed out that at Vita Needle he could have those same kinds of relationships with other men: "Well, they're similar ages, similar problems, similar things with what we're interested in and, I mean, it's a lot of sports talk that goes on. There's a lot of things that happen there that it, there's, it's a different interaction between men and men and men and women."

The men's lunch corner exemplifies the relationships among the men at Vita Needle—like a "men's club," the term Charles used to describe the company. At lunchtime five or six men gather on stools in a corner where the wall art consists of nearly nude women; here they eat and talk about sports, grandkids, the job they were just working on, politics, the weather. Whereas the racy wall decor might be frowned upon elsewhere, here it seems to go unmentioned, except for the occasional joking comment. I got the distinct impression that rules of decorum are different inside Vita Needle. I even heard that when there had been required workplace sexual harassment training, one of the older Vita women had jokingly said to a male coworker, "Oooh, harass me!"[15]

Vita's men have been able to continue work-based social connections in their retirement years. They are quick to joke that they are here because their wives forced them out of the house—a joke that perpetuates stereotypical gender roles of women as the behind-the-scenes rulers of the home. I would hear the humorous expression that the marriage vow counts "in sickness and in health, but not for lunch," or that these men seek refuge at Vita in order to avoid membership in the "Honey Do Club": "Honey, do this. Honey, do that." We see here the carving of single gender space within the workplace, a process that may parallel a gendering of space at home, where the living room or garage may be coded as men's space and the kitchen and laundry room as women's. And it certainly seems to parallel earlier notions in U.S. society of workplaces as men's spaces and home as women's (for a representative portrayal, see the popular contemporary television series *Mad Men* and its depiction of 1960s office culture).[16] These Vita Needle men like being able to spend time with other men, away from their wives, near pinups—this is a chance to just be men again.

Father Figure

Jerry and others evaluate Fred as a positive father figure, though at 56 he is younger than most of his employees. One worker mentioned Gertrude the sleeper and said that Fred's permissiveness shows how he keeps an eye out for the workers. This worker interpreted Fred's care to be "like caring for a grandparent." Obviously Fred cannot be both the father and the grandchild, but both analogies were useful to workers for describing how Vita is like a family. The father analogy goes further too. One worker who is especially close to many of the women workers is jokingly referred to by a coworker as a father confessor—a reference to the Catholic notion of a priest as someone in whom one confides. Here this concept of father confessor (and, below, den mother) does not refer to biological family but to roles that are family-like in American society. There is a certain view of protective masculinity that this notion of fatherhood implies.

In terms of gender roles, men seem to feel protective of the women, and want to help them, as we see in Fred's attitude toward Gertrude or in Jim's daily frequent trips to the sidewalk to feed Esther's parking meter. Sam Stewart's wife, Barbara, told me that Sam "likes to help the old ladies." He clears the snow off their cars if it snows during the workday. She proudly noted to me, "One lady got sick at work and he was very helpful to her. Another one fell and he called the ambulance." I have seen many cases of men helping women in such ways. On the negative side, a father figure could connote patriarchal authority and the tendency to be abusive or ignorant of alternatives. In this regard, I did sometimes hear concern that Fred is too focused on the bottom line and that he does not really listen to workers' ideas. And yet I much more frequently heard a more nuanced discussion of Fred's business acumen and the benefits to all of making money for Fred.

Mother Figure

Though Rosa at 99 is the eldest, she is referred to with terms such as "mascot" and "national treasure," whereas 82-year-old Flo is more the mother figure. (This may not be a contradiction; at 99 Rosa is more than a mother—she is a treasure.) Flo is the "den mother," as one male coworker says, using a Boy Scout analogy. This may be because it is Flo who invariably purchases cards and gets them signed when someone is ill or has experienced a death, including the death of a pet. As Arthur remarked, "It's like a family that way." And women are "nest builders," keeping the home clean—though they tend to just focus on their own work areas, which they make homey with artificial flowers, stool cushions, and photographs. Rosa also tends the potted plants hanging in the window. Women's "care work" at Vita tends to be in the area of kin work.[17] In this sense the care work has conventional gender dynamics, though both genders do participate in forms of care: men do the physical work (both in terms of caring for each other and in terms of the factory work) and women the affective work. The anthropologist Micaela di Leonardo has described how women in Italian American households tend to be engaged in kin work, which includes sending letters and cards and organizing holiday gatherings—these are critical forms of work for the social reproduction of families.[18] Scholars have also shown how women in many workplaces create work cultures in which they "bring the family to work" or "humanize the workplace" by creating rituals like baby showers and retirement party celebrations that connect workers to each other.[19] And women's and men's friendships at Vita Needle seem to have different dimensions. Whereas three of the women have dinner together every Friday night (I have many times passed Rosa's house and seen her being picked up for dinner by Flo at 4:45), I have not heard of any Vita men or mixed-gender groups getting together outside work, except to pay a visit when someone is ill.

Multigenerational Relationships

James Corrigan, 78, who is not a Vita worker, told me in an interview, "I believe in associating with people younger than myself at all times.... Because, first, you're mentally stimulated all the time. Second, it puts you in touch with modern vernacular and what's going on." Though he is not at Vita, James sums up some of what I hear at Vita. As one worker put it, "Having the young people around keeps things interesting." Charles told me that he felt that the multigenerational nature of Vita is good for the younger people, "I think that younger people can get a sense that when you get old you don't die. I mean you're not the living dead. You still have ideas. You still do things. You still have things to contribute." Charles (age 75) also spoke about Rosa (age 99), who was old enough to be his mother. He said that Rosa reminded him of his mother, but he wouldn't say that to her. "I would mean it as a compliment, but it wouldn't come across as one." The media covering the story of Vita group the workers as all old, but even within the older workers there is generational difference; just as the media erase this difference, so workers tend to in their efforts to create a sense of sameness.[20] Though Charles understood this, he also wanted to tell Rosa how much she reminded him of his own mother. There appears to be an attempt among the workers to homogenize themselves to help cement community; any awareness of difference is in a sense backroom conversation. We will also see this later when Mike, the production manager, warns the young workers that the older workers may say things that younger people might find offensive. In these warnings we see a managerial attempt to control difference.

Multigenerational relationships do have negative connotations, especially given the common notion of a generation gap in U.S. society. I would sometimes hear older workers wonder about younger workers, especially those with rings in their noses and chains on their trousers, and I did hear some concern that the "kids" were too involved in their iPods to fully engage with coworkers and with the work. Also, the presence of young people at Vita Needle often was a springboard for older workers to draw comparisons and to remember what distinguishes them from the younger people: they often cited a superior work ethic, though I did also hear them speak positively about the work ethic of some of the younger workers. So while at times older workers may cement their own bond by drawing distinctions between themselves and the younger workers—using a common technique of community building by making a distinction between "them" and "us"—this is not always the case. The shop floor dynamics are actually much more complicated than this us/them dynamic, and there are ways in which vast age differences are rendered insignificant on the floor.

In interviews with me, workers in their teens, twenties, and thirties invariably reflected positively on working with older adults at Vita. Nineteen-year-old Steve Zanes, who had often visited his grandfather in a nursing home before coming to Vita Needle, noted that Vita Needle allowed for more authentic and comfortable interaction across generations because they were all "in it together." By contrast, he found that "for some reason I just could never talk to the people in the nursing home. I don't know that it was, like, the environment we were in. I felt like I was in their territory.... There's something to be said for the fact that you're all kind of doing something together." Another teenager, Chris Hart (age 18), told me that he prefers being at Vita to being in school because there is no social ladder he has to climb or worry about at Vita. He explained that whereas high school students are always trying to place each other in a social world occupied by cliques and status positions, at Vita the older workers do not even attempt this: "There is no social ladder, because we're just different than them." It is in being different that Chris feels that he belongs.

It is common for the younger workers to compare their interactions with co-workers to relations with grandparents. Ben Freeman, who is 29, works on the production floor. Ben did not know any people in their nineties before he came to Vita, and his interactions with older people were confined to those with his grandparents, in their seventies and eighties. Ben commented,

> The one thing I can say I've learned [from working here] is that...my grandmother is, like, she's kind of a tough lady to talk to. It's kind of like, "How is it going?" and she's quiet. Good, good? Okay. If the conversation goes on with asking a question, getting a yes, no, maybe.... But here it's like everybody is pretty much happy. Like you can sit there and actually have a conversation with them, and it's so much different like from what I was used to....
>
> ...But that's kind of what I got used to, and it's a little different to see everyone come in [at Vita] and go like, "Hey, how the hell are you?" and stuff like that, and Grace making jokes, and David making jokes and stuff like that, and it's different from what I'm used to seeing. So it's nice.
>
> ....I'll be out back with David, I'll be like, "Turn that old, turn that stupid old guy stuff off." I'll be like, "Turn that old music off, dude." Just like playing around with him. And he'll be like "Get the hell out of here, you young bastard." And that's just how it is. I'll be like, "You're holding up the line, old man, you've got to get going. You've gotta get going. I've got work to do." It's just back and forth, like "Get the hell outa here, you young bastard. I don't care."

Though Ben's understanding of older adults begins with his grandparents, his interactions with David and others have expanded that understanding. He jokes with David, and to me he expresses surprise at the authenticity of these relationships. As with the older workers who value their work family over their real family relationships, these young workers positively evaluate their work relationships. And in Ben's example, I note the irreverence from both sides. We see David and Ben both deliberately call attention to their differences, perhaps as one might do when using a racial slur in banter with a friend whose race differs from your own. In the process of calling attention to difference, this teasing seems to erase it. Also, as we will see later when I discuss the prevalence of jokes about aging, the ability to joke and tease seems to indicate a sense of sameness and closeness and a concomitant sense of trust.

Emotional Bonds

Family connotes emotional involvement, and this is where the family metaphor seems to be the strongest. We hear about Vita as a family in reference to the distribution of cards when someone is ill. We also hear about care in multiple everyday ways: calling or driving to the home of someone who unexpectedly does not show up at work (usually that is done by Mike, the manager); collecting money for a grieving coworker's groceries; scraping snow off a coworker's car or feeding a coworker's parking meter; helping out when work piles up or a work operation is not working out properly. Negative emotional involvement related to family in the broader society includes fighting and violence, sibling rivalry and bickering, estrangement, divorce, and death. At Vita there are certainly instances of conflict over work: frustration when someone leaves a mess or does not indicate where they were when they stopped (making it difficult for the next person to pick up the work); quiet complaints about too much talking or snacking; whispered concern that perhaps Fred profits too much or that some workers do not pull their weight. But the profound negative emotions of family such as estrangement, divorce, and death are of course not found within Vita (though death of coworkers does evoke mourning).

Sameness on the Shop Floor

For all the apparent sameness and mundanity implied by the family metaphor, the world that Vita's workers create on the factory floor is extremely rich. Though the workers' demographics may suggest that their work culture is the 1950s redux, there is great depth to how Vita's older workers in the process of work create new worlds for themselves. (This is also true for Vita's younger workers, such as Ben, Chris, and Steve.) A powerful sense of belonging emerges out of a shared experience that is enacted and created daily on the shop floor, from conversations, daily joking, and games to diversions about histories, memories, and current experiences both inside and outside work. The sense of sameness at Vita Needle is about shared historical experiences, a shared history of living in this suburban Boston community, shared current experiences related to aging, and shared socioeconomic status. I take each in turn.

Generational Sameness

Grant Harvey is a 68-year-old former General Motors assembly-line worker, now at Vita Needle after his plant closed down to relocate to Mexico. He described how he ended up at Vita Needle, having spotted the "Help Wanted" sign on the door:

> It wasn't that I wasn't looking for work. I was sort of, you know, not really intently. It's not like I was desperately in need of the money. So it's, that's not the primary driving force. But it helps, it's nice. So, anyway, I go upstairs and, gee, I'm curious. I remember this when I was a kid. The theater used to be across the street and we used to go to the movies. And I remember seeing that sign. A trip down memory lane! [Laughs.] It said, "Seniors wanted" or "Seniors preferred." So I said, "Oh, okay. So we'll see what this is." So I walk up there and it's like, "Oh my God, this is a museum!" [Laughs.] All this antique machinery and antique people. Wow, this is really weird.... I am an antique, certainly, I've been an antique for a while. So, what the heck.

Grant's narrative of arrival at Vita Needle echoes comments I heard from others, which also told of serendipitous encounters and nostalgic impressions. Ninety-four-year-old Grace thinks her brother and father—lifelong factory workers— when she works the Vita machines: "I work on a drill press, which I love, and I think my father used to do that, because he was a machinist. And when I'm working on the drill press, I think of my father. And my brother, they both were machinists." Others say the shop reminds them of factories they went into in their childhood. Allen compares it to "Edison's workshop."

Nostalgia for a time past is quite common in descriptions of the physical plant and of its interior social dynamics, as in this example from the *Boston Globe*:

> Time stands still at Vita Needle. The hollow pins, tubes, wires and gauges manufactured by the company are state of the art and bring in $3 million a year in revenue. But from the furniture to the employees, the business

is as old-fashioned as they come.... The 72-year-old chairman fetches the mail every day, the wooden stairs creaking beneath his Hush Puppies; there's no elevator from the street level below, where the company is identified only by a tiny sign on a metal door in the retail district of this suburban Boston town. "It's a step back in time, there's no question," said Frederick Hartman, the 45-year-old president of the business, which was founded by his great-grandfather in 1932. "There's great comfort in the routine, in the character."[21]

The Associated Press article from which this quote is taken was reproduced in newspapers across the United States in 1997 and 1998 with titles that played on nostalgia and a sense of stopped time, such as "Good Old Days Are Right Now," "Time Has Stood Still at Still-Vital Vita Needle Company," and "Time Put on Hold at Needle Factory." Such nostalgia for time past as we see in Grant's comments and the media coverage has a strong role in the everyday creation of sameness at Vita Needle. Nostalgia in some ways seems to animate (or reanimate) antique people and their antique machines—these people are very much alive and creative, not really antiques at all, nor is the machinery in this workshop that produces needles for very modern use in brain and heart surgeries or on NASA's Mars Exploration Rover Mission.

There are many instances of workers invoking a sense of comfort enabled by the old ways and setting, but there is also a sense of sameness related to the shared generational histories. Allen recounted that he tells Fred if he thinks the sales price for a part is too low (for instance, if the job requires using up a lot of expensive materials), because otherwise, "you're not making any money." When I asked Allen why it is important to him that the job makes money, he replied:

> That was just part of the way we were raised. I mean, when you went to work for a company, you did your best for a company. And if a company goes out of business and you're working for them, you're out of business, so...so maybe it was still part of the Depression ethic. I don't know. I mean I was not involved in that but still, the people who taught us were. And we probably picked up a lot of it from that. But, you know, I'm a capitalist at heart. I like to see people make money.

Allen (age 84) and his coworkers were all mostly born in the United States between 1910 and 1950. Although they span a couple of generations, these workers share a sense of common experience of important moments in U.S. history from the first half of the twentieth century. When I asked 72-year-old Arthur (born in 1936) about the difference between volunteering and getting paid for work, he said, "You know, my background, my family went through a lot of economic difficulty. There was a time when my father couldn't work, and my mother had to work. A lot of people here have gone through the Depression and other kinds of economic difficulty. And so we attach meaning to being paid. We have a sense that we are being appreciated." Although Allen notes that he was not an adult during the Great Depression ("I was not involved in that"), its effects were felt in how his parents raised him. In these ways, workers who do span different generations elide this difference in order to create a sense of sameness among themselves. As we will see, they also do this with socioeconomic class.

I often hear reminiscences on military service or vivid memories of war. Men served in the military in World War II or the Korean War, and women worked in factories making equipment for the war effort (Grace, for example, worked during World War II in a factory that converted covered rubber thread into giant elastic bands that would stop an airplane when it landed on an aircraft carrier). And I quickly learned that if you have to ask "What war?" you know you are too young. As Abigail said, " 'The war' means World War II; all others pale in comparison."

This generational sameness also is manifest in the Dee Dee Game through its shared songs and in the shared history of living through much of the twentieth century in the United States. I have even heard a discussion of the proverbial topic "Where were you when JFK was shot?" (akin to similar questions about 9/11 or the 1969 moon landing). Such questions prompt discussion that uncovers and creates connections among people through the shared memory of personal experiences of a national tragedy or victory.

A sense of nostalgia for the past is palpable in daily life, and I categorize it here as old-fashioned but not in a pejorative sense. While Vita's older workers have no doubt changed in attitudes, perspectives, and physical ability as they have aged, they also have witnessed many changes in their lives—and in some instances they feel more comfortable with values and practices that are not the current vogue, a point we saw in critical references to "political correctness" (this is a *Christmas* party, not a *holiday* party). On the outside, political movements that postdate the births of many of the workers include feminism and civil rights. There has also been a rise in immigration from non-European countries and in the use of English as a second language. But inside Vita Needle things are different, for some workers at least. Feminism appears to not have hit yet, as evidenced by the scantily clad pinups are on the walls and the numerous comments I got on my appearance ("Hello, pretty lady!"). As for civil rights, the summer I worked there was the summer of the 2008 Obama presidential campaign, and I certainly heard from some people disparaging racial remarks during the election; when one worker returned from a hospital stay, I heard some genuine surprise and earnest discussion about the high quality of the primarily racial minority immigrant staff there.

Small-Town Sameness

I live in Needham, where Vita Needle is located. Compared with the many Vita workers who have lived here for sixty, seventy, or even ninety years, I am a relative newcomer, having arrived only seven years ago. A Needham friend responded to a description I had given her of the company. Her response offers not only insight about the meaning that work can bring people but also an implicit understanding of the type of community that Needham is—a middle-class community where neighborly engagement often is done with children as the focus. In an e-mail my friend described Vita Needle as like a "supportive community,"

> the way that it feels when one is living in a neighborhood/community among friends who are helpful, interested in your life, etc. My guess is that these folks in their 80s and 90s feel somewhat isolated in their homes or apartments. They don't have kids in school to provide a social and supportive community. They don't go to the gym or do other sports (skiing, baseball leagues, etc.). Perhaps they go to church and/or play bridge. But their supportive community outside of work might be small. Thus, Vita Needle is their community.
>
> Think of all the ways that you come into contact with friends, who are interested in you and are willing to help in any way. Now think of yourself as a very elderly person. Would you still have such a strong and vibrant community? Vita Needle provides this for them. Similar to sitting at the dinner table with friends and family. Lots of conversations, helping, listening, etc.

I hear a lot about sameness enabled by community and connections at Vita Needle. Because Needham is the hometown of the majority of Vita's workers, there are numerous longtime connections among people, and the workers are able to relate to each other in reference to the many threads they have woven through the community over the years: they know each other as their kids' coaches or schoolteachers, fellow parishioners or coffee shop regulars, friends of friends, or parents of their children's friends.

Perhaps because of its proximity to Boston and the tendency for young professionals to move in and commute to the city, this is a town where roots are valued. One longtime resident remembers being told as a newcomer that "it takes seventeen years to feel at home here." Now, nineteen years later, she says she understands how it takes many years to develop the connections that make people feel part of a community, connections formed through common affiliation with organizations and institutions (church, schools, sports leagues); joint participation in community events (lighting of the Needham holiday tree in the town center, ordering Girl Scout cookies from neighboring children, voting for school committee members); using the same businesses and services as others nearby; and witnessing of life-cycle events such as births, graduations, weddings, and funerals.

There is a palpable sense of small town inside Vita Needle when one maps the connections among workers, and it is reminiscent of the blend of family and factory in a traditional New England factory town.[22] A few examples show the variety of town-based ties among workers. Everyone knows 99-year-old Rosa as a famous waitress at the longtime downtown Edie's Restaurant. On her birthdays the chief of police (her former busboy at Edie's) stops in to wish her well. Sam has coffee at Dunkin' Donuts with Grace's son, and Grace's daughter-in-law works at the pharmacy around the corner from Vita Needle. Two of the Vita former schoolteachers taught many of their coworkers' children. The son of one worker is famous in town because he just missed playing major league baseball, and the high school girl's basketball coach worked at Vita Needle when she was in high school in the 1970s. When 18-year-old Ryan Pierce first got a summer job at Vita Needle, his grandmother said, "Flo works there!" Flo, at 82, is his grandmother's best friend, and Ryan had known her since he was 7 or 8 years old. Now he enjoys seeing her at work and makes sure to say hello to her whenever he comes in. He said that Flo "watches out for me." For example, he says that when there is cake being shared for someone's birthday, she will bring him a piece and say, "I know you wouldn't go and take the cake, so I got a piece for you."

When I first started this project, one teenage grandson worked here alongside his grandfather; another worker's grandson came a subsequent summer. Some workers live within a few houses of each other. Some see each other at church, the grocery store, or at senior center exercise classes. The brother of one 85-year-old Vita worker volunteers at the hospital coffee shop, working alongside the wife of another Vita worker. One of the local elementary schools is named after a Vita worker's grandfather, a famous town doctor back in the age of house calls. Finally, the ties to Needham are also ties to the Hartmans: two workers joined Vita Needle after hearing about it from Mason Hartman, the former owner and Fred's father, who was a member of the Needham Retired Men's Club. Other workers have children who went to school with Fred Hartman.

Even for those not from Needham, there may be deep personal ties. The wife of one worker babysat for a manager's children many years before her husband joined Vita Needle. And from the window of her office at a nearby IBM plant, one woman watched Mike, the manager, grow up—after school Mike used to go to a small shop near the plant that his uncle owned. Workers expend considerable effort to discover their connections: one teenager told me that when she first started to work there, the older workers tried to place her in the community, asking who her parents are, mistaking her for someone else. In my very first conversation with Pete he asked me about my last name and about which of the many Needham Lynches I was related to (the answer is none). When a new worker arrives, some workers rush home to the "nosy book" (the town's street list, which includes name, age, address, and occupation).

Sameness of Aging Experiences

The sameness is manifest in instances as mundane as the sharing of food. There is a counter in the shop where people bring in food to share—"food offerings," as one man jokingly calls it. The offerings may be cookies left over from a grandchild's visit, cake to celebrate a birthday, fresh garden vegetables. But I often heard that the food that goes over best is sweets—and more than one person told me that old people have a sweet tooth due to age-related changes in taste buds.[23]

A central tie that creates a sense of sameness at Vita Needle is a commonality of age that pervades work and social relationships (and accompanying economic and medical experiences). Many are in the group American society labels old, though Rosa, at 99, is old enough to be the mother of the many coworkers who are in their seventies. Vita's older workers attribute common experiences and attach shared attributes to being in this same cohort.[24] Some are positive, such as a shared work ethic and wisdom. Some are negative, such as the stigmatization of older adults in U.S. society. For example, one woman told me that she distinctly remembers the first time she realized that after she had spoken to someone, the person responded to her daughter "as if I wasn't there."

Older workers at Vita share the experience of being "disabled" (or being *considered* disabled) outside work but "able-bodied" inside. Outside they may need help carrying groceries or shoveling snow, climbing ladders to clean rain gutters in the fall, or changing a light bulb. They may also receive or be offered help when they really do not feel it is needed, and I often hear workers' stories of being embarrassed, frustrated, or angry when strangers and family members, assuming that a gray-haired person requires assistance, offer aid outside work.

Inside is different. Walking canes and hearing aids provide two striking material symbols of the difference between inside and outside. Two people leave their canes at the coat closet: in the close quarters on the shop floor there is always a table to grab on to if needed. Some men turn hearing aids off at work—a better solution to block out loud factory noises than earplugs or noise-blocking headphones.

With a group of people all facing physical disabilities, help is naturally given and received, with hardly a word exchanged. One person might carry a box for another, or someone might move a chair to let a coworker squeeze by. Often it is the men helping the women, and often the men in their twenties, thirties, and forties helping the older people. (When Rosa and Grace clock out and leave to-gether, two men will stop their work to escort them down the stairs. "Where's my man?" I once heard Grace joke as she waited at the landing.) But needed help can come from all directions—and coworkers seem to know when not to help, in contrast to what happens outside work. Inside Vita Needle, people are respected for what they can do and what they want to be able to do. As 19-year-old Steve told me, "There are some things that I offer to help with. A lot of them actually say 'I don't need help, don't worry about it.' ... Like, if someone drops something on the floor I'll want to try and bend down for them. A lot of times they're 'no, no I got it I got it I got it.'" Jim Downey described to me the dynamics related to this very subject:

> *Jim:* When you get older and you're less flexible, you may dump some-thing on the floor and say "Well, I'll wait until I have three on the floor. Because I only want to get down there once." [Laughs.] ... "I'm going to get down once instead of four times." [Laughs.]
>
> *Caitrin:* [Laughs.] But then if you have some young whippersnap-per walking by, they're going to get it before you get your four accumulated.
>
> *Jim:* That's all right. ... And I've had people pick things up for me. You know, the thing would shoot under the table and Donald [75 years old, and who himself uses a cane outside work] was already down there, he'll pick it up because he could reach it.

Here I suggested that Jim bring in a grasping device designed for picking up things after hip surgery without bending over. "You should get one of those, and bring it," I joked.

> *Jim:* Well, yes and no. I don't think it's designed to pick up tubing and that sort of thing. But it's good for a lot of things and, in fact, when Gertrude was working there, she was 92 at the time, she had a little thing with a sticky tape on the bottom of it to pick things up with. So it was like a stick. She rigged it up herself, it just picked things up. Because it was hard to get stuff and it involved quite a process of get-ting down off the chair, and most ladies that age, they don't bend at the knee, they bend at the waist and you know, you got to watch your blood pressure in your head and a few other places when you're get-ting older. [Laughs.] Or you'll fall over.

Health is central to the shared experience of aging at Vita Needle. When I asked Grace what she liked about working there, her response was punctuated by two age-related health concerns, arthritis and macular degeneration (the latter has forced her to stop reading). And yet she perseveres: "I enjoy going to work because we're all elderly, and we have the same aches and pains. We talk, you know? Somebody will say, 'Oh, my fingers.' And I'll say, 'Look at mine!' You know? And they'll say, 'Yeah, they hurt don't they?' I'll say, 'Yes, they do.' And we seem to have the same, same things to talk about. What did you watch on television, and did you like it? And have you read any books lately? And, I, now I can't read, and I miss that horribly."

Continual sharing of information about health is likely advantageous to the workers, a point consistent with research in other contexts that shows how social networks can have a protective influence on health.[25] In the Vita case, this would be true because of the positive influence of peers on health behaviors, which includes the ability to share information about health-care providers, medication, Medicare policies, and the like. One employee who had a hip replaced told me that several coworkers have asked him about the experience, as they prepare for their own or their spouse's surgery. After one employee had surgery for prostate cancer, three coworkers asked him to share an information booklet he had on the topic, and one asked what he should expect in a biopsy. There are frequent discussions of cancer, eyesight, arthritis, diabetes; there is much people learn from each other through discussion or by seeing the progression or cessation of illness in others. As Jim once said, "We can see what can happen. Hal lost his toes from diabetes." And they are also able to consult each other with concerns about bodily changes. For example, do I have Alzheimer's or is this forgetfulness normal? Am I depressed, and what should I do about it?

Although Vita's workers share in painful life experiences— such as retirement and the accompanying loss of purpose, the social stigma of being old, and the death of spouses or children—the experience of being old is itself not all negative for them. Working with other older people can make them feel affirmed and alive. This is in part due to making money for Fred (being productive makes me feel valued), but it is also due to having better health as a result of staying active and the positive influence of seeing dynamic examples. As Jim once said, "seeing Rosa makes you feel alive." They also share pleasure in the births of grandchildren or great-grandchildren—they bring in photos and news clippings about both. They often study shared family experiences as lessons for themselves. Some stories, like Allen's about a woman named Hannah, become symbolic of what can happen (positives and negatives):

> *Allen:* So there was one woman she just died last summer, she was
> 104. . . . She hadn't worked there in some years. Her . . . kids made her
> quit. . . . She was in her nineties and one day she was sitting on one
> of these higher stools and she must have done something—they're

not too stable. She just fell right over backwards. And I just said "my God," you know, because I knew how old she was. And I was about from here to the window from her [five feet in distance]. By the time I got there she was on her feet and straightening the stool up and she was more embarrassed at having fallen over.

Caitrin: Wow. Now this isn't Gertrude? I heard about a woman named Gertrude.

Allen: No, no. Gertrude was feeble. She was going down. This woman was even, after she quit, why, they'd go by and she was painting her house, she was mowing her lawn....It was too bad that her kids made her quit....She got hit by a car one night going home [walking home]....So her kids said, you know, "That's enough. We're not going to drive." They were driving to work. They're not going to drive, so you've got to stay home. But it was too bad because, God, she worked. She worked. She was a nice person, too.

Allen here expressed admiration for Hannah: a nice person, energetic, and a good worker. And he also noted the frequently discussed problem of children making their parents stop working.

Humor is pervasive at Vita Needle, and there is definitely a shared sense of humor about aging. Anthropologists have long studied the ways in which humor is embedded in social relationships and in which jokes require shared context, participation, and relationships to be funny.[26] A sense of belonging and closeness influences the people with whom one is able to make jokes as well as the content of the jokes that are considered acceptable. Humor in fact is itself a social practice—for example, when it helps build connections and create norms.[27] As philosopher Simon Critchley writes, "The simple telling of a joke recalls us to what is shared in our everyday practices. It makes explicit the enormous commonality that is implicit in our social life.... So, humor reveals the depth of what we share."[28]

The vast majority of jokes I have heard at Vita Needle are about aging, though there are also jokes about other topics, such as the work process and physical plant (Sam's three-finger-job, the meat locker), as well as politics, sexuality, and gender. Some people will bring in copies of jokes from home and post them on the wall by the time cards; the mere act of posting seems to signal their sense of sameness—these are people with whom I feel comfortable joking.

Of the age-related jokes that are posted I once saw a long list of pithy phrases that included "Old is when an 'all nighter' means not getting up to pee!" and "Old is when 'getting a little action' means you don't need to take any fiber today." One time Pete shared the following joke with me, which he said he had made up on his own: "Did you hear about the woman whose urinary tract problem was resolved? She went off the deep end." I must have looked confused, so he explained. "She went off the Depend, meaning the Depends adult diapers." I laughed and jested that it was a bad joke, to which Pete said, "I think I'll call my wife with that one." An hour or so later, he came over to where I was working next to Flo and said, "I called my wife to tell her the joke and she told me that she had told me that joke last week." When Pete, Flo, and I laughed, it was with a shared understanding that memory loss itself is an appropriate topic for humor in this context where the specter of dementia looms large.

I also hear sexually suggestive jokes about aging, such as this one, recounted by Arthur, who told it to me in an interview but said that it is representative of jokes people tell at work:

> It's about a couple who are 80 years old in an assisted living place and they decide they're going to get married and so they sit down and they're going to have a prenuptial agreement. And so they're sitting there and the woman says, "I want to keep my house." "That's fine with me," he says. And she said, "I want to keep my Cadillac." "Well, that's fine with me," he said. [She said,] "And I want to have sex six days a week." And he says, "That's fine with me too. Can I sign up for Friday?"

Jokes (and serious discussion) about death are also common, such as Grace's relieved joke about being glad she would be dead when someone used embalmer's needles on her. Seventy-seven-year-old Larry Clifford once told me of trying to convince his coworker that when Larry's casket went by in his Catholic funeral, everyone in attendance should make an OK sign to indicate "OK, Larry made it to heaven." Here it is irreverence about church traditions that is the source of humor.

Socioeconomic Sameness

We have heard some Vita workers describe the comfort of being in a group of people like themselves, reminiscing on old times, stories, and songs. It is also important that this group is like them not only in age but also in race (predominantly white) and religion (primarily Catholics and mainstream traditional Protestants).

With very few exceptions, Vita employees are nonimmigrant (or, in one person's case, the immigration occurred ninety-two years ago) white Christian Euro-Americans for whom English is their first (and often only) language. When I show my students a photo of the staff at Vita Needle, they usually comment first on the sea of white hair, but then I sometimes hear someone comment on the fact that the workers appear to be all white. Some say they expected factory workers to be young racial-minority immigrants.

So how could it be that all these workers are white nonimmigrants? A German magazine article noted that the manager "only hires people from the area, and most already know a few of their co-workers by sight, either from the church or the neighborhood. This makes the new beginning easier for everyone."[29] Needham's population is 90 percent white, and the managers prioritize the hiring of locals—so the race of the workers is in some sense predetermined.[30] And it may be that nonwhites and nonlocals rarely apply, since Vita usually advertises job openings only by means of the sign on the front door. Thus sameness (and the sense of family) is produced through a selection process that happens before workers even enter but also, as we have seen, in relationships worked out every day at work.

In some important ways, current experiences may differ among the workers, particularly in terms of housing and economic circumstances. Almost all Vita workers live in Needham, but some are renters and some are homeowners; some are in public subsidized housing; some live alone, some with a spouse; some live in an in-law apartment with children. Some are lifelong factory workers, with barely a high school degree and living paycheck to paycheck. Some live in homes with paid-up mortgages; some are retired professionals with pensions and savings; and some own summer homes. However, although there is certainly some class diversity among workers, I often hear them dismiss such difference as irrelevant and note that inside Vita Needle they are all workers. For example, when I told Jim that some of my students had been curious about the presence of class diversity among Vita's workers, he said, "Socioeconomic status may be more important to young people than to us who are not particularly worried about it, or we wouldn't be there. Steve Jamison drives a Beemer [a BMW], but I keep my 1996 Ford wagon going—and neither of us worries about it." And in an interview, Jeffrey, the 74-year-old retired engineer, told me, "I'm a worker bee. I'm not a supervisor. I'm not a manager. I'm not any of the things that I was before." In the *Pensioners Inc.* documentary film, Joe Reddington, a 78-year-old retired physicist said, "I'm a worker. We're all workers here."

In these quotes we hear men who had previously worked in high-status white-collar jobs describe their current positions as simply workers. They were endeavoring to emphasize that there are no distinctions among the workers—instead there is homogeneity in position and process. Vita workers do not seem to find it important to highlight the distinctions between themselves and other workers to preserve their identities, whereas we can imagine quite the opposite in other situations where there are educational disparities among workers doing blue-collar work, such as professionals who have had to take low-paying factory work because of the recession.[31] Is there something about being older retirees that leads to a lack of interest in marking such distinctions?

There are two ways to think about this question. On one hand, management purposefully cultivates some of this sense of sameness. Mike tells me he tries to determine in an interview if someone would be concerned with status and unwilling to do jobs he or she thinks are demeaning. Mike says he tries to hire people who have the maturity to not care about such distinctions. On the other hand, some of this sense of sameness comes from the workers themselves, who understand it as a feature of their stage in life. For this, I offer a quote from Jim Downey, who e-mailed me after reading comments from my students about Vita Needle. Jim touches on issues of family that are pertinent to this chapter but also foreshadows issues of freedom and flexibility that I will discuss in the next chapter:

> There are definite generational differences in attitude. Many of us grew up during World War II, when the whole country was in fact mobilized for a common purpose, and no job was beneath notice. Each of us felt that we had to contribute something of our best, or someone else would suffer as a result. Also, there is personal satisfaction in producing something useful and valuable, that it fulfills a drive to be responsible for success of the enterprise, or at least their contribution.
>
> Remember, each of us has a different set of needs ... —personal, economic, and social—that might be met in a conducive workplace. But the value of time is different for retirees and young people, where the investment in work may interfere with play, or workouts, or whatever social milieu provides more satisfaction. Yes, the job is much more than money, but how many young people actively seek to meet so many of their needs at work?

Jim, 74 years old when he wrote this e-mail, several times refers to age and generation. In so doing he both assumes and creates a sense of sameness (community, shared values) among the workers. Jim was responding to analysis by my 18- and 19-year-old students, so he reads their thoughts in terms of differing age perspectives. We see a cultivation of sameness in two ways in Jim's comments. First, he points out the significance of being children of the World War II era, thus invoking an understanding prevalent in the United States today that that was a time when citizens joined together for a common cause, in a way not since replicated. As Jim sees it, he and his coworkers are people for whom it is natural to roll up the sleeves to work for a common goal. Second, we see this assumed sense of sameness when Jim ends by drawing important contrasts between what work and time mean for younger people and older people: "The value of time is different for retirees and young people, where the investment in work may interfere with play, or workouts, or whatever social milieu provides more satisfaction." Here Jim comfortably contrasts retirees and young people. Jim's coworkers make a similar move in their everyday lives: they draw clear boundaries around their own work community and in so doing make claims about what it means to belong.

Outside, Looking In

When Esther describes "sitting on the outside, looking in" at family events, she evokes anxiety about a transition as one ages from being the center of society to living at the margins. She and her coworkers describe a sensation of shrinking social circles: as Jim once said, "As you get older, your world gets smaller." Theater studies scholar Anne Davis Basting's wonderful work to create meaningful care environments for people with dementia includes a creative storytelling project called "Time*Slips*," in which participants jointly create stories based on visual prompts. Basting has described the end of one energizing and fun-filled session where a participant pronounced, "Hey, we're a group here! And we're really good!"[32] While a dementia care facility is different in many ways from a factory staffed by cognitively intact people, the similarity in the two places has to do with what it means for people considered the "living dead" to experience a sense of belonging.[33] Exclaiming that "we're a group here" is an incredibly important assertion of self-awareness and agency for people otherwise written off by society.[34] This sense of belonging, of connection, and of agency is what Vita Needle provides.

Figure 1 schematically represents the meanings that Vita workers attach to inside Vita (the inner circle) and outside Vita (the outer circle). I have not arranged the terms as polar opposites because the experiences inside and outside are not completely dichotomous. There are many more possible words that could go in this figure, but these suffice to give a quick sense of the profound difference that work makes in the Vita workers' lives.

This visual representation of the meanings of inside and outside (which is not an actual mapping of a cognitive schema) is a useful heuristic even though there is, of course, more complexity than a single figure can connote. For example, the inside is not all positive all the time. There are people who do not get along with others, disagreements over work process, concerns about differential treatment of salaried and hourly workers, and hurt feelings. And the outside can have many positive attributes for workers, such as love from spouse and children, pride of attending a grandchild's ballet recital, excitement of a Caribbean cruise, or pleasure in watching *Dancing with the Stars* on television.

The border between inside and outside can be somewhat permeable (hence the dotted line), and there are certainly instances of the outside penetrating the inside: when a coworker or loved one dies or falls ill, when an argument with a daughter is

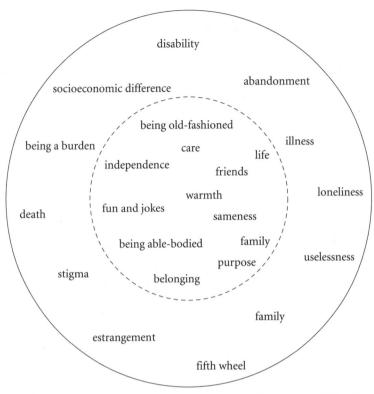

FIGURE 1. Meanings of inside (inner ring) and outside (outer ring) Vita Needle, from the workers' perspective.

fresh in mind when someone arrives at work, when new health problems require a new job assignment, and when workplace regulations imposed from outside have to be followed (such as sexual harassment training, OSHA safety procedures, income tax withholding policies). And likewise, the inside can permeate to the outside. In several homes I saw that workers have the most recent Vita staff photo on their refrigerators or mantelpieces. Three of the women have dinner together every Friday night, and they speak to each other by telephone on the weekends. Some bring work home: Pete coils tubes at his kitchen table while watching the Red Sox, and Rosa did a little Vita work at home while recovering from an injury in order to keep her arthritic fingers nimble and her mind engaged. And when someone is ill or grieving, coworkers send cards, groceries, or flowers, attend wakes and funerals, and visit at home, in the hospital, or in the nursing home.

In these many ways, the inside and outside are copresent in the workers' lives, and as such they provide them with continual reminders of the contrasting worlds they inhabit. Each world can also provide the worker with tools and strategies to cope with the other—especially with regard to the ways in which workers learn things on the inside to bring to the outside (such as treating health concerns, spending meaningful time with grandchildren, accessing social services).[35]

This figure does not include the category "old" because, in truth, old is the wider context for all the other sentiments. I considered adding to the inside circle "not old" or "new old." And in the outside circle, I could have listed "old" or "old as stigma." The concept of and experience of old permeates life both inside and outside Vita Needle, and yet, as we have seen, the meaning of the term is profoundly different inside and outside work. Inside the factory, old means a depth of shared history and experiences, shared values and way of life, shared contemporary health and family experiences. Outside the factory, it means stigma, loneliness, and a world that has passed you by. In the process of navigating these two worlds the Vita Needle workers redefine aging and create positive lives for themselves.

When writing this chapter, I received an e-mail from a management consultant named Jessica Margolin with the following powerful list of the "emotional challenges" (as Margolin put it) that older adults can face.

- Contemplating the end of one's life; regrets, things one hopes that they can hang on long enough to see, etc.
- Having friend after friend and eventually people younger than you die; feeling your social circle shrink, having less ability to connect with people who have shared experiences. Sometimes if you live long enough you outlive your child.
- Increasing levels of anxiety because of not being able to navigate well but also because things seem so disorienting compared to how one lived when one was "in the flow" of young adulthood.
- Anxiety exacerbated by not really understanding one's medical situation, difficulties in managing it (i.e., pills GALORE), and one's children's best wishes being annoying and intrusive.
- Conversely, anxieties about being burdensome to one's family, either in life or during the course of dying.
- Feeling increasingly marginalized (this happens to women who base their social power on their attractiveness and men on their athleticism as early as their mid-30s; definitely by their 40s), with no real hope of success in a social power struggle—it's not a "social justice" issue in the way a marginalized ethnic group might feel....this can be evidenced by being spoken to as if they were a child, or just subtle cues or feeling overlooked. I remember being in my 30s and being "ma'am-ed" for the first time. It didn't feel like matriarchal power, it felt like young attractive men saw me as "other."

- I'd suspect this is magnified for populations of people living far from home (first-generation immigrant groups), who would also have a difference in attitude towards the aged, and different expectations of services to contend with.[36]

Margolin's insightful list of the emotional challenges of aging covers an important range of experiences—some are outward-oriented, and others are related to self-reflection. It refers to experiences I hear about every day at Vita Needle. I hear stories about health and impending death and about friends and family who pass away; comments about being lost, confused, or unable to do something one used to be able to do; concern about health conditions and about nagging children; worry about having to stop work and become a burden for their children; disquiet over feeling useless and betrayed by health and bodies with changes they cannot control, especially those related to memory loss. In a life context such as this, imagine what work must mean.

In the United States, we sometimes hear adages about the strength of family bonds—"An ounce of blood is worth more than a pound of friendship" or "Blood is thicker than water." These are moral claims that appear as idioms. They assume the primacy of blood ties, and they are a call for action: to preserve family relationships. But we also hear the adage "You can choose your friends, but you can't choose family." This refers more broadly to the notion of making the most of what you have in circumstances where you cannot choose, but it also implies that we should choose friends with care and that we need to make the best of our families. These different adages call for the significance of preserving family bonds at all cost. Vita Needle shows us that elders desire family—people they can care for who will also care for them, and they want a place where they can belong and where they have something in common with others.

Conclusion: Sameness as a Means of Labor Control?

Working across from Donald one afternoon, I heard a faint odd sound that I couldn't quite identify. Fingers scraping against rippled metal? A purring kitten? A broken blender? I looked around and realized that it was the sound of Donald snoring. Donald had been inserting metal tubes into larger plastic tubes, and the plastic tubes were now jumping up and down slightly, as if alive, because he was still doing some of the repetitive motions even though he was asleep. I didn't know what to do, and I felt embarrassed for him. I looked around for help from someone, but then Donald woke up, shook his head, arose, and walked to the refrigerator for a glass of cold water. A few weeks later, I was in the same spot, sitting across from Donald, and I heard Dan come over and say to Donald, "How are the cracks, Donald?" When I looked up and said, "What? What are you talking about?" Dan said, "Oh, Donald knows." Later on Dan told me that Donald had been falling asleep, and his head was positioned as if he was looking at the cracks on the plastered ceiling.

Donald was definitely sleeping during the workday. Gertrude used to do the same. Flo gathers signatures on greeting cards during the workday. Friends ask for recommendations about vacations and biopsies during the workday. Friends show off photographs or newspaper clippings about grandchildren during the workday. Some of this happens during the morning coffee break and the lunch break, but much of it does not. We saw Pete and Flo both put down their work to play the Dee Dee Game. Larry leaves his work station to tell a new joke to Jeffrey, and in chapter 1 we saw the great effort that Sam went through to set up his three-finger job joke for two sets of coworkers. The many ways in which workers create and enact care work and family bonds on the shop floor are enabled by managerial policies that allow talking, visiting, and, in some cases, sleeping.

Why would the managers allow these behaviors, which are clearly not aimed solely at the production of needles? There are many ways in which the managers and also the Hartman family support the workers and ways in which they cultivate the notion of Vita Needle as a family. An Argentinean newspaper review of the film *Pensioners Inc.* mentioned the contrasting experiences for Vita's workers inside and outside work. The reviewer uses the family metaphor after hearing workers invoke this concept in the film: "Many there believe that in other places they feel out of place [*desplazados*] because they have to interact with people of other ages, but in the case of this factory, they created a big family, whose members— whether employers or fellow employees—understand each other and back each other up when someone needs it."[37] The reviewer raises the notion of feeling out of place among younger people and points to how their mutual understanding is brought into the work processes. He also points out that it is not only employees who understand each other and back each other up, but also the employer.

When new workers come to Vita, they go through a morning training program in which Mike imparts basic information on the work process and product and also safety information ("There is the fire escape"; "Wear closed-toed shoes"; "Use these safety goggles."). In these sessions, Mike has special words for new workers in their teens and twenties. He tells them, "You are working with your grandparents. There are certain things you wouldn't say in front of your grandparents." And he also advises them that the older workers are from an entirely different generation, with a different outlook, and some prejudices. They are not politically correct. He warns, "You will hear some things you are not used to hearing." He once mentioned this to a group of my students, and he explained that hearing these things used to bother him but it does not anymore. He knows he is not going to change them: "Some are embittered, the world is leaving them behind. I don't want to change them." It is remarkable that Mike attempts to sensitize his younger workers to the different social values that some older workers may have. Mike is sensitive in his desire to make the workplace comfortable for the older workers especially, since they are Vita Needle's primary workforce.

Family is created not only by workers but also by managers and the owner in their practices of hiring locals and people not concerned with status, warning young people that older workers will not be PC, enabling workers to stay on even when growing frail. From one perspective, this creation of family every day at work is good for the owners and managers because it guarantees them a captive and loyal workforce. Is this your classic case of management turning the workplace into a family atmosphere as a mode of labor control? The anthropologist Louise Lamphere has shown how women's cultivation of family on the shop floor can serve management's interests rather than those of workers, and there is a vast literature on the ways in which managers often cultivate a sense of family at work.[38] But how do we read this at Vita Needle?

The workers so often and in so many ways note how Vita affords a sense of freedom and membership in a happy family, and they show that they find in Vita Needle a sense of place and comfort that contrasts starkly with their nonwork lives. This is why Vita workers are so apt to draw strong contrasts between inside and outside work (those famous stairs—the gateway between these worlds) and why they want to return to this workplace day after day. In some cases they sign up to work on weekends and lament forced days off on national and family-focused holidays like the Fourth of July and Christmas. They use the term "family" because it is a readily available term, but in many ways Vita is more than family. The sense of belonging and caring and being cared for at Vita Needle challenges us to think about the value of friendship and to rethink the idea that it is family whom we have until the end of life. It is belonging and caring and having a sense of purpose on which Vita's workers thrive.

The negative aspects of Vita Needle (sometimes excessive heat, low pay, part-time hours, no medical or health benefits) may immediately strike us, but one answer to the question of what keeps workers coming back has to do with their goals for working. As I will argue in the next chapter, they appear willing to tolerate some aspects of work now that they might not have tolerated when they were younger because work enables them to feel productive and useful, to belong and to care, and to access a way of life. In fact, work enables them to live a fuller life. In the simplest terms, if the workers are OK with it, is it exploitation?

Cutting labels. Photo by Caitrin Lynch.

NO CHAINS ON THE SEATS

Freedom and Flexibility

In 2008 the German business magazine *Brand Eins* ran a feature story showcasing Vita Needle as an example to prompt German employers to think more creatively about hiring older workers. Entitled "Staircase of the Willing," the article by Mathias Irle treats the Vita Needle stairs as a symbol of possibility. As this excerpt makes clear, it makes central the notion of flexibility:

> Joe Reddington, bald but for a wisp of white hair, wipes oil from his hands and seats himself at his workbench. The 78-year-old engineer has already come out of retirement twice before. He has to finish the custom order for an industrial client and then hurry to the eye doctor.... The average age of the employees here is 74 years. This was the case ten years ago, when Reddington signed his employment contract. The physicist had a sales career in computers behind him, then a couple of years in his son's business. He was officially retired. Then he happened to learn about Vita Needle, a nearby business. They were said to employ elderly people there, and they could be very flexible.
>
> ... Since 1998 he has worked 30 hours a week at Vita Needle, where he helps to fabricate custom multiple-use syringes for industry and veterinarians. For the most part, he can decide when he wants to start, whether at 4:30 in the morning or not until the afternoon. If his wife isn't feeling well, he only needs to call and he stays at home. He considers his work a combination of a craftsman's challenge and a kind of recognition, although he earns only slightly more than the minimum wage of

> 8 dollars an hour, which is a fraction of his former earnings. "Well, I've
> already made my money," Reddington explains.[1]

With the brief reference to Joe hurrying out to the eye doctor or staying home to
help his wife, the author here focuses on the employer's flexibility in adapting to its
workers' varied work schedules. Elsewhere in the article we hear that the employer
also requires flexibility from the employee—such as flexibility to be assigned to different tasks or to come in at varied hours each week. We hear that the manager shies
away from hiring people who have had long careers at large corporations because
they find it "particularly difficult to accept the flexibility at Vita Needle. Worse, they
often aim to 'optimize the organizational structure or the work process.'" Irle thus
describes flexibility as an advantage for the worker as well as the employer.

Flexibility refers to the quality of being adaptable or variable. It is an important
concept in contemporary business, as the book jacket of one human resources
textbook makes abundantly clear: "How can managers pursue their goals for labour productivity and organisational flexibility in socially acceptable ways?"[2] In
this regard, flexibility is the topic of positive policy and scholarly assessment of
the ways in which flexible employment policies can benefit employers but also
employees who seek to balance their work and family lives. We hear of job sharing, of women's reentry into the workforce after having children, of paternity
leave, and of phased-in retirement.[3]

Flexibility is a central focus for policy analysis of elder employment. The
Sloan Center on Aging and Work at Boston College, a national leader in elder-
employment policy studies, highlights workplace flexibility for older workers,
whereby "employees and their supervisors have some choice and control over
when, where, how work gets done, and what work tasks are assumed by which
employees/work teams."[4] This center has conducted numerous studies that show
the importance of flexible hours, tasks, and scheduling to retirees and to the
masses of baby boomers as they prepare to retire.

But scholars have long examined the downside to flexibility, and there is ample
documentation of how flexible labor policies can put workers at a disadvantage
because they cannot rely on consistent wages and they are at the mercy of employers who may change employment policies or, worse still, shut down operations
to relocate to locations more advantageous to the business.[5] One employee at a
McDonald's in Detroit has written incisively about the contradictions inherent in
her flexible job, getting to the heart of the critique about flexible labor:

> McDonald's is great for stay at home mothers because of the flexibility
> of the hours/shifts. I do not work when the kids have a school holiday,
> can take a day off to attend a child's field trip/class party, and do not
> work during the extended Summer, Winter and Spring vacations. I am

also at liberty to call off if one of my children [is] ill. I basically dictate my schedule, and the managers oblige. That part of my job is absolutely wonderful because I can still be a full-time mother to my children while working outside the home.... BUT, the incredible amount of work expected of you for the paltry salary given is despicable. It's like slave labor. It is slave labor.[6]

Given such criticism of the combination of low pay and high workload, as well as the unreliability of work under flexible regimes, these labor practices are a key target of activism on behalf of workers considered exploited by and vulnerable in the capitalist marketplace.

But as the German article "Staircase of the Willing" and other analyses show, flexibility itself is one of the reasons that Vita Needle has garnered such international attention. This chapter builds on the two preceding chapters to show how for Vita's workers, the opportunity to feel productive (chapter 1) and to be a member of a family (chapter 2) converts what some observers may consider exploitation into freedom and flexibility.

Willing Exploitation?

In chapter 1, Jim reflected on whether Vita Needle is exploiting old people: "I don't mind being exploited. I know that I could get paid a lot more for things I do. I am not in it for that. This is work I like to do." For Jim, in a relatively comfortable socioeconomic position, his work provides such a critical sense of purpose and belonging that the level of pay is not material to him. We see the same sentiment in Joe's comment above: "I've already made my money." But even for people who report needing the money more than Jim and Joe do, their desire for purpose and belonging are great motivations to work in a place few would have described as their retirement dreams.

Former automobile assembly-line worker Grant Harvey was the one who referred to Vita Needle's antique machinery and antique people. Grant is a quiet, intense 68-year-old man whose sparkling blue eyes complement hair that is so lightly gray it makes one think it must have originally been blond. When Grant is working, he is deeply engaged and a bit difficult to distract, but I found out in my first interview with him that when he is invited to talk, he is a storyteller. It is common to find Grant and his coworker Jerry Reilly after the end-of-break bell has rung in the morning, still sitting with their coffees and deep in conversation. Both have years of union experience, Grant in a General Motors plant, Jerry in a Raytheon plant. Grant will usually be the first to get up and turn back to work.

Grant had worked for thirty years on a GM assembly line, until the factory closed down in 1989—one in a series of GM plant closings in North America.[7] Grant attributes the closing to cheaper labor costs in Mexico, thus narrating a common story for workers in America's now dwindling manufacturing industry—factories closing down as they race to the bottom after cheaper and fresher sources of labor.[8] Grant was able to take early retirement with a pension, and so before coming to Vita in 2006, he and his wife had been living comfortably off his pension and her income as a dental office receptionist, and he had occasionally taken part-time seasonal post office jobs during the holiday rush.

At Vita Needle, Grant usually works on the bench staking needles. He works part-time and sets his own hours, leaving room for gardening and volunteering in his church. He noted, "It's perfect for me. It's a win-win. For them, for us, and I get a little extra money, and I don't use up all my time. I don't like spending eight hours a day at a place, and I don't need to work intently like that. Like I did before." Grant used the word "serendipity" to describe finding his job at Vita Needle, a chance occurrence when he was walking in downtown Needham one day. He drew a parallel between finding this job and finding the house that he and his wife raised their children in: "An accident of history, or an accident of something."

At the time of this interview, Grant had been at Vita Needle for one and a half years. He was thoughtful about why work is important for him personally but also for people more generally. As he said,

> I very much appreciate the culture of work, the quality, and the community idea of work.... I think there is also going to have to be a place for senior citizens more in the future because as the baby boomers begin to retire and as long as we're living longer, you can't just sit around and do nothing. And, you know, it's nice to sit around and read a book, but in some ways you still have to feel a need that "I'm creating some wealth that really matters." I can't just keep collecting my checks and going to the store and buying stuff from China the rest of my life because pretty soon, we're all going to go down the tubes. We can't do that.... You have to kind of keep working at something and creating wealth, even if it's just to still be engaged in the wealth-creation process somehow.

I was struck by Grant's reference to "buying stuff from China," this from a man whose own lifetime career ended prematurely so "stuff" could be more cheaply made in Mexico. Impressed by Grant's image of a world that cannot sustain itself in the current direction, I managed to slip in a word and asked Grant, "Why do we have to be working and creating wealth?" Grant explained his rationale:

I think that we have to be. I think that you can goof off for a while, but if we're going to retire for twenty years, that is not realistic. And the economy is not going to be able to sustain us. The money is not going to be worth anything because there's not going to be anybody to do the work that we won't be doing anymore. So who's going to be running all these factories? So I do think that we'll be reentering the workforce but coming at it from a totally different perspective of maybe not so much the money. And maybe we will have learned something—that it isn't about the money.

Here Grant went on to provide a definition that describes work as more than just earning money, referring to the very same kind of care work that we know is critical at Vita:

It's about community and caring and meeting human needs. And, as much the need to consume but also the need to produce so that we can consume. So going to an adult day-care center is an option for some people, sit around and play.... We have senior centers around, and people go and they find something to do, you know, play cards or play pool but, somehow I haven't wanted to do that.

Grant then pointed out that while sitting around at an adult day-care center, older people could also be working—he was basing this idea on a model he had seen of developmentally disabled adults producing small parts for local companies (a practice that Vita Needle itself engages in, but perhaps Grant did not know this). As he describes it,

They bring work in and they in-source stuff that nobody wants to do but it gives these people some dignity. So it's not just a charity, but it actually creates work....I understand the concept of having some place to go...and part of having a place to go everyday is also the camaraderie to be able to hang out with people and talk about the Patriots [the local football team] or whatever it is. And you meet friends and you have friends. Because if you stay at home and watch the tube, you go nuts. So you want to go out and do something and it's nice to be able to go out and socialize with people, work at something that might be marketable and somebody's willing to pay you for it....And so you make a little money too. But the combination of, it's a right balance where you're doing something useful, you feel dignity for yourself, and you're also experiencing the social life of work because I think one of the things I missed the most when they closed the plant was break time and hanging out with guys at work. And things you talk about. And having that social dimension of work is very important.

Grant summarized work as providing dignity and social engagement, and he went on to describe working at Vita in the same way: "The idea that if I can do what I really like doing, and I can have fun doing it, and somebody's willing to pay me to do this, that's great. I mean it's like, you know, mashed potatoes and gravy." When I asked him what this food analogy meant, he laughed and said he was referring to a GEICO car insurance television commercial that depicts the performer Little Richard enthusing about mashed potatoes and gravy.[9] Grant explained, "It's like having your cake and eating it too, I guess."

I was always swept away by my discussions with Grant, a man who had gone directly from high school to General Motors, self-educated but for a few community college courses paid for by GM. He says that on the assembly line he was able to intersperse work with snippets of reading ("work a little bit, read a paragraph or something") from books or magazines—perhaps the *Economist* or, as he says, anything in "politics and economics and sociology and culture." I was struck by his clear articulation of the joint social and economic value that work provides. Grant was adamant about the importance of enjoying the company of friends while engaged in productive activity. He joked that work that one enjoys and gets paid for is like that mashed potatoes and gravy, a stereotypically traditional all-American hearty meal with two elements that go together harmoniously—enjoying work *and* earning money for it. He rephrased this combination as a matter of both having *and* eating the cake. In other words, you are not merely producing something for someone and getting nothing out of it yourself. That cake is also for you to consume! And Grant envisioned a future in which older adults would not be going nuts watching television but would continue to participate in the creation of wealth, and through that they would not only sustain the economy but also get personal economic and psychological gain. In his imagined adult day-care workshop "you're doing something useful, you feel dignity for yourself, and you're also experiencing the social life of work." Vita Needle provides all of this for Grant already.

Like Grant, 73-year-old Jerry also commonly reflected on the socioeconomic position of himself and his coworkers. Jerry explained that with his Raytheon pension and Social Security checks and his wife's income from her job as a day-care provider and what with living in a house that has long since been paid for, he does not need the money he earns at Vita in the same way some of his coworkers might. As he put it, some of his coworkers may be living in subsidized senior housing and may need to augment a pension in order to keep bread on the table. Bearing some of Grant's ideas in mind, I mentioned that one might think of senior centers as an alternative to Vita Needle, but Jerry disagreed, adding,

> Going back to what Mr. Hartman is doing, he is providing a public service. Maybe he doesn't think of it that way but I think he's thinking about

it that way now maybe more so, I don't know. But the realization that he is providing a vital service.... He's not exploiting.... Being in the union background you think at first, "Well, he hires all these people because you don't have to pay them health insurance. And he's exploiting these poor old ladies." ... You could look at it that way, but, in fact, he is providing a vital opportunity for them to come and socialize and they could knit or crochet but.... They could go to a senior care center or someplace and play cards but, coming and moving some cannulas around or doing something and then having somebody pay you to do that because that's valuable. And I'm passing that on and it's going to get shipped out and somebody's going to pay for that and...so I think there's a very useful value.

Jerry explains here that in his own analysis of Vita Needle, he moved from the suspicion of exploitation to an understanding of this job as a value-making opportunity for the "poor old ladies." I then suggested that it seems like Vita Needle is "convenient for the two parties." Here is the exchange that followed. Note how astoundingly savvy Jerry is with his helter-skelter storm of brilliant observation:

> *Caitrin:* So it's a deal for, Mr. Hartman, right?
>
> *Jerry:* I think it's a good deal.
>
> *Caitrin:* But it seems like also a good deal for the "little old ladies." [Laughs.]
>
> *Jerry:* Yeah, and it *is* a deal. And of course there's a combination, knowing that the turnaround time might not be as fast. And he knows that. And he's not going to jump out and bite the market the way a more aggressive corporation would be, to go for the bottom line, constantly increase, make it go better and faster and cheaper. And you could automate that place and throw all these people out of work. So you say, "Why don't you bring in a new machine?" Well, unless you, you don't really want to replace Esther or Grace or Flo. So this whole thing of a corporate world of maximizing return on invested capital.... When that began to happen, our world is being taken over by the corporation and that's destroying the kind of community connections that we had in the small communities, families are all over the place. You have to commute all over the world to get to [jobs].

It was here that Jerry referred to Fred as a father figure like the biblical Abraham, providing a service by employing people. Jerry went on to explain that in contrast to Fred, corporate CEOs do not care about the workers; they just want to see the stock of the company increase. Jerry labeled Fred's work as a "good service" and a "public service." As he sees it, rather than automating the work process and taking the poor old ladies out of a job, Fred provides them with work that produces value for Fred and for the ladies.

These comments from Jerry and Grant nicely sum up dynamics in the world of Vita Needle. Both men attempt to integrate their value as workers with their value as community members. Both explain that work offers much more than just a paycheck. Both bring past unionized factory experience to Vita Needle as they make sense of the differences between this and their past places of work. Jerry reflects on how a family business is so much more human and connected than an anonymous corporation like the one for which he worked for twenty-five years. We can hear in both their voices a sense of indebtedness and gratitude toward Fred, the employer, and a sense that work today for them is not the same as it was for them during their careers.

Born respectively in 1940 and 1935, Grant and Jerry are white Christian men who profited from the post–World War II economic prosperity in the United States. The anthropologist Jane Guyer has described the "predictable solidity of this architecture of life" in that era: "pensions, insurance, 30-year mortgages, un-employment and disability benefits, student loans for career development, and so on, that produced personal security at a new level."[10] But Jerry and Grant are men who have seen this architecture crumble in front of them, especially Grant, whose factory closed down to find fresher fields. Grant was raised in the era of "Fordism," which the historian Victoria de Grazia describes as "the eponymous manufacturing system designed to spew out standardized, low-cost goods and af-ford its workers decent enough wages to buy them."[11] In this era, we often heard the phrase "What was good for our country was good for General Motors, and vice versa. The difference did not exist."[12] Social theorist David Harvey describes the contrast between this Fordist phase and a phase of "flexible regime of accu-mulation" that began roughly with the 1974 recession.[13] This new phase, in which we are presently, is characterized by flexible labor and capital, with corporations moving operations internationally by aid of globally connected communications and financial systems. The ability for workers to afford the commodities they pro-duce is the exception rather than the rule, and lifetime pensions and affordable benefits are elusive to many. Instead, there is a prevalence of part-time workers ineligible for health and retirement benefits.

Grant's "antique workshop" is populated by people raised in the Fordist era, people who likely would once have believed that what is good for GM is good for the USA. In some ways, they are still attempting to live in that bygone era, and Vita Needle enables this to a certain extent. Some of these workers know that their firm grasp on the American dream was a weak illusion: Grant lost his GM job to Mexican relocation; one man lost his life savings to health-care expenses for his wife; one woman lost her standard of living when her husband died and there was no provision for her to receive his pension payments. At Vita, even these workers mostly believe that they do not need to worry about losing their jobs to automation or outsourcing. As we saw in chapter 2, Vita is a workplace connected to this particular community in many ways, and the workers understand it as firmly rooted on American soil—a point eminently clear from the massive American flag that hangs high above the shop floor, a bumper sticker on the refrigerator that reads "Buy American, While You Still Can," and another above the time clock that announces "Unemployment: Made in China." But these workers are part-time, and they receive no health or retirement benefits from their employer. They and their employer rely on that same architecture of life they all expected as they grew up in the postwar United States economic boom: Social Security and Medicare for all, private pensions and retirement savings for many. Some of this architecture (such as pensions and savings) eludes many Americans today, and even the government-provisioned safety nets are under threat in the current economic climate. When we see the vitality of life at Vita Needle, it does make us wonder what we will lose if this architecture of life crumbles in the near future.

Freedom and Flexibility

The German *Brand Eins* article describes what the managers look for in workers at Vita Needle, and it includes a list of five types of applicants as described by the production manager, Mike La Rosa. I also heard about these five categories directly from Mike on the first day I met him, when he took me on a plant tour, and he repeated them to my students during a classroom visit. As Irle writes,

> La Rosa has been responsible for hiring employees for more than 18 years. In that time he has learned to distinguish five types of applicants. There are those who are again seeking work because they determined shortly after the beginning of retirement that they could endure neither the inactivity at home nor the ceaseless time together with the spouse. Others want a supplemental income. There are many who have experienced "volunteer-burnout," and after unpaid volunteer positions they long for a normal, paid position. In addition, there are those who are fleeing either the loneliness of retirement or the stress of their grandchildren.
>
> When older workers apply for a position, La Rosa always asks if they can recognize themselves in this typology. When they cannot, the production director becomes suspicious. Especially whenever someone wants to know right away about salary, or suggests that he is only

interested in certain kinds of work, or when someone had worked for a very long time for a large corporation.... Not bringing any industrial experience... is considered a distinct advantage, explains La Rosa.[14]

Irle adds that there is a downside to flexibility, from an employer perspective: "The flexibility also results in specific demands for the older workers. When it snows in the winter, a large percentage of the personnel don't even show up for work, out of fear of falling. La Rosa then has to figure out how he can maintain the distribution schedule for his nearly 1500 customers."

These paragraphs include a rich portrayal of the employer's ideals. Mike wants to employ people with the right intentions, which typically are encompassed by these five expected motives for work: boredom or loneliness, too much time with the spouse, a little extra income, volunteer burnout, or grandparent burnout. He becomes suspicious when they ask about pay rate early on, as this obvious concern does not match with his own ideals for what his employees should seek from work. Mike looks for workers for whom work means something different than it did at earlier stages in their lives when the size of the paycheck was, by necessity, their prime motive. And—related to his attempts to weed out the status-conscious—he worries about someone only interested in certain kinds of work.

In general, Vita workers' goals match the goals that Mike assumes. Important to the employer and the employee is that this work does not feel like work to the employee. Vita Needle employees describe work today as different than at earlier life stages, and its key features are freedom, flexibility, and choice—in short, it is about *agency*, being in control. Agency and control: these adjectives may not typically be associated with older adults in American society. Whereas they are important values in the United States, we seem to assume stereotypically that old people do not have agency: their bodies are failing, they are not in control, their life choices have already been made, and they are just finishing up their years.

I have many times heard workers say they do not want a job that they have to bring home. They do not want a job that causes them stress. As one worker put it, the minute he steps onto the sidewalk he forgets about work—and that is how he likes it. Another told me that his ideal retirement is what he has at Vita: "It's to have... employment, during acceptable hours, without a lot of stress, job stress, let's say, in a collegial atmosphere. And I guess with a certain amount of flexibility in regard to time."

Vita workers want to be in control of their time, they want to be able to clock out in a moment of frustration or when a grandchild needs them, and Mike has expertly designed the production process to allow that (a surprising feature in an assembly facility). As Grant said, "It's a win-win. For them, for us, and I get a little extra money, and I don't use up all my time." Unlike many of their previous workplaces, where work used to take them away from their families, this work brings these (mostly) men to a new and in some ways more ideal family, but it also allows sufficiently flexible scheduling so the workers can (when they choose to) be with their non-Vita families for babysitting, accompanying a spouse to the doctor, school performances, birthdays, illness, holidays, funerals, and the like.

Back on the production floor that summer of 2008, I was working on the flaring machine, busy trying to outwit the infrared light that would trigger the machine to turn off if my hand got too close. Charles came over, fiddling with a small coil in his hand, and said to me, "You like this job, don't you?" I did like this job because I loved the social interaction, the sense of accomplishment when I finished a batch of work, and also the sense of future accomplishment because I knew the job was providing me with rich fieldwork data for my career as an anthropologist. I replied that I did like it but was glad it was not my permanent job. Charles responded that he agreed, that he enjoyed the job very much but probably would not have felt the same if it had been his career. He explained to me that back when he was working as a sales manager, he had worked for a week on a site visit at a factory that made cast letters for printing presses. The production process involved making molds and then casting letters by pouring molten metal into them. He said that at the end of each day, feeling like he had black lung disease from breathing metal fumes, he was reminded that he was glad that this was not his job.

After relating this story, he said, "But now," and he looked up and around the room, motioned toward the space around him with his coil-free hand, and shrugged. He then said, "I am glad I didn't follow in my father's footsteps," and he motioned again toward the space around him. He told me that his father had been a lifelong factory worker, making stainless steel sinks. Charles explained that he made sure all his life that he could avoid following his father, aiming to get a master's degree in business and to stay away from a factory. But now he was here, which he would not have expected, doing a job he enjoyed greatly, as he told me over and over again in interviews and discussions. Charles is the one whom I quoted earlier describing this as a men's club, actually *better* than a men's club because you get paid: "I think of this as a men's club. You come in, get some exercise, talk, do something, and get paid."

Charles is like many of his coworkers who are doing work that is entirely different now, in their retirement, from the work they did as they raised children, paid off mortgages, and saved for college educations. Former factory workers like Allen, Jerry, and Grant are the exception rather than the rule. There are a few former schoolteachers, engineers, and investment bankers but also a postal carrier, a waitress, an architect, a janitor, and a lab technician. Former Vita employees also included a retired circus performer and a woman who had spent her career as an administrator of a renowned opera house. But even those who did factory work describe feeling very different about this work now than they did about their earlier work. Recurring themes are their willingness to be here, the lack of obligation to family members (they no longer have kids to support), their ability to quit if they want to, and the ability to use their time as they choose. This vision of old age is in stark contrast to stereotypes about a time of life when people lose control of their lives, unable to make decisions and live independently.

Many workers describe the sense of freedom that the Vita Needle job allows, partly as a result of the scheduling flexibility. I repeatedly heard them talk about being in control of time. Sam, who can be found building wooden furniture in his basement workshop when he is not at Vita Needle, once told me the following, referring to the sign on the front door that boasts part-time flexible hours:

> Well it's part of what it says on the front door [referring to the "Help Wanted" sign]. You come in and make your own hours. But, I mean, I'm retired. I don't want another job that I have to retire from. I want another something that will occupy my time, that I don't mind doing, that I get paid for. If somebody said to me, "I want you to come and teach woodworking for 35½ hours, 35 hours a week and get paid," I'd get more money and I'd be doing what I really like to do. And time would fly.

Men pointed out that they can come and go when they want and clock out early if they want to, for whatever reason: "If I'm late I'm late. And if I'm sick, which is very, very rare, I don't feel too guilty." Pete Russell tells me sometimes he leaves early: "I mean, some days I just say, 'Eh, I'm gonna go home.'... I can go in whenever, as long as I get my work done, and get the work out." Workers often described their sense of time as different than it used to be. Recall Jim's comments about the difference in the value of time for younger and older people. As he put it, for younger people, "the investment in work may interfere with play, or workouts, or whatever social milieu provides more satisfaction." But retirees can choose to spend their time as they like—and so work does not have to interfere with play. I definitely heard Vita workers describe being in control of time, in stark contrast to young professionals who repeatedly complain about having no time for anything.[15] A pervasive sense of busyness envelops much of American culture today, with everyday expressions such as "too busy to breathe," with the media proffering the newest solutions for busy moms, and with scholars asking how to understand this "explosion of busyness" in the United States.[16]

In my efforts to figure out what is distinctive about Vita Needle by interviewing many people of conventional retirement age who do not work there, I met Tim Collins, a retired pediatrician who spends most of his time on the golf course. He offers a striking example of how time is viewed differently before and after retirement. Sixty-seven-year old Tim, whom I interviewed eight months into retirement, told me that he no longer wears a watch. Shortly after he retired, he started to put on his watch and said, " 'I don't need a watch.' And I was really happy I had a tan. There was no tan line! I'd say to people 'look at that' [and show them the absence of a tan line where a watch would have been]." Tim had previously known what day it was from the day stamp on his digital watch, so at first he did not like the feeling of sometimes not knowing the day. But now, six months after shedding the watch, "I love the fact that I don't know what day it is." When I asked him why he likes this he explained that it was a change after having been "driven by" the day of the week for fifty years. "I left home, I graduated...I had just turned 17, I graduated from high school in late May and around the first of June went into Boston and started working and I've just stopped. Almost exactly fifty years...yeah, fiftieth high school reunion coming up...so I just don't feel I need to care anymore about that."

Vita workers, by contrast, do at least need to know what day it is so they can know if the factory is open. Allen Lewis, the lifelong factory worker who considers himself semiretired at 84, found he had to buy a "retirement clock" (which shows the days of the week but no times) because "I was just having trouble remembering which damn day it was." He described what happened one day when he had gone to work: "I get there and the door was locked. So that happens sometimes that the lock, it gets bumped and it locks the front door. So I got out my key and opened the door. What the hell, so quiet around here? [Laughs.] Yeah, it was Sunday."

The first time he told me about the clock, Allen had not told me this story of showing up to work on a Sunday, so when I asked him why he bought the retirement clock he said then that he thought it was funny. He added,

> *Allen:* Well, I just liked the idea because that's basically the way my time is. I get up in the morning and I get up when I get up....I had an alarm clock and that blew up a month or so ago. I never used it. I disconnected it probably ten or twelve years ago and I put it up on the shelf and the only time I'd use it was if I was going to make an appointment or a plane flight or something like that....
>
> *Caitrin:* So you don't have to get to work at a certain time when you're working at Vita?
>
> *Allen:* No, no. When I get there, and the same thing when it comes to leaving. But most of the people there, if we know something is needed, we'll work on it....The other day, I saw a job was there and I knew they didn't have anyone who was going to do it so I came in and took care of it. So it, it works out. They're reasonable. We're reasonable. You know, and we get along fine.

Allen is describing a situation where both worker and employer are reasonable about their expectations, obligations, efforts, and hours. Allen told me that he once received a week's paycheck for seventy-nine cents because that was a week when "I came in and I punched in and I walked around. I looked. There was nothing to do. There was nothing I wanted to do. I just said 'ah,' and I stopped and went home....Nothing to do there....I hate 'making work.'" Allen did not return again that week, so his paycheck was for those few minutes when he had clocked in, looked around, found nothing worth doing, and clocked out.[17]

Allen describes here the opportunity to make his own decisions about what to work on and when. He says he and managers are reasonable, and he personally hates making work, though he does concede that managers will find him something to do if necessary. So for Allen, there is an obvious advantage to schedule and task flexibility. I asked Allen about the downside to flexibility, that workers might not be able to rely on steady work. And I asked him if perhaps the workers are being exploited by only being given near-minimum-wage-level work at part-time hours. To this Allen was adamant in his reply: he argued that the scheduling flexibility that this job enables justifies the relatively low wage, with some people starting at minimum wage. "Take Esther. She sits there and mostly she is just putting needles in the box. She's talking. She used to have people to talk to. She doesn't have so many now.[18] She'll get a phone call. Her daughter-in-law wants her to babysit, sometimes during the day. She'll just punch out and go along, you know. You pay for these things. The convenience of just being able to drop your work and go babysit for your daughter-in-law and then come back the next day and go to work." Allen ended this story of Esther by saying, "there are no chains on the seats." He added, to explain the analogy because I had misheard him, "slaves chained to the oars." Allen emphasized that everyone is here of their own free will and that they are making conscious choices about what is important to them: flexibility, yes; high pay, no. Unlike the McDonald's worker, they do not feel they are slaves.

Allen's, Pete's, and Jim's comments about schedule flexibility are just three examples of many positive remarks about scheduling flexibility that I would hear in interviews, on the shop floor, and as a consistent topic in media coverage of Vita Needle. These comments invariably cite the concept of flexibility in positive terms, whereas flexible labor is the subject of considerable analysis by labor activists and scholars who are concerned with businesses' increasing reliance on flexible labor forces, people who can be hired part-time or temporarily, who are easily fired, and who therefore cannot rely on regular work and are not eligible for benefits and certain labor rights.[19] But Allen, Pete, and Jim all argue—and I heard similar things from their coworkers—that they are willing to pay for their flexibility—they will sacrifice higher wages and other benefits if they can maintain a lifestyle where work is qualitatively different than it used to be for them.

Flexibility of their current work schedules allows both the fostering of family and social ties at work and the chance to spend more time with their real families outside work when they, as freely acting agents, choose to do so. They like flexibility also because it allows them to engage in activities they used to not have time for and especially because they feel that they are *in control* of their time. In this way they distinguish between their current work and work earlier in their lives, sometimes using the term "career job" as opposed to "retirement work," but often not even describing their jobs at Vita as work.

Another distinction that some of Vita's men draw between work today and work at earlier life stages is that their former jobs were aimed at financial gain, while the ones at Vita are not. But even if they do need the paycheck, all Vita workers invariably cite the importance to them of social contact. I characterize this difference as one between "I work because I like the social contact" and "I work because I need to, and oh, yeah, I like the social contact too." We see this distinction in the following joint interview exchange with Jim and Charles. Here these two men, both in their seventies, discuss what brought them to Vita Needle. The exchange is rich because it shows how they both weigh the economic and social value of their work. Jim, who is often absent from Vita on exotic overseas vacations with his wife, says he thinks of his work at Vita also as vacation. By contrast, Charles needs the money to pay his daily bills.

> *Jim:* I tell people I'm always on vacation. It's the only answer I can give because work is a vacation for me. I'm doing it to relax, I do it because I like to work, it's not because I have to work. I could leave the whole thing behind.
>
> *Charles:* Oh, gee, we're totally different. I'm doing it because I have to.
>
> *Jim:* Yeah, there are lots of different reasons that people are there. I mean Grace said she couldn't even stay in Needham if she didn't work [because of expensive real estate taxes and cost of living]. I don't know how true that is, but, I mean, she has a need to work. I have a need to work, too.
>
> *Charles:* Yeah, it's just a different... it could be financial, could be emotional, just keep busy.
>
> *Caitrin (to Jim):* Is that what you mean when you say you have a need to work?
>
> *Jim:* I like the social contact. I miss the contact.
>
> *Charles:* I like that too.
>
> *Jim:* The social contact is a very big thing for me. You don't miss it all when you're younger but let me tell you, being home with yourself, working for myself at home is not what I want to be doing. I'd much rather work in a place like this.

> *Caitrin:* Do you think it's different when you get older than when you're my age [41] or their age [indicating college student research assistants who were present]?
>
> *Jim:* Yeah, because I'm not under somebody's gun, I'm working essentially for myself; I could leave there any time. It doesn't matter but I'd rather be there, I want to be there....
>
> *Caitrin (to Charles):* So Jim is saying, "I could stop if I wanted to." You couldn't really stop if you wanted to.
>
> *Charles:* No, I can't.
>
> *Caitrin:* I'm wondering how that makes the everyday work feel different? Like if you got mad at Dan you couldn't just quit, could you?
>
> *Charles:* Well, I could just quit. It's just I would now have to start living on my savings and since the savings are tucked away in the stock market, this is a bad time.

Jim and Charles hail from vastly different economic circumstances, but they come to agree on the importance of social contact; they seem willing to overlook certain differences to have a sense of sameness, as we also saw for differences of age (Rosa is old enough to be Charles's mother) and gender in chapter 2. I draw the reader's attention to the ways in which they interact—how their realization of economic difference is navigated in a friendly tone. In a society where class differences can be tense to negotiate, it is striking that they simply move on—and perhaps this is reminiscent of family dynamics where one sibling is better off than another. They also both emphasize that they are in this voluntarily, that "I'm not under somebody's gun," and "I could just quit." There would be different consequences for these men if they did quit, with Charles experiencing the economic effect in more stark terms but both feeling adverse social effects. But both men emphasize their agency in working at Vita Needle. These men are from similar socioeconomic backgrounds—white-collar educated professionals—but Charles met with bad luck in the stock market some time ago. Nevertheless, I have seen instances of workers of different class backgrounds referring to everyone simply as "workers" rather than pointing out if some have more status than others due to past work experience or current work responsibilities or skills.

Some Vita employees were eloquent on how work today feels much different than before, when there was a heavy sense of obligation about the role work had in terms of supporting a family. Pete is just one example, and he invokes the concept of freedom:

> *Pete:* What I do, I like to do. And I feel like I'm contributing and I feel appreciated. And if they don't like it, they can [laughs a bit, as he

obviously omits a curse]. But I have the freedom to say, "see ya."
[Pauses.] But the obligation to be there and to do the work is still
there, but I can always get out of it. It's not like there's seven kids going
to college. Or anything.

Caitrin: Oh, so earlier, when you did have seven kids who needed to go
to college, work felt different?

Pete: Ohohoho, yeah. [Laughs.] Work felt like "huuhuhuh." [Makes a
groaning sound.] Like that.

Here in the interview Pete indicates that something is bearing down on his head
from above and he is fending it off—as if the world is about to fall on his head.
Pete is emphatic that he could get out of the work if he wanted to; yes, there is
an obligation to show up, since the employer and coworkers expect him. But this
internally chosen obligation is much different from the obligation to work when
raising a family. Choice and control are key to Pete's assessment of his job.

One of the several former schoolteachers at Vita, Ron Crowley, described the
difference between his past and current jobs to me in this way:

> For so many years, much of my job revolved around making sure that
> people, kids, were doing what I wanted them to do and what they should
> be doing. So I was in a supervisory role.... But, you know, when I first
> got [to Vita], I was like "What's he doing? What's she doing?" Just simply
> because that was how I, as a classroom teacher, you know, you want to
> make sure that some kid isn't doing something wrong. And all of a sud-
> den it sort of dawned on me that these people are just doing their jobs,
> as opposed to my saying, "Are you doing that the way you should?" or
> something. You know, it was just "okay, I'm one who did whatever job I
> had in front of me" kind of thing. It was just sort of, I don't know, it was
> just sort of a little lightbulb kind of idea. "Hmm, this is how the other
> half of the world lives."

Ron here was showing the transition he made, the "aha" moment when he realized he did not need to be supervising. He had gone from being a teacher to a
doer. He described this further:

> You know, what I had been doing, I enjoyed, but it had run its course,
> and I was quite happy to be retired.... I enjoy the fact that... I can say to
> myself, whether it's true or not, I'm no longer a part of the dog-eat-dog
> kind of world, I can just do this work, and if they don't like it, well, I'll
> find something else. Now whether that's true or not, I don't know. But I
> feel as though, OK, I went off and I had my career, and such. And now
> I've got a job. And I'll try and do the best I can, and... please those who I

need to please and hopefully enjoy doing what I'm doing, and if it comes to the point that I don't, I'll stop, because I can. You know, I haven't arrived at that point yet. [Pauses.] I don't feel I need to stop. I don't feel as though I have been stigmatized by doing that kind of work, which is, as a matter of fact, I, it's almost the opposite. I feel as though, instead of trying to get others to do something or investigate something, or whatever, I'm the one who's now able to…to, you know, I, as part of that old "Those who can, do; those who can't, teach." I'm "doing" now, you know, I'm sort of "doing"…um, so, it's sort of the opposite of this, I realize, an upper-class, upper-middle-class town that the idea of a factory, being a factory worker, might be off-putting to some, but I don't feel that way, and I don't know that I have ever sensed that from any of my coworkers.

I admire Ron for working out what this job means to him, what it means to not participate in a dog-eat-dog world. He enjoys the chance to do something new and even something that has a vastly different social status. Later I asked Ron how he envisions the rest of his retirement. Here he is at 64, with plenty of time to make plans. He had earlier expressed to me some frustration about feeling pressure to get the work done at Vita Needle. I am struck by his explicit discussion of the creativity of his life at this stage: he is not so clear about where he is going, and he is OK with that. There is a definite sense of freedom for him, freedom to eventually figure out what is next. And he also notes the freedom of doing what he wants for himself, not out of obligation to climb a career ladder. Here is Ron on his plans for the remainder of his retirement:

> *Ron:* Part of my answer is "I don't know. I haven't the faintest idea." It's an ongoing redefinition every day. "What do I want out of this job?"…Because I'm still not sure, in my own mind, what I really want. Because I don't mind being there. But then when I do mind being there, I want to be out, I don't want to be there anymore. Because…in my career, because I started as a teacher and ended as a teacher, I never had an administrative job. I guess I wasn't climbing the ladder then; I never did. And I'm certainly not climbing any ladder now, I'm not trying to get to the top of the rung of Vita Needle. So, I don't know what I'm really, really looking for. And I guess I sort of hope that twenty years from now, when we are reinterviewed for your next book on Vita Needle, that I'm still working there, and still wondering how I should shape my retirement years. [Laughs.] And since I [would be] only eighty four, or eighty five, I plan on working for another twenty years, I should be…I should come to some sort of resolution maybe about this.

Caitrin: But you would imagine that maybe you'd still be there in twenty-five years.

Ron: Yeah, I mean, yeah, I can see that. I find that it's entirely feasible that…I remember making a comment to someone, saying "Well, geez, I hope I'm still working here and in as good shape as David Rivers [age 90]."

We see Ron and his coworkers endeavoring to articulate how work feels different now than before, in a range of ways including freedom and flexibility of scheduling (time itself feels different). We also hear of a pervasive sense of responsibility and duty to self only and not a world-is-falling-on-my-head responsibility to provide for a family. These men articulate a sense of acting and being for themselves, with the power to quit, to say no, to choose a new path if they desire. This is different from how they would have experienced work before, when they were raising children and when they seem to have felt yoked to work because of mortgages, college tuition payments, school supplies, and birthday parties. Their comments echo those of the sociologist Robert Weiss, who once said to me about the people at Vita, "You don't want to retire to a rocking chair, you want to continue to matter, but you also don't want to continue to be out in the competitive world scrambling to make a living."[20]

Like Ron, other Vita workers in their sixties or seventies often speculate about whether they would want to be like Rosa, Grace, or David, working at 99, 94, and 90, respectively. So when we see Ron compare himself to David as he tries to imagine his future, we see how his membership in this group of workers affects his own sense of self, of possibilities, and of what he may want to do in his life. As with a family, the younger members of Vita's older-worker cohort have elder role models from whom to learn as they make their own plans.

Conclusion: Corporate Loyalty and a Way of Life

Vita workers consider Vita a sanctuary, an oasis; they experience it as a place that is comforting and caring, where they can belong. As Grant's evocation of antique people and antique machinery suggests, for some it is a world reminiscent of the past—and many workers value it for its familiarity. In her study of Walmart, historian Bethany Moreton describes the ways in which the Ozarks occupy a place in the imagination of many Americans as an "imagined homogeneous yesterday; America's yesterday."[21] Walmart, today one of the world's largest and most profitable companies, strategically crafts a corporate history that appeals to a sense of place and identity of its workers in its nostalgic origins in the Ozarks, America's heartland.

There is a long history of companies immersing themselves in their local contexts to better conduct their operations, and the history of manufacturing in the United States famously involves dynamics of family and factory, where factories connect to the community through family connections and through playing a family-like role in communities. We have already seen how Vita Needle's workers have deep and varied ties to each other outside work. A second German magazine article explains that building on community connections is a managerial strategy. After noting that Mike hires only locals because "this makes the new beginning easier for everyone," journalist Stefanie Hellge continues:

> But there is another reason. As a rule, there are already medical records in the local hospital for the people from the area, in the event that something really does happen, in case someone falls or becomes ill. La Rosa, who is 50, ensures that each is up to the task he or she is assigned, and he has long since become something of a social worker. If someone doesn't show up for work, he will telephone. If no one answers, he will drive to the employee's home and knock on the door until someone answers. "We have a social responsibility for these people," La Rosa says, "and we pay attention to that." That also means having to accept that his employees become slower as they age or having to overlook someone falling asleep on the job, such as Marion, 96, who nodded off on her stool at the end of each day until her children forbid her to keep working at Vita Needle. Her last day was a Friday. On Sunday she was dead.[22]

Here we see several motives behind the managerial policy of hiring locals, which we already know contributes to the workers' sense of sameness and belonging. On the social end, Mike wants people to "fit in" (a term he has used in discussions with me), which they will if they already have connections to each other. But on the more logistical end, he wants workers who are already registered at the local hospital and who live nearby so he can check in on them (like a social worker) if they do not show up to work.

A team of researchers has written about how at the Lansing Grand River (LGR) General Motors plant in Michigan, the values of the rural community benefit the plant. The workers have a sense of responsibility to the community outside work to keep the plant going, and this loyalty to both plant and community benefits both parties. Whereas analysts often find that workplace loyalty is a "top-down" phenomenon (workers feel loyalty only because it is drilled into their heads by management), these researchers find something quite different:

> Our conceptualization stands corporate loyalty on its head: loyalty also may emerge from below—from the generations of rural and farming

families who comprise the LGR workforce. Loyalty springs from a geographically situated, "moral" community of these employees, and from there it is transferred to LGR via a system of team-based work practices that share certain features with farm work (e.g., flexibility, discipline, dedication to hard physical labor and long hours). The workforce, in turn, obtains "loyalty" from General Motors in the best way they know—with outstanding, globally competitive work that yields return on investment. In this scenario, the employees receive more than wages; they retain a way of life.[23]

At Vita Needle, Fred and his family as well as managers cultivate loyalty through policies such as the Christmas bonus and flexible scheduling and through their daily responses to workers' needs (attending funerals, visiting in the hospital, checking in when someone who lives alone does not show up at work, letting someone sleep). But as with the GM plant, employees receive much more than wages by working there. They *retain* a way of life (an imagined bygone homogeneous American 1950s-era life), but they also *create* a way of life in which one can be vital, valuable contributors to a wealth-making process, *even when old.*

I once discussed with Jim Downey why Grace works, and I mused that some observers might have negative impressions of working at the age of 94. Jim quickly and emphatically replied, "She wants to work. She wants to work. And the social part of it is, to me, is as important as doing the work. Both are satisfying for different reasons. Both...say 'You exist, you're important.'... Or, 'I'm alive...I make a difference.'" Yes, work provides much more than a paycheck for Vita's employees. We may at first wonder "How can anyone consider working here to be an ideal retirement?" But Vita builds on its workers' histories, localities, and emotions such that many hope to work here until they die—and some, like 64-year-old Ron, are not quite sure what they want, but they appreciate the examples they see in their older coworkers. Sam Stewart once told me,

> Fred used to say, "I hope you stay with us for twenty years, Sam." And I say, "I hope I stay longer," which is true. I want to, but I'd be upset if I was released, let's put it that way. And I wouldn't want to have to leave for physical reasons like some people, you know, they just can't go to work anymore because I have cancer or Alzheimer's. I would not want it to end that way....If my working career at Vita Needle ended abruptly for something that I couldn't control, I would have a tough time dealing with that.

Here we see Sam express a desire to feel in control—this is the sense of freedom this work affords for older people when so much in life is not in their control.

And with his reference to cancer and Alzheimer's we hear a desire to be in control from someone who frequently worries about health. Sam and his coworkers know that their futures are unpredictable. They know from personal, family, and peer examples that health fortunes can change without notice, a point some Vita workers even raised as a concern when 73-year-old John McCain ran for president in 2008.

A sense of comfort and family is what Vita's workers constantly return to when they describe the bargain they get from Vita: friends, sameness, belonging, nostalgia, mad money. When I first began to appreciate the sense of ties, vitality, and connection at Vita, I was not entirely surprised that a factory could provide this. From my own research in Sri Lanka and from other scholarship, I knew that factories are not merely the ennui-generating institutions we may expect.[24] Yet the depth of the ties and the nature of the worker's bargain are especially interesting here. These are people who feel marginalized in society, and Vita provides a stark contrast to the sense of invisibility and uselessness. It is a place where pariahs feel important and needed.

So here I am in suburban Boston, and the theme song from the famous Boston-based television show *Cheers* (which aired from 1982 to 1993) keeps popping into my head. Entitled "Where Everybody Knows Your Name," it reminds me of the life Vita offers its workers. Here is an excerpt:

> Sometimes you want to go, where everybody knows your name,
> and they're always glad you came.
> You wanna be where you can see, our troubles are all the same....
> You wanna go where people know, people are all the same,
> You wanna go where everybody knows your name.

As corny as it may seem, this song raises concepts of critical significance. As in the local neighborhood bar of bygone years, many of the people at Vita Needle are the same (old, white, Christian, nonimmigrant men—and some women); they know your name (you are not invisible); their troubles are the same (illness, widowhood, invisibility, loneliness, uselessness). Whereas a neighborhood bar may have provided this atmosphere in the past, we know from sociologist Robert Putnam's book *Bowling Alone* that there are fewer and fewer sites for community building in today's society (at least for older adults; the Internet may provide it for younger people and for Internet-savvy older adults).[25] In the Vita case, rather than a bar or a bowling alley, it is a workplace that provides this sense of meaningful sociality. In 1997, the sociologist Arlie Hochschild argued in *The Time Bind* that there has been a gradual process since the late 1960s in which home has become work and work has become home. That is, people want to go to work to relax and escape the chaos of a home stocked with crying children or a nagging spouse.[26] But an important difference from this wider U.S. social phenomenon is that in the case of Vita workers, the people who feel that work is a sanctuary experience themselves as marginalized, or even invisible, in society. Charles told me in an interview, "One of the nice things Vita Needle has is that it's sort of a *refuge for older people.* We come there, we can talk to each other, we can kid each other.... We can make money at the same time."

Using data from her study of workers at a large corporation in the American Midwest, Hochschild argues that these workers use work as a way to escape from home problems, "never quite grasping the link between their desire for escape and a company's desire for profit."[27] In parallel vein, invoking Jerry, we may ask, is Fred exploiting poor old ladies—and poor old gentlemen too?

It's true that Vita managers endorse the many practices of connection, same-ness, and care work among workers and that they depend on workers' flexible labor. If these policies and practices translate into worker loyalty, in whose inter-est is that loyalty? Does loyalty look different if some workers clearly self-identify as having no sense of belonging anywhere else in their lives or if they crave the freedom of a flexible schedule? Vita's example suggests that a practice that can be good for business (fostering a sense of family, requiring flexibility) can *also* be good for workers—it is not always that family and flexibility serve management's interests *rather than* those of workers. Is this exploitation? In a strict Marxist defi-nition, it is exploitation if there is profit for the employer, that is, if the employer is extracting surplus value from the workers. (Surplus value is the difference be-tween the good's price and how much the laborer was paid to produce it.) So, yes, in a strict Marxist sense, Vita workers are being exploited. We know the employer extracts surplus value from them—they are making money for Fred. But this framework is not very helpful. It would lead us to label as exploitative any profit-able business situation. Exploitation is colloquially understood as a situation in which one party takes unfair advantage of another. Working from this under-standing, the political philosopher Alan Wertheimer would lead us to consider whether the parties have consented to engaging in a fair transaction. Wertheimer distinguishes between "harmful exploitation," in which the exploited party is harmed, and "mutually advantageous exploitation," in which "the exploitee gains from the transaction as well as the exploiter. It is the advantageousness of the transaction that is mutual, not the exploitation."[28]

In the Vita Needle case, the employer is taking advantage of the workers' abil-ity to work, but this seems to be clearly a case of mutually advantageous exploi-tation. Both parties gain something from the transaction, which is why some workers refer to it as a win-win arrangement. We know that at earlier life stages, these very same workers would not have been able to afford the kind of flexibility that working at Vita requires of and enables for them. Work needed to be very different for them back when they were supporting a family, paying mortgages, saving for their own and their children's futures. In addition to their accumulated savings (in real estate and otherwise), it is in large part the government social welfare programs of Social Security and Medicare that enable the workers to survive in this flexible labor market and allow the employers to offer jobs on these terms. The Vita example does not lead to an argument for flexible labor across the board. But what we do learn from Vita is that what makes the exploitation acceptable to the workers is the successful building of community and creation of purpose.

But in the end I am reluctant to us this term "exploitation" at all because of the value judgment it connotes. When we hear the term we immediately think of something negative that must be eradicated; nuance, particularity, and perspective become irrelevant. If we can move beyond "exploitation" to describe the worker-employer relationship we will be better able to describe and analyze the complex meanings of work in a world where flexible labor may both entice and worry workers in a variety of contexts.

Part II

IN THE PRESS

I did not plan to be filmed on the shop floor. Honestly. My intention was to give a brief off-camera tour to my colleague Robert Weiss, a published authority on retirement, and for him to be filmed afterward at my university a few miles down the road. The plan. I had connected the German documentary filmmaker with Professor Weiss, who I knew would have great insight into questions about what was significant and interesting in Vita Needle. I had my hunches and was willing to share those on camera but only in my office—away from the direct gaze of Vita's workers. I never would have wanted to be filmed on the floor. Who was I to waltz around the shop floor on film, as if I were an expert? Awkward. How presumptuous it would look for me to speak authoritatively about Vita. Embarrassing. Some of these people had been there for thirty years. I had known of it for only three, and for two of those years I had been trying to connect with the workers as a friendly, interested person, not as an expert intent on being in the media spotlight. And this was back in March 2007, when I had not yet worked on the shop floor. Camera rolling. I had neither the time nor the courage to express my misunderstandings and concerns, and I did not understand my own feelings anyway.

I had canceled an interview appointment with a Vita employee named Marty Rice in order to bring Professor Weiss for the tour (and for what turned out to be a film shoot). I struggled over canceling, but I understood the sometimes last-minute nature of filmmaking and knew that the Germans were on location for only a few days. Marty, I reasoned, would be here indefinitely. Wrong decision. Marty was angry that I had canceled, and he refused to be interviewed; our interactions after that consisted only of polite exchanges on the shop floor.

So here I was, escorting Professor Weiss, with the film crew glued to us: cameraperson, boom microphone operator, and director. We squeezed through the factory, bumping into tables and moving chairs, fans, and lights; we interrupted people from their production rhythms, and anyone who did not notice us must have been asleep. I introduced Bertram Verhaag, the director, to a few workers whose stories I knew, providing a tidbit of information and giving Verhaag a chance to ask his own questions. At one point we stood near the shipping desk, and I awkwardly and unsuccessfully tried to get the attention of Ron Crowley in shipping, who was busy on the computer, then on the phone, then back on the computer and over to the shipping label printer.

In 2007 and 2008 I met with several groups of European directors, producers, writers, assistants, and photographers who were covering Vita Needle. Summer 2008 was the summer of European visitors, apparently a snowball effect of the airing of Verhaag's film, *Pensioners Inc.,* on German and French public television. Between May and August, journalists visited from Italy, France, and Germany. A pair of German tourists even came by that summer, having seen the film back home and wanting to see Vita for themselves. A pair from the Boston office of IDEO, the international design firm, arrived to do a photo-essay about Vita for a series on global aging; they were there at the suggestion of someone in their Munich office who had caught the film on German public television.[1]

I made an effort to meet as many journalists as possible. I saw the meetings as a two-way street: they could learn something from me (if they wanted), but I could also watch them work, learn about their interest and the European contexts for their coverage of Vita, and see how people at Vita interacted with them. That summer was also when I was working at Vita, and on a couple of days I showed up to work on needles and never managed to do so—instead I observed the shoot, went out to lunch with the crew, and set off to see filming at a worker's house. But my field notes are replete with anxiety about my interactions with the media. Why did I let myself get filmed? Should I have gone out to such a long lunch when I should have been packing needles? Did I ruin my efforts at establishing rapport? Did I say anything that I would regret when it came out on film or in print? Did I scoop myself by revealing my understandings of what kept workers coming back? Did I violate the confidentiality of my research subjects? Did I get what I wanted out of the conversation with the journalists? What would the journalists do with what I told them?

As I write in 2011, five years into this project, I realize that the moment that created the most anxiety for me was that very first interaction I had with the media, when I was filmed on the shop floor. Why had I been willing to be filmed in my office but not on the shop floor? I must have thought it would be OK for me to be portrayed as an expert on film if the interview took place off site—the film would come out months later and perhaps never be viewed by Vita's workers. But I did not want to be seen as an expert when I was in the presence of the people with whom I was trying to connect on common ground and whose own lives I would be representing. It was early in the fieldwork encounter, and I was trying to establish connections, not create distance, between the workers and me. And I also did not yet feel comfortable enough with the material to be in full control of my representations. Accustomed to writing—which allows me to revise, delete, and share with colleagues for feedback—I was uncomfortable with documentary film because I was not yet comfortable with my own role as fieldworker at Vita Needle.

Today I have had more experience speaking about Vita Needle in the presence of its employees. In March 2010, I spoke to an audience of two hundred people from Needham, including three Vita Needle workers and their families and friends as well as the production manager. I worried that the employees would not recognize themselves in my descriptions or that the manager would find my analysis offensive. I felt the weight lift when one of the employees came up to me afterward and said, "Thank you for the publicity," and later I received complimentary e-mails and cards from the others. Stakes were upped in June 2010 when I sat with Fred Hartman and an employee on the set of WGBH, Boston's public television station, for a live interview. Fred had already expressed concern about the kinds of questions we would get, worry about being ambushed on live television. And I definitely fretted about saying something that would be confusing, negative, or incorrect about Fred's own business while I sat near him and later would drive him back to work. But in the car on the way home his one point of criticism (other than my rush-hour route choice) was that I had missed an opportunity by not mentioning this book by its title, a small point that made me laugh with relief. But I was still concerned about what authority I had to represent Vita Needle in my work.

Today, viewers of the hour-long version of the German documentary film *Pensioners Inc.* will catch sight of me walking around the shop with Professor Weiss, discussing the employment model with Fred Hartman, chatting with the production manager about scheduling flexibility, and visiting a few workers. The apparently simple interactions captured on film belie a complicated experience for me as well as for the many Vita Needle workers who are caught on camera and those who are not.

If my own interactions with the media evolved over time, so did those of Vita's workers, who responded in a variety of ways to the media attention, which had begun in late 1997. While they might have had experience in front of an audience (singing in a choir, acting in a church play, speaking at a conference, teaching social studies to sixth graders), there is only one worker I can think of who might have been accustomed to something like celebrity before coming to Vita. I am thinking of Roland Hickok, who has since passed away, a former circus tightrope walker who is referred to in much of the late 1990s and early 2000s media coverage. But for the others, being interviewed and followed by newspaper and television journalists and documentary filmmakers would have been a definite novelty. I heard often from workers that CBS television's Morley Safer had been at Vita Needle in 2003 to film a segment of the newsmagazine *60 Minutes*—a definite point of excitement when first reported to me. But then I began to hear more. I learned that I would never succeed in my attempts to match names and faces from a *New York Times* photo to people I was meeting because some had insisted on using fake names in the photo caption. I saw Frederick Hartman, whose unofficial job is media liaison, instruct journalists before letting them loose in the factory by pointing out people who refused to be interviewed or captured on film. I heard from some that the journalists were "nosy" or a "nuisance." Frederick expressed concern to me that he and the workers didn't really have time to do interviews, and he worried that the presence of so many film crews would "affect the mystique."

I heard stories of fluctuations in how people felt about the media, a clear sign that making sense of their celebrity was an ongoing process. For example, I heard that because David had regrets about appearing in the 2002 Dutch documentary film *Age No Problem,* he thereafter refused to be interviewed or caught on camera. As one coworker said, "I think he felt that he was being overexposed or something. There's a certain shyness that comes from people who are not used to being in the public eye...because it's unfamiliar territory." But in 2008, David connected with one of the European journalists; my distinct sense is that something just clicked between him and the journalist, and again he was featured in a story.

One day when Larry and I were next to each other staking needles, Fred came over to me, nudged my shoulder, gestured with his chin toward Larry, and said, "Did you hear that this guy is an ex-con?" Indeed I had. Larry had told me that he refused to be in any of the early media productions. He proudly told me of his ability to resist even the likes of Morley Safer by making up a story about being an ex-con: "CBS wanted me to be interviewed. I asked for twenty-five dollars. They said no. So I asked Fred to pay me. He said no. I kept refusing all week, and they wouldn't leave me alone. Finally, to get them off my back, I told them I was on parole from prison and didn't want to be seen on television. They agreed, and when it came out, I didn't even appear in the background." Larry was a bit of a star among his coworkers for this refusal and ingenuity, and it was a story told always with accompanying laughter. But there was a serious side to it. "I wasn't saying this for the money, just for the principle. Someone is making money off this, and we all should benefit." Another of his coworkers, Tom Conroy, insisted on being skipped over by the early wave of journalists. Yet Tom was a star of *Pensioners Inc.*, featured for several minutes in a humorous and warm scene that I always hear about when I show the film in classes or presentations. European viewers referred to Tom by name in some of the laudatory e-mails that came in, such as this one from France: "What moved me the most was the personalities of the employees interviewed, Rosa, Ann, Paul, Tom....Each was so sincere and responded so naturally, with such honesty, that I felt I actually know them."

Vita's workers continually try to figure out how to balance the media, their work, and their everyday lives. I got a sense of this balancing act one day when I helped Ron package up a batch of two hundred-pound boxes. Ron had asked me to hold the boxes shut while he sealed them; to do so I needed to get up so close that the sweat dripping off his face would sometimes land on my hands. My head was not far from his underarms, and he apologized for the closeness. I replied that I did not mind and I joked that this was what an anthropologist would call an "authentic experience," to which he laughingly replied, "Yup, that's right. The sounds, sights, and smells of life at Vita Needle." A few minutes later, still wrestling boxes, Ron apologized to me for the time more than a year earlier when he had not come when I summoned him over to the German film crew. I was struck that he remembered this and raised it now; obviously our shared experience of sweat, hard work, and jokes had made him comfortable to raise the topic. "In retrospect, I should have come over, but my worktable had been stacked high with work and I had no time for a conversation with the media." He said he found it difficult to balance getting work done and taking time out to talk to journalists. This sweat-induced discussion with Ron brought to mind an earlier comment from one of his coworkers: "By working here you are agreeing to be filmed. It's part of the job."

At work in the men's lunch corner. Photo by Caitrin Lynch.

RIDING THE GRAY WAVE

Global Interest in Vita Needle

In October 2002, a television viewer named Martina wrote a lengthy e-mail to Vita Needle. It was 8:00 a.m., and the previous evening she had watched an interview with Fred Hartman on German television.[1] One can imagine that the first thing Martina did that morning after she awoke was to turn on her computer and log her support for Vita Needle. Her missive was entitled "Mail to the company I never thought that could be possible!" Apologizing for her imperfect English, Martina described her situation: "I am, like people in Germany from beginning 50 until 65, now unemployed and living with the money from the unemployment fund. There is no chance to find a new 'job,' you live until you can get the retirement-money from government, unemployed, there is here in Germany, nothing to do. Companies send elder people home." Martina explained that among other things she spent her time going to literature classes at a university, "to give my time, some say, 'waiting for death' meaning. Our government should have seen this report.... Sometimes I think business in Germany is as bad as it is because they send people like me to watch TV on the sofa. Your company seems to me is a wonderful example and this report should be on video for the 'school to learn how business really works,' so that our land could also start to learn from experiences elder people could bring to them." Martina explained that she had been to the United States and would like to return, but now with less income she had less opportunity to travel. She asked whether Vita Needle would employ her, though she knew she needed a visa and a Social Security number. "I like the States and now to know there is a company who never throws old people away like garbage, is one reason more!"

Martina's letter captures a spirit evident in many of the European letters and e-mails that have come to Vita Needle in response to media coverage. Martina admires what she understands as a forward-thinking business sensibility in the United States. She refers to German social and employment policies that expect retirement at an early age. She worries about a scarcity of things to do and she characterizes this phase of life as one of "waiting for death." She wants to do more than watch television. Strikingly, television is a recurring motif in letters to Vita from Europe and the United States—never seen as positive, it is understood as an always too-easily available activity (a fact consistent with the 2009 finding that Americans 65 years and over spend almost 30 percent of their time watching television).[2] Perhaps ironically, it is because she caught an interview with Fred on television (that reviled medium) that Martina was able to learn of Vita Needle and imagine an alternate future for herself. Martina makes sense of her own personal experience of being relatively young and unemployed in a wider social context. Rather than imagine her situation as a personal failing or injustice, she places the blame on business practices and government policies that do not value the experiences and contributions of older people.

Martina's is only one of many letters I analyze in this chapter as I delve into the role Vita Needle has in the imagined futures for societies undergoing critical social and economic transformations: an economic crisis that may require more elders to work coupled with greater longevity and the social changes these bring about. While some commentators see inevitable crisis (a "silver tsunami"), others see opportunity to ride this "gray wave." It is in this latter configuration that Vita Needle has had a role. Many people have seen the company as a model from which we can begin to envision a future where older adults can be employed and engaged, where they can continue to contribute to the economy, and where the economy can continue to grow.

This and the next chapter examine the media coverage in three dimensions. I consider perspectives of the *producers,* who include the journalists as well as the Vita Needle owners, managers, and employees, who may choose whether or not to participate in media visits. I analyze the *content* to understand how Vita Needle is represented. And I examine the *reception,* gauged by the audience mail sent to Vita Needle; since most of it is positive, I refer to it as "fan mail."

Media can affect the self-understandings of media subjects and audience. The interplay between audience responses to Vita Needle and worker response to journalists and fan mail reveals how a mediated self-understanding can take multiple directions. For subjects (as discussed in the next chapter), their sense of self shifts when their daily lives are performed on screen or in newspapers, and when they learn how audiences interpret their lives. On the other side of the screen or the newspaper, the sense of self for some audience members shifts when they read about or see on television lives they may not have imagined as possible. An unemployed 50-year-old German viewer of *Pensioners Inc.* stated that she would go see her unemployment counselor because the program "gave me a bit of hope and energy for another try!" She noted, "In Germany—and I'm afraid in most European countries—people are out of everything once they are 40! If they lose their job, no matter whether it was their own fault or not, they won't get another chance, which is not only a personal disaster but also a big loss for the social system in general." A 28-year-old woman in Belgium wrote that *Pensioners Inc.* made her cry when she thought of her recently deceased grandmother: "I'm 29, maybe a long life in front of me…and if I have the chance to become a grandmother, I just want to be like you, ladies. You really touched me inside." And a 40-year-old in the Netherlands wrote in about the earlier Dutch documentary film, *Age No Problem:* "I hope I grow old the way you do."

As the anthropologist William Mazzarella has written, "The power and attraction of particular forms of media depend on their close distance, that is, their ability to appeal at once to the intimately quotidian and the compellingly distant."[3] Mazzarella explains the concept of close distance: "Mediation produces and reproduces certain configurations of close-distance, mediated self-understandings that depend on the routing of the personal through the impersonal, the near through the far, and the self through the other." We definitely see audience members interpret the Vita Needle story in terms of what they see as close and familiar and also as distant and unusual. Audience letters and e-mails reveal a shift in understanding as they make sense of their own situations in terms of what Vita Needle represents for them.

Vita in the Media

When Martina wrote to Vita Needle in 2002, the situation for elders that she describes had already gotten the attention of policymakers in the United States and Europe, and there was already discussion about the socioeconomic and health effects of the expectation that people should retire in their sixties. Vita Needle provides a compelling story for Martina and media consumers and producers throughout the world because it resonates with issues that are uppermost in the minds of many. While Martina vividly describes personal experiences of "waiting for death" and being thrown away "like garbage," the implications extend even further than an individual's sense of personal self-worth and contribution to the economy and to society. If people are expected to retire in their sixties, then various forms of subtle and overt age discrimination and assumptions about age also affect their ability to retain a job in their forties and fifties and to locate new work if necessary. Whereas the official retirement age varies across countries and the prevalence of working after official retirement age varies widely, the global trend is that people are expected to retire from full-time work in their sixties.[4] Yet a retirement age of 65 or so was developed in Europe and the United States at a time in the late nineteenth and early twentieth centuries when life expectancies were not much longer.[5] Today, those who retire at 65 may still have one-third of their lives left to live. Does it make sense, both from an economic and a social perspective, to be retired for twenty or thirty years?

While the United States is facing important demographic changes, Europe, by many accounts, is at the forefront of the changes to come. Journalists from France and Germany have expressed special interest in Vita Needle. In both countries the picture of an aging population looks profoundly different than it does in the United States. Both countries boast sophisticated social welfare systems that support retirees, with the expectation that one retires in one's early or mid-sixties to enter a new phase of life.[6] This notion of a new life phase after retirement—a third age ("troisième age") in many parts of Europe—that does not include work is so common that it is accompanied by a vast tourism and lifelong learning industry.[7]

Table 2 focuses on countries key to the discussion in this chapter: Germany, France, and the United States. It also includes data about Japan to show the stark differences in population figures and percentages of elders working there, a country with one of the highest rates of older workers in the world.[8] Among the many revealing statistics in this table, we see that while 15.94 percent of people over

TABLE 2. Retirement, work participation, and population

	FRANCE	GERMANY	JAPAN	UNITED STATES
First eligible pension age[a]	N/A	63	60	62
Full pension age[b]	60	65 (67 for those born after 1964)	65	65 for those born before 1938 (gradually increasing to 67 by 2025)
Percentage of people who are 65+ and work[c]	1.68	4.02	20.04	15.94
Percentage of population 65+ (2008)[d]	16.50	20.06	22.11	12.72
Projected percentage of population 65+ (2030)[e]	23.39	27.79	31.83	19.30

[a]For Europe and Japan, see http://www.ssa.gov/policy/docs/progdesc/index.html. For the United States, see http://www.socialsecurity.gov/pubs/10147.html.
[b]Ibid.
[c]OECD 2010b. Based on 2009 data. OECD provides figures for total population (by age categories) and total labor force. It also provides a demographic breakdown of the labor force into age categories. The figures in this row were calculated by dividing the number of people 65 and over in the labor force by the total 65 and over population.
[d]OECD 2010a.
[e]Ibid.

65 in the United States work, only 1.68 percent of French people in the same age group do so. According to figures from the Organisation for Economic Co-operation and Development (OECD), it is expected that the French will spend more of their life in retirement than will people in any other country.[9]

When Fred Hartman issued a press release about his company's sixty-fifth anniversary and its policy of employing older workers, the result was immediate and widespread. An Associated Press feature article was picked up by at least thirty U.S. newspapers, including major national papers like the *New York Times, Boston Globe,* and *San Diego Union Tribune.* Other media outfits soon caught on. Media coverage has been a feature of life at Vita Needle since late 1997—hence the employee comment, "By working here you are agreeing to be filmed. It's part of the job." The coverage occurred in three waves (1998, 2001–3, and 2008–present) and continues as I write in 2011. The first wave was initially from the United States, while the second and third waves were centered in Europe and have spread as far as Japan, Australia, Canada, Indonesia, Brazil, and Chile (see table 3, which is not exhaustive). The coverage included programs like *60 Minutes* and the *Today* show from major television players in the United States and programming in Europe on television channels like France's TF1 and M6, the Franco-German network ARTE, and the Dutch station VPRO; these included two lengthy European documentary films that aired on television, in theaters, and at film festivals worldwide.

The media coverage and the audience responses touch on a number of points but include two recurring themes that I describe with phrases intended to

TABLE 3. Summary timeline of Vita Needle media coverage

1998: At least forty newspapers around the United States reprint two long feature articles about Vita in the last days of 1997 and early 1998. These stories are followed quickly by a segment of *NBC Nightly News* and the *Today* show and short articles in other national newspapers (such as the supermarket tabloid the *National Examiner*) and the *Economist* magazine. A story also appears in the Japanese magazine *Silver Tochigi.*

2002: The Dutch documentary *Age No Problem* airs in the Netherlands and Scandinavia.

2003: *60 Minutes* episode airs and is viewed nationally (and in at least one international locale, as evidenced by a viewer letter from the Philippines).

2008: The German documentary *Pensioners Inc.* airs on television in Germany and France and on television and in movie theaters in Spain, South America, Korea, Canada, and Australia (continuing up to the present). Other European news outfits soon arrive at Vita: French television (TF1 and M6), German magazines (*Brigitte* and *Brand Eins*), and Italian television.

2010–2011: PBS television in Boston (transmitting throughout New England) produces a show on WGBH (*Greater Boston with Emily Rooney*), and NPR's *Morning Edition* broadcasts a feature throughout the United States. Brazil's Globo television network broadcasts a news story, as does Japan's *Diamond Online* magazine.

evoke the emotional weight that both themes carry for Vita workers and media consumers.

1. *Rosa would be dead if she had to stop working.* At 99, Rosa, the retired waitress, is the eldest Vita Needle worker and the star of the media coverage. A recurring theme concerns the life-sustaining importance of community, purpose, and meaning as one ages and focuses on how work can provide this sustenance. We see repeated references in the media to Vita Needle work as "therapy" and to workers who value being with people "in the same boat" as they are. We hear workers profess that working at Vita keeps them alive—for example, in this excerpt from *Pensioners Inc.*:

> *Tom (age 72):*[10] I think by working here I am further away from death. If I was sitting at home, I'd most likely die in a year. But I am here and I have fun, make a few bucks, and have nice people to work with. So I continue to do this until I can't walk up the stairs.
>
> *Paul (age 71) interjects:* It would be the same thing as if Rosa could not come here. She would be dead in a very short period of time. This is her *whole* life, and I have become very, very close to her. I'll do anything to keep her coming here. Because of the fact that it is that important to her. There are many who have the similar situation in here. That if they don't come here—like Ann and Sally, and some of the other ones—if they couldn't come here, the same thing would prevail. They would be gone in six months or less. Because they have no reason to be here [in the world]. They have no reason to live. So, pfft, fold up your tent, bye-bye. And that's an important part of being here [at Vita].

The many stories that focus on this theme that Rosa would be dead are of human interest and focus on the social and health benefits to the workers themselves and on the quirkiness of the people and the place. We hear about the sense of connection and community among Vita's workers. For example, the German women's magazine *Brigitte* includes a feature on Vita Needle that focuses on the workers' families and on the depth of amity among coworkers: "Each works at his or her own pace. It is anything but hectic. Now and then there is time for a little chat about the grandchildren. Joe tells jokes to Tom and Zina clasps Bob's shoulder as she passes. Their attitude toward one another is marked by respect and a great feeling of camaraderie. It's almost like a family." And we hear some of people's motivations to be paid: "Zina Zambito, 66, is also here to make money. But it is not a matter of her survival. 'I like to spend money,' she laughs, 'for new clothes and to go dancing, gifts for my grandchildren and whenever I see something pretty.'"[11]

2. The second media theme is that *Fred is not a good guy but a good businessman.* We often hear an emphasis on the business model, and we hear that a

business gains important economic advantages by employing old people. Morley Safer from *60 Minutes* noted, "Hartman says he seeks out the elderly not because he's a good guy but because it's good business." Audience letters and comments from journalists praise Fred Hartman for how his forward-thinking attitude about aging has been leveraged as a good business model. For one American woman who wrote in after the *60 Minutes* episode, her strong conviction about the rationale and potential of this company translated into an investment inquiry: "I like your understanding of the older people you employ and your honesty in saying it not only keeps them productive and happy, but also is good business. Do you sell stock in your company?"

We see repeated in media coverage the apparent surprise that a successful and growing company is staffed by people 75 years and older. Since the media coverage began in the last days of 1997, nearly every single journalist and filmmaker has referred to the profitability of Vita Needle. Some of the stories coming out of media outfits in the United States, France, Germany, the Netherlands, Italy, Chile, Argentina, Japan, and elsewhere are primarily business-oriented; they tackle the feasibility and replicability of the model and explore the advantages and disadvantages of employing older workers and of managing a multigenerational workforce. For example, Irle from the German business magazine *Brand Eins* asked in November 2008 whether septuagenarians could make a business profitable. He continued, "This might sound absurd, but it is an indication of something we need to take very seriously. Here in Germany the workforce is also aging. The high-birthrate Baby-Boomer generation is now nearing retirement age.... The lack of an experienced workforce is creating problems for companies in struggling regions. This will reach a crisis point if companies are unable to reactivate a retired workforce."[12]

Of the vast collection of media pieces, I have picked out below just a few representations that highlight these two themes and merit further exploration.

"Time Stands Still Here"

In December 1997, a reporter named Jon Marcus wrote an article about Vita Needle that was published throughout the United States.[13] The article emphasized the firm's outdated nature, even though its applications are "state-of-the-art" and its revenues great. "But from the furniture to the employees, the business is as old-fashioned as they come." The concept of old times was repeated in titles that appeared in newspapers across the United States—from Florida to Ohio, Tennessee to California.

The article quoted Fred on the advantages of such a "loyal, very dependable, and highly motivated" workforce but pointed out the drawbacks, such as older people's concern about change and the unfamiliar. It cited worries among employees about the newly installed microwave and fax machine and about a possible future purchase of a computer—we hear that the secretary was reportedly "horrified at the prospect." The article ended with a quote from then 79-year-old Bill Ferson, "who worked for 39 years in a machine shop, managed to stay retired for only about six months 'with my wife getting after me.'" The story's final words are Bill's: "Retirement isn't good for anybody."

Within days of Marcus's article, an article by the *New York Times* reporter Julie Flaherty ran in the *Times* and was reprinted in papers elsewhere in the country, including the *Chicago Tribune* and other top papers.[14] This business-section article was originally entitled "A Company Where Retirement Is a Dirty Word," and it placed emphasis on the business model. Reprint titles included "Where Seniority Counts" and "No Need to Lie about Your Age Here." This article was quick to point out the business benefits of the workforce: "Not that Mr. Hartman, who is 45, is just being nice. He says he recruits older people because he finds them loyal, responsible and eligible for Medicare—eliminating the need for company-paid health coverage." The article emphasized the benefits to the employer of this loyal and cost-effective workforce, and it referred to one widow who used her income to cover basic housing expenses. It quoted one worker who referred to the job as therapy. "This work is kind of like therapy. . . . Getting up early, getting dressed every day, not sitting around in your pajamas. It was too boring to be at home when no one's there. You clean your house for two days in a row, and then what?" To contextualize this eldersourcing model in the wider economy, the article also provided figures on the numbers and percentage of Americans over 65 who were employed.

The *60 Minutes* story in 2003 focused on a few workers and also on Fred's motivations. Fred and the workers said on television much of what had already been quoted in print.[15] Rosa Finnegan, then 90 years, explained why she was there: "Because I would be bored to death sitting and doing nothing. Beside that, I'd be all stiffened up. My fingers would be all stiff. No way. I tried it and I did not like it." Bill's attitude was similar. "My wife wasn't used to having me home another eight hours a day. Well, I couldn't find enough to do. I saw this little ad in the paper, Vita Needle. . . . So I went home and I told my wife. She says, 'Good, you get out of my hair.' Best thing that ever happened to me, 'cause I lost her last year. So this—this is quite a place . . . 'cause I have people my age here and they're in the same boat I am. A lot of them don't have their spouses and it's a place for them to go. My doctor told me, 'Don't you ever quit working, Bill.' That's therapy. It keeps this occupied, your—your hands and your body and your mind."

When we meet Fred on *60 Minutes,* he discusses the business model: "People are here for life. As long as they can climb the stairs, be productive, get along with people, I will promise to find them something to do." It was here that we heard that Fred had adopted this eldersourcing policy "not because he's a good guy but because it's good business." Host Morley Safer continued: "And like any business, it's subject to strict government standards....His employees don't need health benefits. They're already covered by Medicare. That's helped the company grow revenues by 20 percent a year." Safer asks Fred to explain this model:

> *Fred Hartman:* Back in the late eighties we had to reinvent the company. And at the time, like it is today—it was a recessionary period—and we needed to find flexible employees who were willing to work part-time. And at the time, that's the only segment of people we could find, people that had been laid off or retired. So we started with three or four people in this age category and then the lightbulb went on, said, "This is better than just a short-term solution."
>
> *Morley Safer:* Lightbulb went on because this was a better class of workers than you would normally get.
>
> *Fred Hartman:* Yes, it was. Not only the dependability, the attention to quality, but there's an old-fashioned work ethic, people work very hard, very conscientiously.

Here we see Fred and Safer in dialogue about how an elder workforce can benefit an employer. Fred mentions flexibility, dependability, quality, work ethic, and conscientious workers. Safer mentioned the health insurance savings because workers have Medicare. While Vita Needle does contribute to state and federally mandated health and pension accounts for the part-time workers (a cost that totals 7.65 percent of an employee's paycheck), for those same workers it does not contribute a higher voluntary contribution that an employer may elect to pay for private retirement and health benefits (which typically averages the equivalent of 29.4 percent of an employee's paycheck).[16]

Pensioners Inc.

The 2008 film *Pensioners Inc.* appears to have reached the farthest and has aired (dubbed or subtitled, on television and in theaters) throughout Europe, South America, East Asia, the Middle East, Australia, and Canada, with broadcasts still occurring in mid-2011. It was the January 2010 "documentary of the month" for a series that appeared in theaters in forty cities in Spain and South America and has been the subject of film reviews and editorials in newspapers in Germany, France, Chile, and Argentina.[17] My summary below highlights how this film, like other media coverage, raises questions about business profitability and ethics and examines what an older worker gets out of work besides a paycheck. As we have seen, this film resonated with viewers, many of whom wrote to Vita and referred in fine detail to people and incidents from the film. Because the depth of character development and the tight connections among the workers obviously spoke to the viewers in a meaningful way, I have tried to capture some of the depth and connection in my own description. My aim is to try to reproduce the viewer experience; I hope my words will bring you onto the shop floor, just as the viewers were brought onto the floor through the film's visual and aural display.

The film opens with the music of a stringed instrument that evokes the sound of a train whistle; we see a "Help Wanted" sign, and the strings begin to play to the beat and tempo of the grinding and stamping of machinery that slowly comes into earshot. We are on the shop floor, following Bill Ferson, who is gathering materials as he makes his way through the factory. "I'm the oldest man in here. I retired when I was 69, and I have been here fifteen years. I didn't like retirement. So I got this as a part-time job. Now it's a full-time job. I'm 85, coming up. I'm 84. Yup. Ayup. I don't know where the years went, but," Bill smiles to the camera, "they're gone." The camera then moves to shots of hands, all light-skinned, all clearly aged, some more so than others. We see hands grinding and stamping needles, packaging and stacking tubes. One woman appears to be asking another woman, who is staking needles, if she wants to buy a lottery ticket together. They laugh, and the would-be lottery ticket buyer affectionately squeezes her coworker's shoulders. When we move to a new set of clearly arthritic hands, the caption tells us this is Rosa Finnegan, age 96.

Rosa speaks as she repeatedly attaches needles to plastic dispensers with the quick twist of a rubber band (the very same job she trained me on in 2008). "You can work fast or slow, whatever you feel like. Some days you feel like working fast, some days you feel like working slow. You really don't have to do one thing all day long if you don't feel like it. You just say, 'I'm tired of doing this, let's do something else.' You know. Which is great. And nobody says 'hurry up, hurry up,' you know. They give you a job to do and you do it. It's good."

Rosa's narrative becomes a voiceover, and now we see the Needham commuter rail train roll by; the train's whistle fades into the whistle-like music of the opening, and we return to the shop floor. While the camera pans through the factory and settles on a man with unkempt white hair and thick glasses who is pushing a long needle into a tabletop machine, the narrator begins: "The small town of Needham, population twenty-seven thousand, a suburb of Boston USA, is home to a company of a very special kind. It's the dream of every happy employee. No one here ever gets sacked or forced into retirement. And yet the average age of the employees here is 74. The place is packed with human maturity and experience and they have turned the traditional firm into a highly successful enterprise. Over the past five years Vita Needle has managed to double its sales."

The camera cuts to Fred Hartman (age 55 and Vita's president, the caption tells us). "I know that is kind of an irony. You're saying, well, you've got senior citizens. Senior citizens are slower and they don't move as quickly. That is just a mistake. That may be true from a physical standpoint, but we overcome that by having more than enough people to get the job done. If you have more than enough people, you can move very quickly. And that's what we do." Only three minutes into the fifty-two-minute documentary film, and we know much about Vita Needle: older workers, successful company, people who did not like retirement, flexible work tasks and scheduling. The film goes on to feature a few people, especially Rosa, and we come away with a keen sense of vitality, comradeship, and friendship among workers. Some scenes show us the obvious consideration that men at Vita show toward the women, and we even hear of one man brushing snow off Rosa's car in winter.

Near the end of the film we see Rosa with her coat on, preparing to go home, fishing car keys out of her purse. "I've had a wonderful life so far, but my whole family is gone now. I am the only one left. And most of my friends are gone. So it's pretty lonesome. So it's good to come here. And you have friends here to talk to, which makes it nice." As Rosa makes her way out of the shop, we see each of her coworkers wish her good night.

We cut to a warm and humorous scene with three men: Ray and Paul are staking needles, while Tom is standing and massaging Paul's shoulders from behind. As the threesome chuckles, Tom explains that Fred always comes to them with problems: Ray laughs at them, Paul solves them, and Tom creates them. Tom laughs but turns a bit more serious when he says, "If I wasn't here I'd be sitting at home, getting in trouble, my wife would drive me crazy." It is when Tom then earnestly shows his ankles, swollen from standing all day at his work in the shipping department, that he mentions how working at Vita keeps him alive. And this is when his coworker Paul refers to the women who "would be gone in six months or less" with no reason to live. Paul's are the final words spoken in the film. The opening music returns and surges, and we cut to two workers exiting down the stairs. The man, whose back is humped, helps the woman, who uses a cane, and when they exit, the door shuts from outside, and the sign that sits above the door, Vita Needle Co., is left on screen as the credits roll and the strings play on.

The viewers are left with this touching scene; the final impression is of people whose bodies are decrepit but whose souls are fully engaged, people who know their value because of the paycheck but also the daily friendships and support.

Greater Boston with Emily Rooney

In June 2010 I joined Fred and a worker named Mary Brassard in a studio interview on WGBH television, the Boston-area PBS station. The program, *Greater Boston with Emily Rooney,* opened with a short video shot inside the factory and

brief worker interviews. Back in the studio, Rooney asked Fred about his employ-
ment model, and she noted that because the workers have Medicare and Social
Security Fred does not need to pay them benefits. "So it works out well for you,"
Rooney mused.[18] To which Fred replied:

> It works out from a business standpoint. But honestly, all sides win. Peo-
> ple are active. They have a place to go. To be able to contribute to the
> company. And at the end of the day, the wild card is that at the end of
> the year we really don't prefer to pay taxes any more than we have to. So
> we divide up the pot. And everybody gets a check. And in a lousy year
> it might be a month's worth of pay. I think our best year we might have
> had three or four months' pay at the [end]. And everybody's guaranteed
> a job. As long as they can come up the stairs, we'll find something to do.[19]

Here we hear Fred refer to the Christmas bonus, and he explains that Vita utilizes
this system (he uses the term "profit sharing" elsewhere) because "we don't prefer to
pay taxes any more than we have to." Elsewhere he has said that he does not want to
give his money to the government and that he prefers to give it to his employees—a
common attitude among business owners in the United States. For example, in one
study of attitudes toward business ethics, the authors found considerable antigov-
ernment feeling among business professionals and students, summed up in expressions such as "Big government is bad" and "Government taxes too high—they
tend to screw small business."[20] In Fred's case, by giving bonuses from profits to the
workers, he pays less in taxes than he would have paid if he had not given the bonuses. As an accountant explained to me, for every $100 in bonuses that Fred pays
out, he might save about $35 in taxes. Thus it is costing him $65 to save $35! This
"savings" might not appear to make sense, unless you factor in that Fred is resolute
in not wanting to give the government too much of his money and in wanting to financially reward his workers.[21] Looking at this in another way, although there is no
tax benefit to the employer for giving workers a year-end bonus rather than higher
hourly wages (all wages, hourly and bonuses, are deductible by the business), one
can argue that paying with a bonus system offers distinct advantages to an employer. First, he can calculate the appropriate size of the bonus when he knows the
size of the year's profits and also has been able to factor in capital and other expenditures, whereas a higher hourly wage would need to be sustained regardless of the
year's profits. Second, there can be managerial advantages to motivating workers
to be more productive by holding out a profit-sharing bonus as an incentive—and
we know that is true at Vita Needle, where the workers delight in making money
for Fred and repeatedly refer to the Christmas bonus.

Fred's opinions and approach resonate with the concepts of the eighteenth-
century moral philosopher Adam Smith, who argued in *The Wealth of Nations*

that the free market is a self-regulating mechanism that does not require external intervention. And when journalists frequently note that Fred is not a good guy but a shrewd business owner, we see admiration for Adam Smith's notion that the public good can be advanced through self-interest: that rational self-interest and competition can lead to economic prosperity and well-being.[22] From many corners, Fred is lauded as an example of this famous claim that the self-interest of the capitalist will benefit society. The Vita Needle website even refers to its position on ethical business practices and flags its elder employees as a key piece of its approach: "The internationally acclaimed work ethic and experience of our team members sustain an environment dedicated to both quality and socially responsible business."

As we will see below, many in the audience read Fred's commitment to older adults and his shrewd business acumen as socially responsible business, even if they do not use this very term. And the ensuing discussions fit into wider debates about whether it is the state's, the market's, or the family's role to provide support for society's older adults.

Viewer Response: A World of Letters

Since 1998, fan mail and inquiries have poured into Vita Needle from around the world. As of mid-2011 there have been roughly four hundred letters (first faxes and e-mails and since 2002 almost exclusively e-mail). In the first media wave, Fred posted newspaper articles and letters on a bulletin board specially erected in the main shop floor area. The board quickly became crowded with handwritten letters, passionate and highly personal. These early letters were posted side by side on the board so they could be read by anyone gathered around. Eventually that board was removed, and e-mails that came in during my research period (2006–11) were posted on a hallway bulletin board in clipped bundles so a reader could take them down and leaf through. Eventually most of the fan mail makes its way into notebooks that are kept with company photo albums on the landing at the top of the stairs. But some of the early letters were framed and now line the stairwell and landing, along with newspaper banners and clippings from the first media wave and shop floor photographs from the 1950s through 1990s.

Some letters are addressed to all the workers, others to individual workers, and yet others to Fred himself. Many invoke workers by name and make personal connections between the viewers and employees featured in the media. Elder-care professionals endorse the importance of staying busy for healthy aging, business owners and managers request details on how the business model works, and customers confirm their loyalty to the company. Some letters contain warm and highly personal greetings and stories (including recommendations on herbal remedies for Rosa's arthritis); many people say they were inspired and energized after watching one of the films. Some letters contain heart-wrenching narratives of loneliness and passing time in front of the television. Indeed, some letters convey pessimism and misery and are depressing commentaries on aging in the United States and Europe.

In general, audience correspondence has been deeply personal, admiring, and congratulatory. The story has resonated with many people, appealing to them for a variety of reasons. Audience members often recognize something about themselves in the story. Sometimes it is confirmation of what they do have; other times it is confirmation of their unmet desires. Business owners and managers recognize a path they have taken or would like to take. Young people see an opportunity they hope they (in the future) or their elder loved ones (in the present) can exploit. With rare (if any) exception, every older adult who responds seems to consider this path unavailable—because of either discrimination (as American audience members describe it) or national policies (for Europeans).

No letters have come in from employed older workers, and I can only speculate as to why. Are they too busy to read newspapers or watch television? Too busy to write? Are they like fish, not bothering to notice the water in which they swim? There have been occasional critical letters (particularly from young people concerned about older people taking their jobs), but these are not posted—since, as manager Mike notes, the posting of the letters is meant as a "morale booster." A November 2010 NPR story includes critical comments on an Internet discussion board that show definite skepticism about this eldersourcing model—a point I return to in this chapter's conclusion.

I now consider the letters according to my two themes (Rosa would be dead, Fred is a good businessman), highlighting representative examples of the passion, concern, and interests of the media consumers who have bothered to write in. I see commonalities in the European and American letters, but below I analyze more closely the French and, to a lesser extent, German responses to Vita Needle in order to show how national cultural and political contexts can affect how people interpret the significance of Vita Needle in their own lives.

Rosa Would Be Dead If She Had to Stop Working: Engaged Aging

The bulk of the letters focus on aging. They come from health-care practitioners who work with older adults (nurses, doctors, neurologists); some reach out because they admire the model and want to implement something similar on their own. Other letters are from young people, who have been prompted by the coverage to think about their grandparents or about their own old age. Old people who are sitting on the couch lonely and bored pen many, and others come from people caring for elders or disabled spouses. We hear of loneliness, a lack of purpose, and unfulfilling retirements.

A handwritten letter that came from Florida in 1998 in response to a newspaper article provides an example. The entire letter is brief: "Sir: Looking for a job and room board. Any prospects? Am 85 years old. Can wash, dress, eat with no assistance. Have diabetes. At present take care of self. What is the results? Bill Regan. St. Petersburg Florida, info from Sunday *St. Pete Times*." There is this brief note from Finland, in response to the Dutch film: "I saw a documentary about your company, it was something great to see that somewhere older people are appreciated." And a 52-year-old with an 85-year-old mother wrote in to say that in France "at 65 you're finished."

A 50-year-old from Wisconsin wrote that watching the *60 Minutes* program "gave me IMMENSE confidence and motivation. Already I had begun to worry about retirement. Those worries are gone and everyday I will remind myself that I will NEVER retire until I am ready. And that may never be. Thank you for your courage and conviction that people over 30 can be productive." With this reference to productivity, this writer, already anxious at age 50 about retirement, invokes a term we see in many letters. There is frequent acknowledgment of the importance of productive engagement for health, happiness, and identity.

An e-mail from Canada, in response to *Pensioners Inc.,* included the subject line "just to congratulate you." Jeanne wrote, "I have just watched a show on your company and just had to find you and congratulate you on such monumental compassion you have for people of all ages. I'm from Canada and can't think of one place where they hire older people." Jeanne goes on to explain that she recently put her 75-year-old husband in long-term care, and she continues, "I spend my afternoons with him and the other people there. It boggles my mind how we shove people into these places and forget about them.... Maybe I will move to Boston if my husband passes away."

And there is this 1998 excerpt from a letter in beautiful cursive script. Hailing from Rhode Island, Hazel referred to the closing down of the textile industry in New England. Her discussion of the significance of work ("something to look forward to each day") is even more meaningful when we read this in the context of the recent death of her husband.

> I am 79 years old and worked in textiles as a drawer-in for years.[23] The reason why I retired was the place I worked went out of business.... I certainly wish I lived in your area, because I would be very happy to work for you, and I would be happy to work 6 or 8 hours each day for you. You stay more alert and it's good to get up early in the morning and have something

to look forward to each day. You see I'm a widow, my husband died suddenly last February and it's not good to sit around. I could work any hours for you and would be delighted and happy to do so. A person gets lazy when they retire, in my estimation.... Always stay good to your help and you'll get more work out of them. You see we do not have to have health benefits from anyone, we have our own Medicare and are happy with that.

Hazel's comments bring to mind those of Bill, who was quoted in *60 Minutes* referring to his deceased spouse and the therapeutic significance of Vita Needle as "a place to go," a sentiment we also heard from Esther in chapter 2 when she described returning to work after she was widowed. Noteworthy also are Hazel's advice to Fred on how to get the most out of his workers and her concession that this is not merely an eager workforce but also a cheap one because employees come with Medicare in place.

Like Hazel's, other letters also refer to deindustrialization in the United States, and we are left with the impression that some of these letter writers are people whose skills are rapidly becoming obsolete because of changing times (in this case, the relocation of much of American manufacturing overseas). In the face of the consequences of out-of-date skills and ageism, the sense of uselessness is palpable. This 60-year-old woman from Ohio says she "was made hopeful for the first time in three years" after seeing the *60 Minutes* segment. She moved from Ohio to Massachusetts to be closer to her daughter, has thirty years of factory experience, and can find only retail work, which she finds unchallenging and unfamiliar. "The body is more than willing still but one look at this grandmother's face and all hope of something more is gone." She ends by asking for suggestions on finding a job.

These letters express a need for purpose and a lamentation about television as the only option for something to do. We hear confirmation about the role of work as therapy. We hear the yearning for an alternative path for elders—a path entailing vitality, purpose, recognition, and visibility, at the very least a hope not to be forgotten. We read of health problems and of ill or deceased loved ones. We see people reconciling their own hopes and dreams with what their society permits and expects. These letters are testimony to the cultural construction of aging. Aging is not experienced and made sense of in the same way by everyone; these people (in their own way) are pleading for a new recognition of what it means to be old and how best to age. At the same time they are reevaluating the significance of work at this stage in their lives, as if they are only now realizing that many people both live to work and work to live.

Rarely do letter writers refer to financial need. Although many older adults do need money for everyday living, in the letters and media coverage the Vita story centers on purposeful aging. This is a story not about filling a critical financial need for impoverished elders but about elders who work primarily out of social need. These workers have already made their money (to invoke the German magazine quote from Joe).

Fred Is Not a Good Guy but a Good Businessman: The Business of Capitalism

A large number of letters are practical and complimentary and focus on Fred's business model, such as the one by the woman who wanted to know if Vita Needle sold stock in the company. These more business-oriented letters come from present customers of Vita and also from potential customers asking for specific products, such as knitting needles or embroidery needles: "I would like to buy something that you make just to feel a connection with what you do." Others are potential business opportunities, such as offers of milling and design service or a private health-care program for older adults.

A number of letters come from European business owners or managers who are thinking of copying the model. For example, a 62-year-old from a German office of a major American international technology firm wrote, "If the people work sometimes slow, how can you define a salary/hour? I am interested to know: What is the salary/hour? And as compared, what is the salary of a regular worker at an equal place? I hope I am not too indiscreet." Some European managers and business owners ask if they can come to visit, and at least one Dutch group did in 2004.

When a finance and human resources manager for a Dutch company saw *Pensioners Inc.* in 2009, he wrote, "I think this is a perfect example of combining commercial and social responsibility of a company." This is the only viewer to use the term "social responsibility," and yet many viewers invoke the concept in their descriptions of what they admire about Vita. Indeed, a recurring theme is the recognition of Fred's commitment to doing well by doing good, an idea (often attributed to Benjamin Franklin) that is a motto in corporate social responsibility campaigns. In this respect, viewers bring together their concerns for creating a positive society for people of all ages and their respect for economic productivity and profit making.

In 2002, in response to the Dutch documentary, a viewer named Maarten sent an e-mail with the subject "great work you do!" It began "Dear sir, madam" and seemed to address both the workers and the owner:

> Living in a country where most people above 60 don't work anymore, it was quite astonishing to see how you guys keep on going. What you do is much better than just sitting in a nursery [*sic*] home behind the flowers near the window, wondering why your children don't visit you more often.

Okay, I understand the pay is low, but that also enables Vita Needle to be competitive, isn't it? It looks like (most of the time) everyone is happy. So why don't you start such a company in Holland also? I don't know much about the needle market in Europe but the closer you are to your customers the better I think. If you want I'll provide you with the first 10 employees as a free service to start with. Also I can hook you up to some institutions who will be able to finance your subsidiary here.

You probably think I'm not realistic and just an over enthusiastic viewer? Okay, just do nothing then. You probably don't have customers overseas anyway? So don't blame me if in the near future you wonder how a small Dutch company seems to be able to copy your philosophy in Europe:-) Be assured, it would not be in the needle business, the skills and craftsmanship for that are in your territory I think."

Maarten described a bleak alternative to Vita Needle (sitting in a nursing home, longing for visits from your children) and praised Vita Needle for offering elders a way to "keep on going." Then he turned practical and asked the question about low pay. But Maarten mused that if everyone was happy, perhaps low pay was excusable. Maarten got to the crux of topics that come up in debates about corporate social responsibility and fair wages. Vita Needle often elicits the question, "Well, if they are happy, can we call it exploitation?" Given that the media coverage focuses on those who emphasize the desire to be busy, have a place to go, and have friends and purpose (rather than those with financial need), we would perhaps more easily agree that work means something profoundly different to Vita's older workers—who may even be willingly exploited.

Indeed, some writers acknowledge the complexity of the topic when they skirt the question of whether the employment of elders is exploitative. They see in Vita Needle a much more nuanced situation—the fact that the employees do not seem to be primarily motivated by money is key to their interpretation of the model. For example, the following three letters all reveal viewers struggling to reconcile their preconceived notions about older workers with what they saw in *Pensioners Inc.*

"Hello from Marseille in the south of France! . . . I was not an optimist when I read the [description] of the program, I thought that if retired people still work, the reason was necessarily money, but when I heard Rosa Finnegan and the other 'young in their head' workers, something hit me in the heart. You all are incredible, so courageous (the horrible stairs!), what an emotion for me. Let me tell you it was a real lesson of life for me. THANK YOU so much. Nathalie Roche, Marseille, France." The life lesson for this author is that she had assumed old people would be working only for monetary reasons, but Rosa and others taught her otherwise. Her understanding of what work means has radically changed, as has her understanding of the desires and capabilities of old people.

In this next letter, the author first apologizes for his poor English and then writes of how this program led him to understand that people may work for reasons other than financial need: "I often hear from older people in Germany: I would still like to do something. But please not such simple work. On my journeys by the USA I often saw old working people. I thought that has to do with the social system. I am now cleverer."

Within moments of the end of the airing of *Pensioners Inc.*, a Swiss viewer e-mailed: "Into a country fully destroyed by ultraliberalisation and overcapitalism, you show that respect of human, of customer, employee, and product is the most important. You are all so beautiful, you all give hope, thank you." In Vita Needle, this Swiss writer sees an alternative vision of a respectful kind of capitalism, one in which a businessman can respect wider concerns than the bottom line. One Argentinean journalist likewise refers to Vita Needle as "humane capitalism," an expression often used to describe socially responsible business.[24]

Vita Needle in Political Context

Now let's turn to France specifically as a way to explore how the story is taken up in a specific political-economic context. We have already seen how people "rout[e] the personal through the impersonal," as an example of Mazzarella's concept of close distance, by interpreting their personal situations in light of the Vita alternative. But we also see that the media provide audiences an opportunity to rethink the wider circumstances in which they live, as evident in the manner that the Vita story has entered French discussions about work, retirement, and pension reform. Pascal, a French viewer, wrote in to Vita after watching *Pensioners, Inc.*, "I wish our French president Mr. Sarkozy would see this program and initiate similar initiatives in France, where many people are sent to retirement before the age of 55, whether they like it or not."

On 22 October 2010, the French Senate passed President Nicolas Sarkozy's controversial pension reform bill. The bill includes three provisions: gradually raising the retirement age from 60 to 62 by 2018, raising the number of years of work required to receive a full pension from 40.5 to 41.5, and raising the age at which pensioners can receive a full state pension from 65 to 67.[25] There had been occasional strikes and protests in France ever since Sarkozy's conservative government began working on pension reforms shortly after coming to power in May 2007. But in September and October 2010, when the government began to move forward on these reforms, strikes intensified. Protesters included union members—strikes by unionized garbage collectors in Marseille led to what the international media described as garbage-strewn streets. And strikes were by college and high school students who, according to some commentators, were participating in an important French rite of passage that marks the initiation of youth into leftist politics.[26] The reforms struck such a nerve and resulted in widespread strikes perhaps because of France's deeply embedded culture of retirement (a mere 1.68 percent of people over 65 work) and also more generally because of widespread discontent with the conservative government's neoliberal economic reforms. Within days of the escalation of the strikes in mid-October 2010 one *New York Times* pundit quickly noted that "we've moved beyond pension as an issue."[27]

Two years before these 2010 strikes, Vita Needle had already been inserted into discussions about pension reform in France. The Vita example has been upheld in France as a vision of productive engaged aging that is critical to the nation's future. On 3 May 2008, for example, the French newspaper *Le Figaro* published an opinion piece entitled "We Should Favor the Work of Seniors and the Return to Employment by the Retired." The author—Jacques Kossowski, national secretary for senior employment in Sarkozy's party—opened his op-ed piece by writing, "Retirement at sixty is one of the cornerstones in the myth of the Republic, appropriately engraved in marble, on the same level as paid holidays and free, secular, compulsory education." But he said now is the time to rethink this practice, and for evidence of an alternative path he devoted the majority of the column to the example of Vita Needle (he noted that the French television station ARTE had recently screened *Pensioners Inc.*). Citing the Vita example, Kossowski proposed that phased retirement might solve the problem of "the sharp break from full-time work to full-time leisure." And he wondered why people over 60 are allowed to do many things in life such as travel and sports, and yet they are forbidden to work. He argued that this prohibition demonstrates a lack of individual freedom and respect, and he called for creativity in thinking about the prospect of people working after age 60.[28]

Le Figaro is a conservative newspaper (aligned with President Sarkozy's government) with the second-largest readership of the French dailies. Kossowski's editorial appeared after Sarkozy had begun to promote his pension reform package to ease the state's financial burden. A round of union-led strikes protesting the reforms started on 22 May 2008, a few weeks after this editorial. Implicitly supporting pension reforms, Kossowski wrote, "[I]n the global context of discussing the thorny question of funding retirement pensions, the voluntary return to the workplace appears to be an interesting avenue to explore."

Readers submitted impassioned comments about the editorial on the newspaper's website, and many wrote in support of the pension reforms, an expected result for readers of this conservative paper. Some readers interpreted the minister's column in terms of their own experiences, whereas others situated it in terms of the country's social welfare and employment policies. Although no commentators referred to Vita Needle, we did read personal stories about middle-age unemployment, as well as praise for the government's reform efforts, criticism of the habits of business owners, concern about the forthcoming demographic crisis, and worry over what the state of the nation's elders meant for the country.

On 23 May 2008, a crew from France's largest television network, TF1, arrived to film a short feature about Vita for its national news program.[29] This was a few weeks after the *Figaro* editorial and only a day after the strikes spurred by Sarkozy's proposed pension reforms had begun. TF1, like *Le Figaro, is* a conservative media outlet aligned both with Sarkozy and with the style of journalism we saw in Kossowski's column.

The two-minute news story that later aired was simply stated and devoid of an explicit political agenda. The segment opens with a view of Rosa walking on the sidewalk outside Vita, wearing jeans, sneakers, and a short and sporty navy blue winter coat. The camera focuses in as she climbs the stairs and then punches in on her time card. During Rosa's entry, the voiceover from the reporter, Gilles Bouleau, tells us, "Of course, the employees are a little less energetic than in Silicon Valley. Before being hired, a candidate agrees to one condition—to be able to climb a flight of nineteen steps that leads to the workshop. The average age of the thirty-five employees is 74 years. In their previous lives they were engineers, nurses, accountants. They wanted to remain active in retirement." We meet Rosa, Jim, and Ann, who each discuss what they do and why they are at Vita. We hear from Fred about some of the ways in which Vita accommodates its workforce: "It's not piecework, it's not a race, but by having more than enough people, we're able to get orders out fast. The hours are flexible. We have people in here at 4:30 in the morning. People that have a key, open the door, they don't need supervision." The reporter closes the piece by commenting that "in the United States four million people over 70 years old go to and from work every morning. Rosa has other ambitions—to have the experience of being the first salaried centenarian in the company. The previous record is 97 years."

More than merely a human-interest story, in the French political context the TF1 feature illustrated to viewers a surprising alternative to French norms about retirement. At one point during their visit, I asked a member of the U.S.-based TF1 crew what had brought them to Vita. He said that their Paris office had suggested the story. Given the proximity to the airing of *Pensioners Inc.,* I am certain someone in the Paris office had either seen the documentary or read the *Figaro* editorial. This crew member explained the idea behind producing the program as follows, a nearly direct quote: "French people are very lazy, they complain, and they have no work ethic. When we show this program, they can realize that they should stop complaining and do something." I was struck by the overly optimistic assumption that one two-minute segment on a nightly news program would have such a direct effect on viewer attitudes (though I concede that this was not the *official* aim).[30]

After first meeting him in person, I later e-mailed the TF1 producer to learn more about the Vita Needle segment the network had aired. I reproduce with permission the September 2010 e-mail discussion I had with Gilles Bouleau (bureau chief/senior correspondent) and Vincent Mortreux (senior producer) for its succinct summary of the issues at hand.

> 1. *Caitrin:* What response did you get from viewers?
>
> *Bouleau and Mortreux:* We got an interesting variety of responses from our viewers. They admired Vita Needle and the work of its employees, and at the same time it was a cultural shock for them, given that the French have a cult for early retirement.
>
> 2. *Caitrin:* Why did you make the program?
>
> *Bouleau and Mortreux:* We did this news story because retirement is always an issue in French politics and society.
>
> 3. *Caitrin:* How do you feel about Vita Needle two years later, and in light of the recent strikes in France?
>
> *Bouleau and Mortreux:* For the French, Vita Needle is like stepping on another planet. Vita Needle embodies flexibility, whereas in France there is a lack of. [In a subsequent clarifying comment they wrote the following:] Regarding the lack of flexibility in France, we meant in hiring practices in France (hiring and firing with unemployment compensation, high unemployment numbers, early retirement practices, 35 hours work weeks etc.).
>
> 4. *Caitrin:* Would you ever see a place like Vita Needle in France. Why or why not?
>
> *Bouleau and Mortreux:* Gilles' response: "Not in my lifetime." Why? (See answer #1.)

Bouleau and Mortreux echo other journalists who see early retirement as such a deep-rooted and even "cult" value in French society that expectations about retirement will be slow to change, if ever. The nature of the contrast between U.S. and French expectations and experiences is captured in their use of evocative terms such as "cultural shock," "cult for early retirement," and "like stepping onto another planet." Bouleau emphasizes the vast difference between the United States and France when he says that he would not expect to see a Vita Needle in France during his lifetime, which we can presume means "not in a very long time," since web photos of Bouleau indicate that he is well under 65. Their discussion about flexibility is revealing because all the examples they provide for lack of flexibility refer to hard-won labor rights ("hiring and firing with unemployment compensation, high unemployment numbers, early retirement practices,

35 hours work weeks etc."). Thus these journalists draw a distinction between the current French context and the kind of economy and society that would support a Vita Needle. Though they clearly think Vita is a model worth emulating, they argue that France is not ready for it. What they would want is a more flexible economy, in the neoliberal sense—an economy that is not burdened by unfeasible demands from the workers but includes staffing by part-time, temporary workers.

The French letters from viewers of *Pensioners Inc.* contrast in important ways with the journalistic portrayals of Vita Needle. In the letters, we see people articulating a reevaluation of norms and meanings of work. Vita Needle has struck such a nerve among European viewers because it has led them to rethink the role of work in older people's lives. They appear to have suddenly noticed that under the right circumstances, work for older adults can be fulfilling and preferable to sitting around, watching television, and feeling useless. In the politically motivated commentary, we see journalists laud work as a solution to the nation's economic ills. The negative portrayal of French workers as lazy also reveals a particular perspective on the nature of work. When the *Figaro* column and the TF1 segment praise hardworking American elders, it is praise in stark contrast to entrenched French norms and values that they seek to change—that they think *must* change for the nation to move forward and prosper.

Conclusion: Vita as a Lens

Between 2007 and 2010 I met with or corresponded with many European journalists covering Vita Needle. I was always struck by their unambiguous intent to use the company as a specific example for political ends. To borrow a concept from communication studies, they seem to have hoped that the Vita Needle story would create a new frame for understanding aging and work in Europe. As we have seen, in the case of France alone, there is ample evidence that some journalistic efforts have joined discussions about retirement and work in that country.

Like France, Germany also is facing important demographic changes that will require more and more elders to work. In Germany, Vita Needle has certainly been put forward as an example worth considering. As author Mathias Irle writes in *Brand Eins,* "One thing is clear. Vita Needle is an extreme case, far removed from the everyday norms of German businesses. Yet it illustrates how productive even older workers can be when the work is not predicated on physical strength, high rates of production or rapid work procedures. Vita Needle serves as an instructive example for how many widespread prejudices it has proven wrong."[31]

On the *Pensioners Inc.* website the film summary tells us about the factory's owner: "Hartman's innovative approach seriously questions attitudes in our society, which treats even people as young as 50 as being virtually incompetent."[32] *Pensioners Inc.* has been shown throughout Germany, on television and in film festivals, and it is available for purchase on DVD. German reception seems to frequently come around to the question of exploitation. A German magazine review about the film describes it as follows, after first noting that "[w]ith this unusual workforce, the company has experienced measurable success":

> The story of the company demonstrates the success that is possible with a highly motivated workforce. Frederick Hartman, the president, highlights this motivation as a key to the company's success. Whereas young people soon tire of the monotonous work and quit, the seniors see an opportunity to escape their own four walls and spend the workday with colleagues. They enjoy being there, and this makes them efficient. It is not clear how much the seniors earn and whether or not the factory profits because of low wages. Drawing principally on interviews with employees and their bosses, the film gives us a reassuring view. The documentary shows us a 78-year-old worker with a mathematics degree who can further apply his knowledge to the factory's machines, and a 96-year-old woman who continues to drive herself to work. They all confirm what a 72-year-old worker expresses: "If I were just sitting at home, I'd have died long ago."[33]

Here we revisit the two themes from earlier in the chapter, about economic profit (Fred is not a good guy but a good businessman) and social vitality (Rosa would be dead if she had to stop working). The reviewer obviously is wrestling with questions about how to evaluate this model: he or she writes that the film "reassures" us about the question of low wages when we meet older workers who are vital and productive and who would otherwise be dead.

The director of the film, Bertram Verhaag, told me that when he screens it in Germany, he invariably is asked about whether the workers receive fair wages and whether they are exploited. He tells me that he responds in terms like these, which I take from an answer he gave a journalist for an Argentinean news blog:

> The employees work half a day. In the U.S. this means they have no sick leave or vacation time. The firm does not provide health insurance because employees are covered by Medicare (the government's health insurance). I do not know exactly how much they earn, but it is similar to others doing the same kind of work. While I was filming, I saw how much they enjoyed the work. The work environment and the compensation satisfy their needs at this stage in their lives.[34]

Verhaag's words succinctly capture the complexity that Vita Needle appears to pose to so many people who either instantly admire the model (as Vita fan mail writers clearly do) or approach it with some skepticism and pensiveness (as we see in the questions posed by German viewers who have not written to Vita).

From the many examples in this chapter, we can see that Vita Needle has a "life" in European media and in European conversations about life during conventional retirement years. The example challenges conversations within Europe because it takes up issues that are as much about culture (when to retire, what is expected of the retiree, what constitutes the good life) as they are about governance (what is labor for a nation, how do we regulate work and work life, what can society expect of work and workers, and likewise, what can workers expect of society). Even if Vita Needle, a small factory on the outskirts of Boston, does not answer these questions, it may at least be a staging ground or lens to begin answering them, as we live longer, are healthier, and re-imagine the meanings of family and community.

In the first wave of media coverage in the late 1990s, the Vita story had reached numerous U.S. media outlets, but it did not quite play the same way as it did in Europe—the audience responses were more about culture than about governance. But questions about governance began to emerge in the mixed response to Vita Needle from National Public Radio listeners in November 2010, at a time deep into the United States recession. In this moment of economic crisis, audience members used the Internet comment board to discuss their perspectives on Fred's employment policy and to debate whether the older workers at Vita Needle should pass their jobs on to younger unemployed people.[35] While there were certainly laudatory comments and listeners who reported feeling inspired by the example of Bill and Rosa, others were critical: "I am betting old Bill is drawing social security, as well as a pension from his retirement job. Pretty good gig to have 3 revenue streams to draw from." And "I wondered how many young men and women who have families to support are locked out because these antiques do not have sense to get out of the way." An astute listener named Janice noted the following:

> It's not the main point of this article but this illustrates how universal, single-payer health care frees both business and labor. Health care as a fringe benefit leaves many millions out and distorts the business model—temporary vs. permanent, part time vs. full time, whom to hire, wages, outsourcing to avoid labor cost, what jobs are worth keeping, the social cost of economic flexibility. Universal health care is the biggest subsidy our international competitors enjoy.

Janice here perceptively notes that this story about work, productivity, and purpose is much more than just that. It is a story that gets to the heart of questions about whether it is the state's, the market's, or the family's role to provide support for society's older adults. Or maybe, we may even wonder, it is the individual's own responsibility?

Rosa Finnegan on her ninety-ninth birthday in February 2011, pictured here with Vita's president, Fred Hartman. Rosa's birthday was celebrated during the morning coffee break; soon thereafter she was back to work on the Rosamatic. Photo by Caitrin Lynch.

ROSA, A NATIONAL TREASURE

Agency in the Face of Media Stardom

My interviews with Vita's workers were often open-ended and free-form. Especially in the two years before I worked on the shop floor, I relied on interviews as a window into a workplace that I could visit only occasionally; I wanted the off-site interviews to bring me onto the floor through the workers' reflections and representations. To these ends, I used a number of methods to get at the texture of daily life inside the shop: I would often bring photographs, word cards, newspaper articles, or needles to spark comment. I would sometimes ask workers to bring show-and-tell items for us to discuss, and I would be led in fruitful directions through discussion of items such as damaged needles, noise-blocking headphones, and paycheck stubs. I was frequently taken in stimulating and surprising directions during long interviews with 84-year-old Allen Lewis—for instance, in his description of Rosa:

> *Allen:* Rosa, Rosa. Everyone takes to Rosa....If you look at all the TV interviews been done there...I think she's got more time on tape than anyone there.
>
> *Caitrin:* Why do you think that is?
>
> *Allen:* Everyone just likes her. She's just a nice, pleasant person and, uh, you seem to sense that....Very obliging. Whatever they wanted, they want interviews, some of the others they say, "No, I don't want to be interviewed. Don't bother me."
>
> *Caitrin:* And you didn't mind being interviewed?
>
> *Allen:* No, you know, I don't know. What's the uproar? [Laughs.]

For one show-and-tell, Allen brought me a photocopy of a foreign newspaper article from that first intensive year of media coverage in 1998.[1] Though he was quoted and photographed in the article, he did not know what it said because it was in a language he could not read. I asked him how he felt when he saw the article. He told me that by the time that journalist had come in, "We were getting blasé about it. The *New York Times* had been in two or three times. And I forget who else." So when this journalist came, "No one else wanted the interview, and it didn't bother me any. I don't know what...a lot of them just have this thing about whether they're going to give some secret away or what, I don't know.... But I say, 'Fine, I don't care.'"

When Allen describes Rosa as obliging and willing to do whatever journalists wanted, coworkers as blasé, others reluctant to be interviewed, and himself as not being bothered, he invites questions of agency and subjectivity. That is, what ability did the workers have to exercise their own willingness or not to be interviewed, and how did their participation affect their sense of who they are and what meanings their lives hold? Whereas Allen's willingness to be interviewed by the media extended to me, this was not the case for everyone at Vita—some consented to interviews with the media but not me, some with me but not the media, and some with neither. Others had on-again, off-again relationships with me and the journalists. In this chapter I focus on workers' agency in the face of media stardom, but I weave their responses to journalists in with their responses to me. There was a variety of responses to us outsiders, as one might expect from people who are busily living their lives and making sense of experiences that might not always be easily summarized. While the journalists and I were there to create representations of their lives, we see people endeavoring to reconcile whether and how to disclose their personal stories. Perhaps some worried that the representations would not capture the complexity of their lives, others may have been nervous that by consenting they would expose their lives to strangers in ways they did not want, and yet others may have worried about what their coworkers would think of them.

While the previous chapter examined the content and reception of the media coverage, this chapter brings the workers to the fore. On one hand, it examines their agency in the face of media stardom and the anthropological gaze. The workers choose whether or not to participate, and they craft the nature of their participation. And these choices may change over time. On the other hand, this chapter analyzes how being media stars affects the workers' sense of self, their subjectivity. So while the previous chapter showed us how the content of media shapes media consumers' lives, here we see how the mere participation in media events by the Vita workers shapes their own lives.[2]

One crucial way that global media shape participants' lives is in following the shift from local, family, and personal concerns—how to age well, how to keep busy, how to get out of the house, how to survive economically—to a global context. Media coverage provides a common language for the workers to understand, validate, and define their personal experiences—it provides their experiences with name and texture.[3] But the participation also affects how the workers assess the meaning of their lives. For those who do participate in the media coverage, we can see in their choices to participate the enactment of their desire not merely for recognition but also to matter at a stage of life often stereotyped as devoid of meaning—a life stage when people need to work at finding meaning. Many older adults likely have previously built their identities and sense of purpose from work (perhaps more so in the case of men) and family (perhaps more for women). But where do older adults find meaning now, when family is shrinking and relationships may be estranged, and/or when work is gone or at least occupying a smaller part of their lives? These Vita workers seem to find meaning both in the process of work (as we saw in part 1) and in their engagements with the media.

The Hall of Mirrors

The media coverage that affects the Vita Needle workers' sense of self infuses their daily lives. As I turn to examine both how the coverage reaches them and what they make of it, it is no exaggeration to say that even when the journalists are absent the media are a daily presence at Vita Needle. Everyday when they arrive at the factory, workers are met with media coverage as many tangible reminders in the form of clippings, headlines, and photos hanging on the walls. Especially during the first wave, workers were confronted with a hall of mirrors each day when they arrived at work to the bulging wall of clippings and letters that were media representations and the audience's own representations (in the form of letters) of lives considered important and exemplary.

But as the years went on, and especially with the coverage from Europe, sometimes workers did not even see what was written or broadcast—or they may have seen it but not fully understood it because it was in language they did not know. Perhaps the Hall of Mirrors had become more like a carnival fun house of mirrors. Some workers sought out copies of the coverage once it appeared. But sometimes they never saw what resulted from interviews—for example, nobody at Vita (including the owners) saw an Italian television program from summer 2008, and this includes me, as I have yet to be able to locate it. (We only assume it exists because journalists came to interview and film that summer.) In the past few years, there have been several instances where people at Vita saw coverage only because I provided it to them—such as translations from German, French, Spanish, Japanese, and Portuguese, or DVD copies of the German film that I made for each worker, with the director's permission (but not all workers could see that, as many only had VHS players at home). Even if they had seen the coverage, it could get confusing: Which reporter was that? What film was she in? What country were they from? Have I seen that film? Bertram Verhaag, the *Pensioners Inc.* director, visited Vita a number of times in 2006 and 2007, and the workers generally knew him by name, but in 2010 one of the subjects of the film said to me, "Who is Bertram? I don't think I met him." This comment we might attribute to age-related memory loss or simply to the overwhelmingly wide cast of media characters coming in and out of the shop.

When they do watch or read the media stories and read the fan mail, they interpret them through the lenses of their own lives and simultaneously absorb them into those lives. Being in the media, repeatedly interviewed, affects what they think about Vita and their coworkers. We can see that media coverage about Vita mediates how people understand each other, even becoming *part* of that understanding. By participating in and consuming the media, workers learn how to interpret their Vita world.

I would sometimes hear someone say, "He is here on his doctor's advice" or "She stayed here after her husband died because it was like therapy." If I asked, "How do you know that?" the speaker might say, "I heard him say that in one of the films," or "I read it in the newspaper" or "So-and-so [a second person] said she said that in the Dutch film." The media coverage even affects daily interactions at work. Charles told me that after watching one of the European films ("at this point I don't know which one it was"), he started to think in a new way about one coworker. "I got an insight into what he was like from the video....I couldn't believe this guy was so articulate. It was just incredible....And I had new respect for him, and I began to see him in a different light, and I just started to help him out. 'Can you reach this for me?' 'Sure.'"

For Vita's workers, their status is elevated in their own eyes by the media coverage itself and by their understanding of the situations of other older adults in the world. Anthropologist Brian Larkin, though writing about an altogether different context—how Indian film is received in Nigeria—introduces us to the very relevant concept of "parallel modernities." He writes that media allow those who are not mobile to "participate in the imagined realities of other cultures as part of their daily lives."[4] This is a process much like nontravelers learning about other countries from watching travel shows or reading travel books.

In the previous chapter we saw this process among the Europeans who write in, but now let us consider this process for the Vita workers themselves. Many of Vita's older workers have not seen much of the world. It's true that some have gone abroad for World War II or Korean War military service, and some have worked or vacationed in Europe, but many have never left the United States. Even those who have traveled earlier in their lives often feel that their traveling days are over because of poor health or lack of finances. But these Vita workers are like the "armchair anthropologists" of the nineteenth century who learned about other cultures from materials brought back to them by traders, missionaries and the like—they have specific understandings of Europe, but these are realities they have constructed from the letters that come in, from brief discussions with journalists, and sometimes also from their own readings about European news and society. Just as Nigerian youth can consider through media what it means to be modern and to situate their society in that modernity, Vita's workers consider what it means to be old, and they consider the role of Vita Needle in a rapidly aging world where people's needs and desires do not match up with opportunities. For all that the media have made stars of Vita's workers, they also provide a surprising and new lens through which these workers can reflect on their own place—the media are a mirror.

Allen recalled some of the letters that came in during the first wave. He described feeling bad for the people who wrote in, such as one person who, as he remembered it, said, "I'm sitting on the sofa all day watching television and I'm only 45." He described this as the situation in Germany: "Retired. And nothing to do but watch television all day.... And you know it's horrible.... You figure, you can see why they're dying off over there." (Allen imagines that Europeans are "dying off," and yet this is far from the actual demographic situation. But for him, idleness would lead to certain death.) Others speculate about the apparent situation in Europe. One person said he gleaned from the letters "that in Holland, after 55 people feel like they're the British equivalent of 'redundant.' In other words, they're useless; they're just a drain on society."

For the workers at Vita as well as the viewers, the media provide a space of "imagined possibilities," a point anthropologist Mark Liechty makes when he examines the role of mass media in the worlds that urban middle-class Nepalis imagine as they make sense of their lives.[5] In the Vita case, the imagining goes two ways: Vita's workers imagine other less attractive possibilities (a Europe, where one cannot be old and work), and European viewers imagine a better world (a United States, where one can). And Vita's workers know that they are being noticed worldwide because they get poignant and highly personal e-mails and letters from around the world addressing them by name and hoping they are doing well, suggesting remedies for ailments, asking for recipes, and more. And they have an anthropologist who corroborates all this by her interest in them. They know quite certainly that they have captured the imagination of people worldwide.

And they even manage to attract visitors, cameras in hand, as when a German tourist couple stopped by the shop that summer of 2008. One day when I was eating lunch with Esther, both of us huddled at our worktables eating our peanut butter sandwiches, she told me that just a few days earlier two German tourists had stopped her and a fellow coworker on the street in Needham. The tourists told them that they were famous in Germany and congratulated them for being an inspiration to others. When I expressed surprise that foreign tourists would come to see Needham (a relatively nondescript suburb), Esther explained that they had been in the area to visit relatives. She told me that their visit made her think how terrible the situation must be in Europe and made her glad she lived in the United States. She wondered what older adults in Europe did with their time if they were not allowed to work.

Esther is not alone in imagining what a European life without work in retirement might be. One person with a number of friends in Europe says they are all sitting at home bored, "doing a lot of wishful thinking." The Vita Needle workers are quite the opposite of the imagined European counterparts. They are media darlings, with names that will live on long past their own lives.[6] E-mails from Europe refer to them by name: "We are very impressed by the working team, especially by Rosa." "What moved me the most was the personalities of the employees interviewed, Rosa, Ann, Paul, Tom." Instead of being at home occupied only by wishful thinking, they are at work, being interviewed by foreign journalists, getting attention from an anthropologist, and being stopped on the street by fans!

The workers also develop a sense of self-importance when they explain to me, to themselves, and to others why there has been such great media interest in them. Journalists are "trying to promote this activity in Europe." Or they are "interested in old people doing useful things." Or journalists are hoping to spread the message that "when you're 60 or 65, you don't fall off the face of the earth" and to show that the European alternative "is a terrible waste." I heard that the media coverage would help society by reducing the number of depressed elders because work groups functioned like a "mutual aid society." And I heard simply that the coverage was "to show other people that they can hire elderly people." As 21-year-old Kimberly Flanagan, a college student summer worker eloquently stated,

> I think it's great that we're getting such recognition, and it's also probably kind of turning around the views of a lot of foreign countries about us that we're lazy and everything else, and that all old people look forward to dying and stuff like that. I think that it's, I don't really know how things happen in other countries, I've never been to another country, but I think that it's probably inspiring older people in other countries to pick up the sword again and keep going. It really is an inspiration to see these people doing what they do everyday.

This is a view of the media from a younger person—someone who has never been interviewed by the media but who is also obviously making sense of the media and of her own involvement in the Vita Needle story. Nineteen-year-old Steve Zanes had only begun work that summer of 2008 and said that before the media blitz, "I didn't know Vita was such a hot item." Steve, also never interviewed by the media, said he found it "hectic" and "stressful" to work with the crews there, always trying to squeeze by camera people, stay out of the way, not interrupt an interview.

Assessing a Life in the Limelight

How does the daily presence of so much media attention affect how workers assess the value of their lives? I am thinking here both of the people who do engage with the media and those who do not. Even the latter would also likely think differently about their lives as a result of seeing the media circus around them. There is no doubt that being observed and noticed affects how the workers think about themselves, not unlike the famous "Hawthorne Effect," the early-twentieth-century industrial study that measured the effect of lighting on productivity in a factory that produced telephone relays (electrically operated switches). The researchers argued that it was not so much the lighting as the effect of being watched that increased the productivity of the research subjects. Although the study's results have been widely debated and in some estimates debunked, there is something to retain about the notion of how attention affects one's sense of worth.[7] Here I am concerned not with the production of relays or needles but with the production of meaning—the sense that knowing you are being evaluated as special and important will make you feel special and important.

In the case of Vita's workers, what is especially interesting and efficacious in terms of subjectivity is that such intense attention and interest (interviews, photographs, cameras, microphones, clippings, fan mail!) is directed toward *older adults*. These are people used to feeling invisible and feeling that the world is passing them by—feeling like a fifth wheel, as Esther put it. In this context, imagine the impact of global visibility and celebrity. I think here of a concept first articulated in 1922 by the sociologist Charles Cooley: that we shape our sense of selves through how other people perceive us. Cooley writes of "a reflected or looking-glass self" by first referring to how we consider our reflections in the mirror:

> As we see our face, figure, and dress in the glass, and are interested in them because they are ours, and pleased or otherwise with them according as they do or do not answer to what we should like them to be; so in imagination we perceive in another's mind some thought of our appearance, manners, aims, deeds, characters, friends, and so on, and are variously affected by it.

A self-idea of this sort seems to have three principal elements: the imagination of our appearance to the other person; the imagination of his judgment of that appearance, and some sort of self-feeling, such as pride or mortification.[8]

Cooley argues that once we imagine how people see us, we then imagine how they judge us, and then we think of ourselves in new ways. In the case of Vita's workers, it is striking to think about how being in the limelight—how seeing fan mail (even if unread) and repeated interest from the media—must affect self-understanding.

The anthropologist Mary Catherine Bateson has built on the work of developmental psychologist Erik Erikson.[9] Erikson's famous 1950 formulation of psychosocial development describes the eight stages humans go through to reach full development. Leaving aside the question of the cross-cultural universality of these stages, I do see value in his approach for Euro-American experiences of aging. Erikson's last two stages are Middle Adulthood (he calls this from age 35 to 55 or 65) when people focus on "generativity," or making an impact, bettering society—and avoiding any feeling of inactivity and meaninglessness. His last stage, Maturity (age 55 or 65 until death), is marked by reflecting on our lives and feeling that they have had meaning and that we have made a contribution—a feeling Erikson calls integrity. Bateson has added a new stage to account for longer life spans (Erikson was writing in the 1940s)—she calls Adulthood II a new phase of life between Middle Adulthood and Maturity. In this stage the focus is on engagement and continuing to contribute to society.

Bateson inserts Adulthood II before the stage called Maturity (which she says starts with "the decline of health and mobility in old age").[10] For some people Adulthood II begins at retirement or when children leave home. It is a time when people ask what is next and reflect on what has been missing in their lives. They have relative health, energy, and productivity—but work is no longer their focus. Bateson has even discussed what work means for those who do work in this phase: work during retirement is not just about money but about the feeling that one is making a contribution to society.[11]

If we think of Vita's workers in this stage, we can see that they are asking how they can contribute and make a difference. We can see that for the people who thrive on the media coverage, participating in it may be one way for them to confirm to themselves both that they are making an impact today and that their lives will have made an impact when they eventually are gone (but their media selves live on). Giving another interview could be considered, in a sense, a service or a chance to leave a legacy. And this is distinct from a world where older adults are treated as invisible. Robert Weiss once said to me about people in retirement, "they just want to matter." It's not so much that they want to be busy as that they want to be engaged in something that matters.

There is a popular saying about "mattering" that is found on lists of "volunteer appreciation" or "inspirational" quotes and attributed to the twentieth-century American writer Leo Rosten: "I cannot believe that the purpose of life is to be happy. I think the purpose of life is to be useful, to be responsible, to be compassionate. It is, above all to matter, to count, to stand for something, to have made some difference that you lived at all." When I think of Rosa and Allen, who always agreed to interviews, or of Abigail, who once came up to me and said, "Thanks for the publicity," I have come to realize that these are not people necessarily pursuing fame for the sake of fame. They may be famous (I will say more about this below), but they do not have a "fame motive" (as the psychologist Orville Brim puts it) or an "urge to fame" (in the words of the historian Leo Braudy).[12] Instead, they are living out their desire to matter and to be seen and heard, to leave a legacy. And maybe for some of them there is a thrill to being famous (to be known by people they do not personally know), but that also no doubt circles back to the thrill of knowing you matter.

The sense of wanting to matter and to give back undoubtedly also affected their willingness to participate in the media and to work with me. When I first met him in 2006, Sam had consistently refused to participate in media interviews. Yet when I showed up, he was very generous with me, initiating our friendship with a phone call to my house. His willingness to meet with me for numerous interviews stemmed from a desire to share some of his insights—as I see it, a commitment to giving back, helping out. As he said in a joint interview with his wife, Barbara,

> *Sam:* But this whole business with adults and senior citizens it's…this country is way behind in our thinking and what's happening to those people because they're going to be there some day and work is one of [the issues to deal with], and health is another one.
>
> *Caitrin:* Right. That's why I'm interested in this topic. It's a big, important topic.
>
> *Sam:* It is an incredible topic. That's one of the reasons I'm happy to share it because of having studied about it years ago in my college life.
>
> *Caitrin (to Barbara):* Did you know that? He wrote a paper about how the Irish and the Japanese treat the elderly, for the most famous anthropologist in the world. It was in a class for Margaret Mead.
>
> *Sam:* I think of it. Since we got together, I think of it often. And of course it gives me a chance to think about ourselves getting older and what are our kids going to do when we get older?

Our interviews gave Sam the chance to reflect back on his life but also to think forward. After we had met for a number of interviews, he began to meet with the media too. I can imagine that his change of heart may have resulted from a developing sense of the significance of his life as he grew older and the significance of his insights for the important topic of aging and society. Sam's case is only one example of how, for Vita's workers, self is constituted in the media and how media life influences the subjectivity of the people in it. Merely knowing that they have a world audience seems to bolster their image. The media coverage seems to amplify the sense of purpose they feel at work, and it changes the sense of significance of what they are doing. It is as if they are thinking this: if others care about my life and see themselves reflected in it, how do I assess (or reassess) its value? In other words, mattering is important on several levels, in a bit of a feedback loop: there is mattering to self, mattering to others, and then the external evaluation of mattering that is provided by the media.

Agency, Self-Fashioning, and Fame

Sam is only one of many Vita workers who demonstrated agency by changing his mind about media engagement. By saying that Vita workers are agents in their media participation, I draw attention to the ways in which individuals act on the world around them but within certain structural constraints.[13] By understanding Vita workers' interactions with the media we can be attuned to their attempts at "self-fashioning," a concept I use following the literary critic Stephen Greenblatt. Greenblatt examines sixteenth-century English literature, both the texts and their wider contexts, to show the process of constructing one's identity and public persona according to a set of socially acceptable standards.[14] Scholars have extrapolated a wider lesson from Greenblatt's meticulous study of the world of Renaissance literature: people do not construct selves as fully autonomous individuals but in the context of the cultural and political worlds in which they live. The concept of self-fashioning seems apropos for a factory setting: by making needles workers also are making (or fashioning) themselves. We see these people in the process of making needles also developing all sorts of ways in which they retain a sense of agency.

Orville Brim defines fame thus: "[P]eople are famous when known by name, recognized by sight, and talked about or written about by a nameless public unknown to them."[15] In this conception, Vita workers are certainly famous. Think of the many people, quoted in the previous chapter, whom Vita workers do not know personally but who know them by name and who send them e-mails and letters with personal comments on marriages, health care, and personalities. Or think of the appearance of Vita workers' names on Internet discussions, as in this critical comment from the NPR website, quoted in chapter 4: "I am betting old Bill is drawing social security, as well as a pension from his retirement job."[16] In this one NPR example we can see how a media story can take on its own life: Bill's personal example quickly led into a discussion about whether older workers such as this were "greedy geezers." As Leo Braudy writes in his history of fame, "being looked at puts you in the possession of those who look."[17] And he argues that there is a loss as well as a gain to the person who is famous because the audience is observer and judge and pays only partial attention to what the performer may have wanted.[18] Moreover, participating in the media affects the relationship that the media subjects have with others around them. As the sociologist Kerry O. Ferris explains, "[F]ame and celebrity develop relationally, and...the advent of fame and celebrity into the life of an individual transforms self as well as relationships to others."[19] We can see from the Vita example that the media have a way of making their own stories, and consent to participate does not guarantee control over content and reception.[20]

For the Vita workers, who might otherwise have thought of work as nothing other than getting up in the morning and having someplace to go, being the subject of so much external interest now makes them think that what they are doing is significant on a global stage. Someone like Rosa no doubt thinks about her self and her value in society differently when yet another journalist interviews her. During the years I have known Rosa, if I run into her shortly after another journalist's visit, she will typically chuckle, shrug, and shake her head with disbelief when I ask her about her latest media appearance. As her coworker Jim once said to me, the presence of the Dutch film crew made him think differently about his own workplace. He had noticed years back, when he was new at Vita, that the crew visited the shop a few times before even bringing in their cameras. "I thought, well that's interesting, because that says that they're more interested in something besides the surface. And they wanted to get to a little different level. And that sort of interested me to start with. And I began to discover as I worked there, it sort of opened my eyes a little bit: that there is more going on than I thought."

This sense of digging below the surface came up in one of many interviews I had with Jim; he made the above comment a couple of years into our friendship when explaining why he had first wanted to interact with me. He saw me as someone who could help him get below the surface—he said this was "part of the reason that I was interested in what you were doing." Jim wanted to learn what I was learning, and he no doubt wanted to influence how I made sense of Vita Needle, but he has also told me that our relationship has opened up his world to new people and ways of thinking. So while Jim's commitment to helping me contained an element of self-interest, I experienced it as great generosity, manifest in numerous ways: in his willingness to connect me with coworkers, e-mail me updates on news from the shop floor, notify me about journalist visits, give me feedback on ideas, meet for multiple interviews, and come with me to events related to work and aging, and certainly to meet my students. All of this happened because of Jim's agency: it was he who did the work to enlarge his worldview.

When I write of agency, I am focusing on the capacity of the Vita Needle workers to tell their own stories to the media. But their capacity for storytelling to the media is deeply connected to their capacity to tell their stories to the anthropologist. Indeed, Vita Needle's workers were agents not only in media participation but also in interactions with me, which fell along a spectrum of engagement. On one end was the consistent welcome and help from Sam, Jim, Allen, Abigail, Charles, and others; on the other end were those of their coworkers who wanted nothing to do with me, such as Marty (who was angry when I canceled an interview in order to speak with a filmmaker), as well as several workers with whom I never spoke more than a polite hello or a question about work process when we worked together. Along the intervening points of the spectrum were the many people in between who were helpful and pleasant, perhaps merely tolerant of me, and others who were simply cool and professional in their interactions. This was a range of responses to my admitted attempts to turn Vita Needle workers into research subjects, to turn the anthropological gaze on them—which I tried to do by integrating in a friendly manner, sometimes as an observer or a participant, other times as a scholar, friend, or a coworker.

In the introduction to this section of the book I hinted at my own anxieties about fieldwork in a media-saturated environment. Jim's remark about wanting to dig below the surface of Vita Needle is only one of many comments that reveal how my ability to connect with Vita workers was deeply affected by the journalists who came before me and those who have visited since I first began this project. On more than one occasion, the workers aligned me with journalists in our interviews. When I asked Charles what the journalists asked him about, he said, "They asked me some of the same kind of questions you have"; when I asked Steve why the journalists were so interested in Vita Needle, he said, "Same reasons you are"; and when I asked one person in her twenties about what she learned from working with older people she said, "I get asked that question from all the interviews." In the first interview-exclusive phase of this research, one worker refused to be interviewed, saying, "I have spoken to enough journalists." Two years later I was working on the shop floor for the summer; by then I had done much to establish that I was not a journalist, and I had been able to develop the necessary trust and rapport with many of his coworkers, yet this same person told the manager on my first workday, "Keep her away from me."

As an anthropologist but also a coworker, I was part of the same drama as the people about whom I am writing, and this became increasingly true the more time I spent at Vita Needle. At times my Vita Needle interlocutors read me as a journalist. But my position was different from that of journalists in that I was both outsider and insider. I like to think that my own anxiety and fluctuating identity in some ways paralleled what some workers might have experienced as they tried to locate themselves in the world of media attention. Ron, Steve, and others told me they had a hard time juggling work and media interviews. Though some workers seemed comfortable with the notion that being filmed was part of the job, even they still had to work out how precisely to live in an environment where their every move might be showcased to others. And in their interactions with me, they also were working out how to live a life that could be meaningful to themselves even while being meaningful to others.

In 2006, when I first approached Fred Hartman for permission to do this research, I had asked him if I could work on the shop floor. He consented to my research, but he refused the request to work there by citing three concerns. One was that I would adversely impact factory productivity; he also worried about liability in case I was injured. His third concern was on behalf of the workers: he explained that some people were tired of media attention and wanted to retain their privacy; they would not want an anthropologist hanging around. Two years later when Fred decided to let me work on the production floor, he had three very clear ground rules: (1) Do not carry a notebook for taking notes ("these folks do not want to feel like monkeys in a zoo"). (2) Do not talk to people while they work. (3) Be sensitive to the workers' feelings. Fred suspected that some might not be happy with my presence because they did not want a nosy anthropologist invading their privacy or because they might think I was taking work away from them. On the latter point, this was in 2008 during the economic recession when workers were feeling a particular financial squeeze, which they might not have been feeling in 2006. Fred said he would alleviate this worry about scarcity of work by assuring people that this was not the case, but also he would assign me to tasks for which they always need workers and he would not provide me with a timecard—which would have given the false appearance that I was on the payroll.

So there it was, my fourth Vita Needle workday. I arrived around 8:30 a.m. and heard right away that a French television crew was already in the shop. A notice posted on the bulletin board the previous day had alerted me to this visit: "French TV in tomorrow." Though I could see the TF1 crew in the back corner filming Rosa at the machine named after her (the Rosamatic), I decided against going back to observe, and instead I went to help out in the shipping section. As we taped and weighed boxes, checked packing orders, and printed up mailing labels, my coworkers talked about Rosa. Harry Simon noted that she had obviously had her hair done. Ron Crowley pointed out that she had worn her Vita Needle seventy-fifth anniversary polo shirt with the company name embroidered on the breast pocket. Sixty-seven-year-old Lou Davis asked me, "Have you followed Rosa around?" and when I shook my head, he said that I would see that she was hard to keep up with! "If she finishes a job, she will right away be looking for the next." But, he earnestly cautioned, "to a fault." He said when she came in on a Monday morning and people asked, "How was your weekend?" she would say, "Awful! There was nothing to do." Lou concluded, "She needs to work." When 64-year-old Ron interjected to say he hoped he would be at Vita when he was Rosa's age, Lou said, "Not me, I have other things I want to be doing then." Ron and I asked in unison, "Like what?" to which Lou replied, "I don't know yet! I'll let you know."

Moments later, the TF1 producer, Vincent Mortreux, came close to our work area, which was near the time clock. He wanted to film Rosa as if she were arriving for the day, so he asked Fred if she could punch a spare timecard. Echoing the question he had posed to me a few minutes earlier, Lou joked to Mortreux, "Have you gotten Rosa on the stairs yet? You will need to keep up. She will probably take two at a time." A blank timecard had been located, so the shoot was back on, and it was time for Rosa to enter the shop floor and punch in. Rosa and Fred engaged in light-hearted banter about Rosa's missing her hair appointment for this film shoot, and Mortreux said he could take her to his hair stylist in Washington, DC. Fred said, "Did you hear that, Rosa? He says he'll bring you to DC to get your hair done." Rosa quipped, "You better hurry up." And then she added, "I might only have a few hours left. You never know." Everyone within earshot said, "Don't say that, Rosa." Fred and Mortreux then talked about how Rosa needed to beat the record of 97, which Fred had told Mortreux about earlier (Fred's great-grandfather Oscar Nutter worked at Vita until age 97). Fred pointed to a photo of Oscar on the wall and then told Rosa, finger wagging at her exaggeratingly, "I told you, we want you in the triple digits."

As the camera and microphone were being readied, Mortreux teased Rosa that they were preparing for her "best supporting actress" role. Rosa was asked to come up the sidewalk, through the doorway, and up Vita's famous nineteen steps. This very sequence is the opening in the televised TF1 news segment that I described in the previous chapter. Ironically, after all the banter about Rosa's short life span, she was hospitalized within a few days of the TF1 shoot and did not return to work for two months. Despite having a sore foot, Rosa had not wanted to balk at the crew's instructions to reenact her arrival at work. The repeated stress exacerbated her foot problem and sent her to the hospital and then to rehabilitation. So perhaps this was not ironic at all—rather, perhaps with aching feet a constant reminder of her mortality, she was led to joke about impending death.

Through this TF1 vignette we can consider Rosa's agency in her media encounters. Allen told me Rosa was "very obliging" to the journalists, willing to do "whatever they wanted," whereas some others would refuse interviews. In the time I have known her, to my knowledge Rosa has never refused a media interview, even welcoming a journalist to her home when she was recovering that summer from her foot injury. Although she may choose whether or not to participate, she also may not feel fully in control—in the TF1 case she felt unable to refuse to walk on a sore foot. And meanwhile, with Rosa busy as the main subject of this shoot, some coworkers were careful not to be caught on film. Frederick had pointed out to the crew whom not to film, almost as though they were in Hollywood. The first time I saw him make his finger-pointing sweep of the factory, I was heartened to learn that some of the camera-shy were the very same people who had refused interviews with me; it was then that I started to understand that their refusals were not merely brush-offs but ways to assert control.

Ann, Rosa, Tom, Paul, Bill. Readers of this book have met these real people in my description of *Pensioners Inc.* These are real people to whom some European film viewers directed their e-mails and letters. These are real people who had made a choice to be in the press. At other times they and their coworkers may have chosen to appear on *60 Minutes,* the *Today* show, or M6 French television or to be interviewed by the *New York Times* or National Public Radio. And other times they may have refused. These workers are agentive in their choices about whether or not and how to participate in the media coverage. How can questions of agency give us insight into control over privacy and storytelling in a context replete with journalists and this sole anthropologist?

Iconic Images, Real Lives

David felt overexposed. Robert refused the media and the anthropologist, and told a French television journalist an interview was "an invasion of privacy." Rosa endured foot pain. Jeffrey was "miffed" because the media passed him over. Larry fended off *60 Minutes.* Steve said the media visits were "hectic." Zina got a voice. Ann never disclosed her age. Abigail thanked me for the publicity. Pete called the TV crew nosy but brought them to his home. Sam refused the media but helped the anthropologist. Fred issued the press release.

A variety of forms of engagement with the media for a variety of lived realities. These people at Vita Needle have become iconic images of how to live a healthy and productive retirement. Their names and stories have traveled the globe (and now their pseudonyms might too, with the publication of this book), to engage audiences in theaters and homes. The story we hear is this: average age 75, healthy in body and mind at least in part because of the depth of friendship and purpose enabled by a continuing work life. But while the media narratives may give a quickly summarized, moving, and heartfelt depiction, they obscure a story of people who are working out how to best live their lives and trying to make sense of their lives in the present and the past. There are subtlety, contestation, and even anxiety about media engagement, and by examining the diverse forms of media engagement we can understand how people continue to attempt to control their lives, narrate their stories, and make meaning as they age. Contrary to stereotypes of aging, older adults are not invariably faceless, nameless, and disempowered people who merely sit by and observe a world that has changed in front of them, a world where they are no longer important.

The variety of forms of engagement show a complex picture of maintaining and asserting control, in this case, control over privacy and storytelling. Of many examples, I offer the following to paint the landscape of engagement and control.

Control over Privacy

There is a particular story of media engagement for every person on the shop floor, including those whom I will not name here because they refused to be interviewed by either me or the media. Often those were women, and I can only speculate about their refusals on the basis of conversations I had with others who referred to their coworkers' desires to retain privacy in the face of hardship. I heard of great financial difficulty, illness, heartbreak; I heard of widowhood and divorce. I heard about a woman from a well-off family whose comfortable lifestyle was lost when her husband passed away and who found community and purpose but, critically, also a paycheck at Vita Needle. Yet this woman felt this was a stigmatized place to be in her retirement years—she was deeply ashamed to be working in a place that she considered far below her station in life. But I never heard this from her directly, and so this may be a story fabricated to explain her reserve and her desire for privacy not only from interviewers but also in daily work life. She would come in, work while engaging in polite but not excessive conversation, and then punch out—an operation that would sever her connections to her coworkers until the next day.

Robert Benedict was another quiet and hardworking person who also refused media and anthropologist interviews—and yet did share with me a few details about his life. One day when I had stopped by at Vita Needle, nearly four full years after first stepping foot there, Robert looked up from his work, waved me over, and said, "You know, I'm sorry I'm a private person and I don't really want to, ah, I haven't talked to you. But I was thinking maybe we could sometime." He then told me that he knew he had a story to tell. He explained that he took care of his grandchildren and knew there were others like him, and that his story might be important to tell. This seemed to be a moment of acknowledgment from Robert that telling a story is a way of fashioning a life. As much as I yearned to, I never did interview Robert—I left it in his hands to contact me. But I did glean that this was only the tip of a moving and complicated story from a person who greatly valued his privacy. And I must confess, I had heard some of his story from his coworkers, who deeply admired him; several of them urged me not to bother him. As Pete said, "For Robert's sake, don't ask him for an interview. Don't."

Robert was only one of a number of workers who referred to privacy or to nosy journalists. And in their ability to fend off would-be interviewers they exhibited great agency. I think of the words of Richard Taylor in his book *Alzheimer's from the Inside Out.*[21] Taylor, who has dementia, has become a vocal advocate for rethinking the caregiving of people with dementia, including Alzheimer's. He describes how dementia sufferers also suffer the loss of dignity and the right to privacy, and they become invisible in social as well as caregiving settings. Anne Davis Basting, a scholar of theater and aging, has called the attitude of many caregivers toward their patients "chronic underestimitis"—a chronic tendency to assume that someone cannot do things, that he or she is best ignored and put in a chair facing a window.[22] Both Basting and Taylor describe a world of dementia caregiving that is profoundly affected by fears of memory loss but also deep-seated ageism, a point that Basting describes beautifully in her book *Forget Memory.*[23] Of course Vita's workers do not have dementia, but they do in various ways suffer from the same ageism that affects how we care for people with dementia. And the diagnosis of chronic underestimitis can apply more broadly to how American society assesses the potentials of older adults. I think of Robert, Larry, the many others I cannot name, and I think of older adults who in their refusals to be media subjects retain something they can control. In effect, I hear them say, "By invoking my right to privacy I show that I am alive and in control; I may have a body that is calling it quits, but I am still a human being."

Some Vita workers who wanted to remain private were able to demonstrate their humanity not only in their refusals to participate but also in refusing to be named. In a 1997 *New York Times* article that included a group photo accompanied by a who's who map for matching names and faces, several people were labeled with fake names at their request.[24] Furthermore, one could maintain privacy by refusing to disclose personal details. One example of this was Ann's consistent refusal to disclose her age to the media (and to me)—while all the reporters invariably wanted to mention workers' ages. In the TF1 story, her coworkers say their ages, but not Ann. Here they each speak to the camera:

Jim Eppich, age 72, I pack stainless steel tubes into plastic tubes.
Ann Poulos, age ancient, and, uh, job title: I'm going to say quality control.
Name is Rosa Finnegan, I'm 96 years old and I've been at Vita now for ten years.

And in *Pensioners Inc.,* whereas all the speakers (including Fred) have their ages listed in a caption with their names, Ann's caption merely says her name. To a viewer it may seem that the filmmaker made a mistake and forgot to include the age, perhaps even forgot to find it out! But this silence speaks volumes about Ann's agency in what she agrees to say and how she retains some privacy in her life.

Control over Storytelling

Ann refused to reveal her age yet was willing to tell her story many times and was consistently quoted in media coverage from the time it began in 1997. Control over storytelling manifests in decisions workers make over whether and how to tell their story. I am sure it is evident that some people met me more than once. Some phoned me, some e-mailed me, and some invited me places. Some left me voice-mail messages about events or news. Some took notes to remember to tell me things later. Others ignored me.

During my time there, I saw some people change their minds about media participation. Early on I had heard that David had regretted earlier participation so was now saying no to interviews. But two years after my arrival, he started to engage again. But he refused interviews with me, so I am unable to say why he changed his mind about the others. And I have already mentioned Larry, in some sense the equivalent of the class clown in the shop, who was jokingly admired for refusing *60 Minutes* by fabricating an ex-convict alibi—and yet he later did agree to media interviews.

Sometimes workers seek the spotlight but are not chosen to speak—"Maybe my hair was not gray enough," one mused to me. Clearly some people want to speak and are confident they have a story to tell. Jeffrey told me he had not been filmed for the 2002 Dutch film: "I was somewhat miffed because they considered me too young or too whatever, and I thought 'well that's sort of funny,' and I just sort of bided my time." But later Jeffrey was interviewed for other coverage; he says a reporter realized "I might have something to say." Jeffrey was so proud of the forthcoming story that he contacted friends in Europe to ask them to look out for it.

There is a certain agency in the choice of stories one tells and in the decisions to possibly edit and sometimes even alter stories depending on diverse circumstances. In an interview I had with 82-year-old Harry Simon, he had spoken for several minutes about his motive for working as one of social engagement. I then referred to a newspaper article from nearly ten years earlier, which said that he was working to be able to pay his property taxes. Obviously startled to hear this, he replied simply, "Me?" Suddenly worried about putting Harry on the spot—in effect making him divulge something he was not yet ready to share with me—I endeavored to give him the chance to tell a different story, my efforts evident in my reply:

> *Caitrin:* Yes, it says [reading], "Harry Simon." It could be wrong. Reporters get things wrong all the time.
>
> *Harry:* Yeah.
>
> *Caitrin:* It says [reading], "Harry Simon, a retired truck driver, took a job here a year ago," this was 1997, "because his Social Security check was not…"
>
> *Harry:* Yes, yeah, true.
>
> *Caitrin* [reading]: "…paying the taxes on his Needham home."
>
> *Harry:* That's true.
>
> *Caitrin:* Right. So, there is, so, there's some financial part of it as well?
>
> *Harry:* Yes, oh yes, yup. And it also increases my Social Security check, which helps a lot.

In this somewhat surreal exchange, an interview from an earlier time descended into a present interview and appears to have disrupted the narrative that the speaker had decided to tell this time around. Here it was, nearly ten years later, and for whatever reason, Harry apparently wanted to present a different self to this interviewer. Maybe he had long ago regretted divulging financial need to the journalist. Maybe his situation had changed, or maybe what had changed was his estimation of the relative importance of the financial and social benefits of work. Maybe he was embarrassed about disclosing to me a financial need. No matter what the explanation, we can see in this exchange an active moment of (re)constructing a story and making choices about what story to tell and to whom—an example of how people may refashion their own histories in light of changed current contexts.

Perhaps an obvious display of agency is simply the act of narrating one's story. The case of Zina Zambito is especially interesting because Zina, an Italian immigrant, could not narrate her story to her coworkers because of her heavily accented English. In summer 2008, the German magazine *Brigitte* sent a reporter and photographer to Vita Needle, and the reporter happened to speak Italian. I was there when the connection was made, and I recall the unmistakable joy in Zina's face and eyes when she could speak to someone at work! I sensed that her happiness was not about forthcoming media recognition but about conversation in a place where she was otherwise effectively silent. Though never actually silent, Zina always tried to communicate—she laughed, she joked—but she was never fully understood.

The journalist went to Zina's home the next day. The slick multipage article about Vita Needle includes two long paragraphs about Zina's home life—and photos!—and her reasons for working. The story tells of Zina's desire to work to make money, not for survival but for dancing, gifts, and, the reporter quotes Zina, "whenever I see something pretty." At this point Zina momentarily switches to English (in the next sentence the reporter refers to her "adventurous English"): "She indicates her wristwatch. 'Here, Gucci. I buy for myself. With my money.'" We learn that Zina lost her job as a seamstress as a result of a factory closing: "In the short time when Zina was at home without a job...she had too much time for reflection. She sat in front of the television and grew more depressed. Her children finally begged her to find another job, and so six years ago Zina came to Vita Needle."[25]

In reading about Zina in the German magazine, I was struck by the parallels between her story and that of coworkers with whom she was unable to communicate, with whom she had not found common ground. Zina had found a channel for her voice—though this channel was published in German and translated into English only when I hired someone to do so. I did provide the translation to Vita Needle, but I am not sure if any of her coworkers would have read it and would have then been able to connect with Zina after hearing her story. So she likely remained voiceless among her peers, though she spoke to German readers. This is a wonderful example of how media coverage of a needle factory enables the fashioning of lives: it enables the circulation of Zina's story across languages and contexts.

The Private Side of Public Lives

What do all these different forms of media engagement tell us? They tell us a story about agency and controlling one's story, sometimes more and sometimes less successfully than others. But they also tell us about people living public and iconic lives in a modern media-saturated environment. We see people struggle over questions such as these: How do I live in this media environment? Is it OK for me to refuse when others consent? Can I change my mind? Why isn't anyone else wondering about who benefits from the media coverage? Is it OK for Fred (and now this nosy Caitrin) to be putting us out there in the media?

We also see skepticism about how the media try to encapsulate a story. Some workers appear willing to be encapsulated and to tell that story; they even retell common accounts in subsequent interviews or sometimes borrow what they hear from a coworker and use it in their next interview. We see instances of repetition of phrases among workers from one interview to the next—for example, the concept of work as therapy, the idea that Rosa would die if she had to stop working, or the notion of retirement as a dirty word. But others resist that summary or change their minds about their willingness to be encapsulated or change the story they want to tell.

We also see people wonder how to tell their stories and how to sort their own truths from the media versions. Sometimes workers consider how the media coverage matches up with reality. For example, some workers asked me how accurate I think the oft-repeated claim is that the "average age is 75." And they would at the same time mention that photographers rarely turn the camera on the people who are well below 75. In another example, I heard various comments about the common media statement that nobody ever gets fired at Vita Needle, a reference to a claim in a lot of stories, including a tabloid article in the *National Examiner* entitled "Nobody's Ever Been Fired at... America's Best Company" (which ran on the front page, alongside an article called "Hubby to Teen: Kill My Wife but Don't Touch My TV!").[26] In reflecting on this claim, one worker said there is a "shade of gray" to it: "I think on the working floor it's pretty much true. They die or can't come back to work, like Ken." Here he was contrasting the situation on the floor to that among the full-time sales force. But then he started to talk some more, came up with some examples of shop floor workers who had left under circumstances unclear to this worker, including one person who took a vacation and then, the story goes, was not allowed to come back: "He wanted to take a summer off and come back but because he screwed up so many things they decided 'No, not doing that.'"

It is conspicuous that media coverage never raises any kind of debate or conflict—except for the reported concern workers had back in the late 1990s about the installation of a fax machine (near "mutinies"), a microwave, and the planned use of a computer.[27] Likely this oversight is due to journalists' wish to paint a picture of how Vita satisfies unmet social needs. But it does not take long on the shop floor for me to experience and overhear plenty of everyday complaints and concerns: so-and-so talks too much, he bumps into me all the time, he doesn't respect the work we do, so-and-so moves so slowly its imperceptible, she did this job so fast that we should check these needles carefully, it's air-conditioned in the office but not out here, etc. In one interview a Vita worker contrasted the film portrayal of a coworker with the reality: "He comes off great in that film, he really does. But he spends most of his time going around like this [whistle sound]. He's whistling." In other words, in this case, the contestation was that the film did not capture the reality—and the speaker was able to use the media representation to reflect on something that he noticed in his coworker that bothered him. Here we see that the people on the shop floor interact with the media accounts; the people's stories and the media's stories begin to mix together and influence each other in a complicated way. Such is the nature of life in a media-saturated world.

I mention these other possible story lines to show that there is more going on here than is at first apparent—maybe I am just doing what Jim set out to do, dig below the surface. In some ways the Vita story is about finding a voice and, as we will see below, in part about purpose found through fame. But it is also a story of daily questioning about how people live the media experience, how meaning and engagement may come in unexpected ways. Maybe meaning comes in part from the excitement and debate that media participation brings along with it. Maybe meaning even comes from the ability to complain (I complain, therefore I am), compare, and reflect—and sometimes it is the media coverage or journalist presence that provides that chance. (In regard to nursing homes and assisted living facilities, we hear that caregivers are sometimes urged to regard residents' continual requests and complaints as an assertion that they are still alive! They just want to be recognized.)[28] I demonstrated in chapter 1 that meaning can be found through productivity and through making money for Fred, and this is a point that has never been discussed in the media. Similarly, the media have not discussed their own role in creating meaning for the workers. Meaning and life are found at Vita (which we must remember means "life" in Latin) *on the floor* but also *in the media* through the sense of mattering that is generated by media attention and the ability to engage or not with the attention. In some ways, we could consider that the media attention—for some workers—may be an added benefit of working at Vita.

Life at Vita Needle is not a tightly composed story of purpose found through work; instead, it is a variety of stories of working out meaning and value, stories of how to best compose a life and live it every day. Among Vita's willing and reluctant media stars, as well as the media-shy and those not even noticed in the media's gaze, there are a multitude of people working out their lives. Through diverse responses to media among Vita's workers we can see some of the contradictions inherent in media. The anthropologist Daniel Miller writes about how media can "create new possibilities of understanding at the same moment that they pose new threats of alienation and rupture."[29] In the Vita case, media coverage offers a chance at storytelling but also opens up questions of authenticity, of representation, of who gets to speak for whom. I will always remember Robert's quiet and reluctant comments to me about knowing he had a story to tell; his comments showed that he saw what stories were being told and had come to assess his own as important—but for him the time to speak had not yet come. For some of Robert's coworkers, who they are today is at least in small measure an effect of media interaction. Robert's self-fashioning is partly an effect of media noninteraction.

By examining the agency of the workers in their engagement with the media and the anthropologist, my hope is to dispel stereotypes of old people as passive, as victims, as followers; these are culture makers. And we learn something from this about the public worlds we inhabit. The public worlds that Vita Needle's workers live in and that are dispersed globally through media representations are not simply prepackaged worlds to be lived. Rather, the public sphere is a world to be made, through debate and experiment, through consideration and transformation—and the Vita Needle example shows us that even old people can be culture producers, cocreating the publics they inhabit.[30]

There is an important literature in anthropology about how minorities successfully assimilate media for their own cultural and political concerns, I think especially of the anthropologist Terence Turner's work on the Amazon Kayapo's self-production, on the use of indigenous media for political ends.[31] Scholars have asked whether minorities are inevitably compromised by the presence of the media, and I also ask whether the older workers at Vita Needle are inevitably compromised by the media coverage of them. Is being in the limelight necessarily negative? How is it assimilated? How is it put to different and sometimes surprising use by its very subjects? How much does media reporting become an aspect of culture's creation if not renewal? But it is evident that although Vita workers are not *producing* the media (i.e., on their own initiative), they do have a role in production through the choices they make about what to say and do and about participation itself. Of course, workers don't have ultimate control over how journalists spin their stories after they leave Vita Needle or over how the consumers interpret the coverage—the NPR comments show us how responses can be contrary to participants' intentions. Of course, I, too, am spinning the Vita story, and my role in creating representations raised concerns not only for some workers but also for me.

Conclusion: The National Treasure

"Rosa is the star of all our productions." "Everyone loves Rosa." "She is a national treasure." "She is our mascot." In these comments from people at Vita Needle we see admiration for a woman whose continued work life, her longevity itself, has become a group project—a project that in itself provides meaning for the participants. Let's recall Paul's impassioned comments in *Pensioners Inc.*, "I'll do anything to keep her coming here. Because of the fact that it is that important to her." The reporter from the German women's magazine *Brigitte* wrote that "Rosa was the measure of things. Living proof that there is still a future even for the elderly, when a 97-year-old can still work a seven-hour day."[32]

This reporter used the past tense because she had interviewed Rosa at home during rehabilitation from her foot injury. Rosa was no longer the measure of things in the workplace. And yet when the reporter went with Rosa's friend and coworker Bill to interview her, Bill also brought Rosa her paycheck and retrieved some work she had completed. Though Rosa was not *coming* to work, she was still *working*. Fred, Mike, or coworkers occasionally brought her small batches of simple sorting or packaging work to do at home while she recuperated—which she greeted with definite appreciation because of the stimulation they would give her stiffening arthritic hands, because of her boredom, because of her sense of uselessness without such work. The *Brigitte* article featured Rosa as well as several other workers but began as follows: "The queen has a bad leg. She sits at home on a reclining chair behind screen doors on her veranda. An insect looks for a way in; an automobile passes. Time goes by, otherwise not much happens. Until eight weeks ago Rosa Finnegan was the queen of Vita Needle. She would complete before noon the work it would take two others the entire day to do." The story quoted Rosa's coworker Tom saying, "Without Vita Needle, Rosa is lost." It continued, "Manager Michael senses that also. For that reason he is giving Rosa some work to do at home, sorting or packing needles, things that will keep her occupied and perhaps even keep her alive."[33]

How and why is keeping Rosa alive a group project? Rosa is the center of all the coworker and media attention because she is a symbol of possibilities—the "measure of things," as the German journalist writes. When a coworker describes her as a national treasure, he makes a claim for her importance to society; her life matters in a big scheme and is a symbol of a bygone way—a treasure to be preserved.[34] In a discussion about why Fred would want Rosa to keep coming to work and in particular to come back after her rehab, one worker in her twenties speculated, "I think he sees more benefit for her than maybe she does, and he wants her to stay active and realize that there is something more to live for." Remember Fred playfully admonishing Rosa about her age in front of the TF1 producer: "We want you in the triple digits." This very command from boss to worker I saw repeated several times over my years at Vita—especially on the festive days when the 10:00 a.m. coffee break was transformed into a birthday party for Rosa (I was there for the ninety-fifth through the ninety-ninth). Here the managerial pressure to perform was in terms of life span and not company productivity. Yet could both kinds of productivity perhaps ultimately be for the sake of the company's bottom line? In what way would a 100-year-old employee benefit Fred and the bottom line, besides her actual labor power?

Some coworkers mused that Rosa could possibly win the Experience Works annual award for America's Outstanding Oldest Worker—an award previously given to a 100-year-old journalist, a 103-year-old real estate developer, a 100-year old architect, and others.[35] Copping this award would certainly bring more publicity to Vita Needle (Rosa would be an icon for the vitality of the business and for the ways in which this business itself is a fountain of youth and well-being). Would this publicity bring with it more business for Fred? But then again, more business for Fred means more work for the workers, and there is always that Christmas bonus.... This is a complicated scenario to disentangle: Does Fred seek media coverage for altruistic or self-interested motives, and does it matter what his motives are?

But what if we realize that the project to keep Rosa alive does not seem to be just for the sake of media coverage? I have heard plenty of other examples of a more generalized project to keep people coming to work, such as Mason's entreaties to Esther to come back to work after her husband died. So what are Fred's interests in keeping Rosa alive until she hits the triple digits? He is clear in interviews that Vita is not a "country club" or "charity" (he uses these phrases in several media interviews)—and that of course brings us around to the repeated journalist comments that Fred is a shrewd businessman, not a good guy. But the workers certainly see him as providing an opportunity they would not get anywhere else. As Rosa said in *Pensioners Inc.*, "It's a wonderful place to be when you get to be my age. Where could I go? I don't want to go to a nursing home yet."

When Larry fended off *60 Minutes*, which would not pay him $25 for a media interview, he later told me he did it out of principle: "Someone is making money off this, and we all should benefit." He and others would muse about the media coverage: What's in it for Fred? Why would Fred want the media there? And I heard many times from Fred, Frederick, and other family members and managers that continued media presence was a distraction from the work they needed to do, that there really was not time to deal with all the media interest.

Who profits from the media coverage? I discussed this topic often with workers, and though one worker said, "It is better for them than for us," others had no problem with the fact that Fred might have a profit motive in seeking or agreeing to the coverage. As one said, "It's his business, more power to him." Here we can see the deep loyalty that has been developed at Vita Needle, and we circle back to the Christmas bonus—more business for Fred means more bonus for us. So do some workers feel pressure from the employer to consent to media interviews? Do they think they owe it to Fred to give an interview? I never heard this explanation or speculation about it. But I can certainly imagine a worker feeling that she or he is obliged to consent. And yet I hope I have demonstrated in this chapter the ways in which the decision to consent or refuse is a deep and complex issue of having a voice and making meaning at a stage in life where neither voice nor meaning is automatically assured. As much as the factory makes needles, it also converts media interest to the benefit of the business and its workers.

The author at work making needles. Photo by Joe Reddington, printed with permission.

CONCLUSION

Vita's Larger Lessons

One time when we were working across a table from each other, Donald Stephens told me that he had come to Vita Needle after his wife died because her long-term illness had sapped away their life savings and put him into debt. While I taped needles into batches to be sharpened and he inserted long metal tubes into plastic casings, he told me some of his story. At 75, Donald's own Social Security "pays for my roof, but that's it." He came for the money but not just that: "I needed purpose because my purpose was gone." He continued, "When you're married, your purpose is living your life with this person." He said it was "really hard" for him when his wife died; he still thinks of her often, and Vita Needle has given him purpose. At the time of our conversation, Donald was looking for a second job because he could not work enough hours at Vita Needle to meet his financial needs, even though he lives in subsidized public housing. Telling me that his ever-increasing medical bills for treating diabetes were especially worrying, he asked me what I thought of bagging groceries as an option. Although Donald certainly felt that he mattered at Vita Needle, he also needed more money than he could earn there. I was left to wonder if any second job would provide the sense of community and mattering that he got at Vita.

Today many scholars are working on understanding retirement, on what it means, on how people live during this period that can constitute a full third of their life. As I write in 2011, governments, health-care providers, investment companies, and many others are focusing on how aging global populations and shrinking economies are putting pressure on states and employers—and what can be done to relieve such pressure.[1] Others are asking about tapping the opportunity in these unprecedented demographic changes: there have long been attempts to "turn gray into gold" by targeting elder consumers, and the aging of the baby boomer generation has intensified such efforts.[2] In addition to economic and business questions, we must also consider questions of quality of life, of social connections, of the meanings we make of aging and retirement. This book has considered how economic and social questions interact.

Retirement is a phase of life that psychologists have long considered a challenge because it is a "roleless role," as the sociologist Ernest W. Burgess famously wrote in 1960 when he described the fate of retirees who find that they "have no vital function to perform."[3] There are numerous scholarly and policy attempts at redefining retirement and at identifying what retirees seek—such as "finding work that matters," to invoke the subtitle of a best-selling book by Marc Freedman, founder of Civic Ventures.[4] This topic also is the subject of a major initiative called "Engaged as We Age," launched in 2009 at the Sloan Center on Aging and Work at Boston College.[5] This initiative includes leading researchers in the field, such as the social work scholar Nancy Morrow-Howell, who examines important questions about what activities older adults experience as productive—that is, engaging and meaningful. It is mattering that is key here—mattering not only for oneself but also for others in one's community. An important scholarly literature examines social engagement and meaningful work, and there has been attention to the ways in which it is not only volunteer work that provides meaning. This literature has given rise to innovative programming such as Experience Corps, which places older adults as volunteers in schools.[6]

Of course, many older adults face age-related health issues, including dementia, hearing and vision loss, cardiovascular disease, and more. A discourse of healthy, positive, productive, and successful aging can tend to ignore or belittle other roads older adults must take because of physical or mental constraints. I do not wish to ignore the realities of the many older adults who could never work at a place like Vita Needle. Listening to the voices and experiences of people at Vita Needle can help us think more generally about purpose and meaning making in the later stages of life. And I know that these larger lessons can lead to improved caretaking for those in need. One example is the transformational programming (including TimeSlips storytelling) that Anne Davis Basting has created for dementia care facilities throughout the United States.[7]

Retirees and older adults—even those in dementia units, as Basting's work so movingly shows—simply want to continue to live and to be part of life, where life itself means community engagement and contribution. Vita Needle is a place of life for people who may otherwise be written off as nonproductive, useless, invisible, and no longer human. When Vita's workers repeat the phrase "working here keeps me alive," they draw a concrete connection between work and life—and in so doing add complexity to the oft-heard expression that gets at questions of work and value in capitalist societies: "Do you 'live to work' or 'work to live?'"

In U.S. society, old people are often in a sense socially dead in the eyes of others. What's the point of old people? The gerontologist Robert Butler's seminal work lamented that through ageism young people "cease to identify with their elders as human beings."[8] The anthropologist João Biehl's book *Vita: Life in a Zone of Social Abandonment* examines a clinic called Vita in Porto Alegre, Brazil. A Brazilian colleague first described it to Biehl as "a dump site of human beings," where people leave their mentally ill, sick, unemployed, and homeless relatives. Biehl writes, "Vita is the end-station on the road to poverty; it is the place where living beings go when they are no longer considered people."[9] Biehl's work is to examine the larger social, political, and economic forces that create such zones of abandonment and to show us how the people in these zones—abandoned and written off—continue to call out and make themselves alive and known. As one reviewer has written, "Latin for life, *Vita* [the clinic] ironically is best defined as a *non-place* where one dies socially and emotionally while physically still embodying vitality."[10] What first drew me to Biehl's Vita was the name, then the starkly different order of abandonment under discussion, and finally the ways in which people in both Vitas call out for recognition. In the suburban Boston Vita, to work is to be alive, and to be noticed by peers, bosses, anthropologists, media producers, and media consumers alike.

For the owners of Vita Needle, eldersourcing appears to be a solution to some of the pressures that have led other manufacturers to flee the United States in search of cheaper costs. Eldersourcing is to Vita's older workers like "homesourcing" is to the many U.S. workers (especially women) who have found part-time flexible work by performing computer- or phone-based service work from home.[11] The homesourced workers are able to have the flexibility to maintain a household while earning an income; the eldersourced workers are able to maintain a lifestyle they seek as older adults who desire freedom and flexibility in how they spend their time. Vita Needle's success at eldersourcing relies on the idea that the income from Vita Needle is *supplemental*. At the same time, the company makes the supplemental nature of its work a virtue for many of its employees, creating a flexible work environment that meshes with the workers' schedules and values.

When manufacturers move from the United States to establish factories abroad, particularly in the Global South (where their workforce will be primarily women), they cite greater worker productivity, women's extraordinary docility and nimble fingers, and cheaper labor costs. So why is Vita Needle able to stay afloat in the United States in an economic climate that has caused so many manufacturers to leave the country? Answers to this question include its small production volume, quick turnaround time, and proximity to local customers in an area that boasts numerous high-tech and medical-device companies.[12] But one reason could certainly be its unusual staffing model: by eldersourcing part-time employees, the company avoids paying health or retirement benefits. Such a financial savings brings their labor costs closer to those of foreign competitors. In cases well documented by scholars, managerial ranks often describe the relatively low wage level of their female workforce in the Global South as a supplement to other significant family income, especially from men.[13] The logic is that if we understand this income as supplementary, then it does not matter whether the income provides a living wage.

Likewise, at Vita, management describes their employees' income as a supplement to other significant income. Company representatives consider the minimum wage, part-time, benefits-free work as a supplement to other support such as Medicare, Medicaid, Social Security, retirement savings, and adult children. Further, as with manufacturers who relocate abroad, the owners and managers here too cite certain attributes of their workers as superior to others: work ethic, reliability, experience, and productivity. As with the assumptions that have led to the feminization of industrial labor across the globe in the past thirty years, Vita Needle operates within deep-held assumptions about the needs, desires, and resources of older adults.

However, there is an important distinction between Vita Needle's practice of employing a targeted demographic and that of the many manufacturers who employ cheap female labor in the Global South. As we saw in chapter 3 with the production manager's list of the five attributes he looks for in a new employee, the meanings of work to the workers *matter* to the employer at the outset. The manager builds the production system around the workers' needs (and thus it can allow for someone to arrive at 3:30 a.m. or clock out early to babysit a grandchild). This is very different from, say, feminized factory work in Asia where employers *assume* that work is merely pocket money or supplemental to family and work priorities, even if workers hold very different meanings of the work. At Vita, the employer's perception of what the employees themselves want and get from the work is actually at the forefront of the hiring process and the design of the work process, so that workers' choice, freedom, and desire for flexibility are built in to the workplace.

Vita workers and employers claim that eldersourcing is a net positive, economically and socially. We have seen that both groups use work to achieve ends other than what is obvious (e.g., for the employers it is not simply profit; for the workers it is not simply a paycheck). Some of the retirees claim to need money; all say they want social contact. Vita's president explains that he employs older workers as a social good—to counter adverse health impacts of isolated old age. Yet he and observers invariably note the success of this business model. Can a business operate according to economic and social logics simultaneously? In her research on labor and value in a cooperatively owned Mexican silver mine, anthropologist Elizabeth Ferry explains that a tension between social and economic logics is apparent in "production policies, labor organization, and profit sharing" at the cooperative mine. As she writes, "The Cooperative and its members employ a social logic that runs alongside and sometimes conflicts with the economic logic of production and the market."[14] I examined a similar tension in my book *Juki Girls, Good Girls,* where I analyzed a state-initiated factory program in Sri Lanka in which investors and politicians explained their social service motivations to participate in this industrialization program—in this case, the service was cast initially as a way of providing jobs to rebellious youth and later as a way to protect village women from the evils of urban life.[15]

From the Vita and the Sri Lankan cases, we see that a practice can make both economic and social sense. The current book has shown that eldersourcing can be positive for employers and employees, though there is plenty of debate and discussion as both sides make sense of their experiences and their goals. By providing a nuanced understanding of the relationships between community and profitability, between social and economic logics, I hope that this book and the Vita story will move analyses of labor and capital beyond dichotomies of exploited and exploiters, victims and agents. Questions of exploitation remain important, but the answers are not black-and-white, and, in fact, the Vita case leads us to think in new ways about work.

Eldersourcing raises important ethical questions. Even if I see many positive and nuanced dynamics in play at Vita Needle, I would be remiss if I did not at least mention the potential downside to eldersourcing more generally. Low wages, flexibility, and mutually advantageous exploitation: these may add up to a win-win for Vita's workers, but from an organized labor perspective, what are the wider implications of the sourcing of labor from older adults? What happens to work across the board when one group of people considers it something other than work or when one group of people is willing to put up with certain conditions in order to get any kind of steady work? Do the needs and rights of other workers suffer?

The anthropologist Anna Tsing has examined the ways in which workers and employers bring cultural difference to the workplace. She shows how workers may contribute to their own exploitation by performing identities (that is, living out certain ways of life) that have nothing to do with the economy. In effect, they tolerate exploitative work conditions in order to hold on to noneconomic factors such as values, ways of life, priorities, and location.[16] Tsing demonstrates that some workers have a competitive edge on the basis of their social identity; their employment is largely due to their specific identities—as so-called nimble-fin-gered women in much of the Global South or white male entrepreneurial chicken growers in the American south—or, I suggest, as flexible older workers in the Vita case. But what are the trade-offs of such an arrangement?

The anthropologist Carla Freeman has demonstrated how Caribbean women in the informatics industry (processing airline tickets, medical claims, and more) enjoy the higher status that these jobs offer by comparison with others. "They feel adequately compensated, in spite of their low wages, by the status implied in more fashionable work wear and travel benefits."[17] Tsing describes Southeast Asian mushroom foragers in California who consider that foraging enables a cer-tain kind of freedom and a Southeast Asian lifestyle characterized by sociability, networking, and more. They do not consider that what they are doing is work in conventional labor movement terms (this is *not* a matter of sacrificing time and effort in exchange for a wage).[18] Tsing refers to the enactments of specific cultures and histories as "performances of niche specificity." Calling for us to rethink cri-tiques of supply chain capitalism that show us the sacrifices that workers make for the sake of capital, Tsing writes:

> The mushroom pickers I am studying *want* to be foraging in the moun-tains. Here they can combine making a living and revitalizing ethnic and gender histories. Supply chains are not always evil. Furthermore, even in the most exploitative situations, nonwork identities are not only about labor discipline; they also open alternatives. James Hamm…describes a man working in Mexico's maquiladora industry whose dreams of becoming an independent furniture craftsman sustain his hopes for a better future….Hamm imagines creative alternatives emerging from within the interstices between capitalist and noncapitalist spaces. Supply chain performances of niche specificity can make such alternatives more evident, as workers endorse projects of identity that move them beyond (as well as, of course, within) the limitations of their workplaces.[19]

Tsing starts off here by asserting that the mushroom pickers *want to* forage in the mountains. But she also cautions that although these performances of dif-ference enable workers to move beyond workplace limitations, they can also dig them deeper into worker-employer struggles and contradictions. We especially see this in the case of the chicken growers—white American men who value en-trepreneurship as signs of their manliness but who ultimately are working long hours for very little pay and at the mercy of the buyers of their "family farmed" chickens.[20]

Tsing argues that many groups of workers today "perform" cultural difference—that is, they bring to the workplace dispositions and values that are important to their ways of life. In Tsing's examples, a day laborer performs brawn and avail-ability; a prostitute performs sexual charm. Tsing explains that "these perfor-mances bring them contracts *and* make it difficult for them to negotiate the wage outside niches for gender, sexuality, and race."[21] Adding age to this list of perfor-mances of difference, I assert that an older worker may perform the differences of old age: flexibility, a work ethic, and a need for purpose and community.

When Vita workers repeatedly call their work at Vita something other than work (vacation, a men's club, therapy, a family, something to do), they assert that they value the job for noneconomic reasons. And their employer knows very well that they are not just in it for the wage; the manager "becomes suspicious" if prospective workers ask about the rate of pay or do not recognize themselves in the manager's typology of five reasons to seek work in conventional retirement years.[22] Vita workers narrate their work in this life stage as remarkably different from work earlier in life. They value it for its flexible hours, the ways in which they can integrate it into family life, the fact that they are recognized for their valuable contributions, and the presence of friends who depend on them. From one perspective, we could perhaps think of Vita Needle as an example of manage-rial strategies for exploiting workers through paying low wages and demanding flexibility. But from another perspective, the workers, managers, and owners are joined in constructing this work as something other than work.

We see a similar dynamic at Walmart. As historian Bethany Moreton writes, "Human Rights Watch calculated that in 2002, Wal-Mart spent only about three-quarters as much on *all* benefits per covered worker as other major retailers aver-aged for their covered workers' health care alone. But for some, it was a bargain they found reasonable. In return for demanding work at underwhelming wages, they got to remain in the Ozarks, integrate work and family, and put a floor of security under their households' diversified earning strategy."[23] There have been important critiques of Walmart for labor policies that render workers only barely able to scrape by. According to an internal memo quoted extensively by activists and media, Walmart provides its workers with such poor health-care coverage that they are forced to go onto Medicaid—as the author of the confidential memo wrote, "Wal-Mart has a significant percentage of associates and their children on public assistance."[24] As Moreton describes it, in the U.S. south, where many people would find comfort in conceiving of work in an idiom of Christian service, Walmart enables a way of life where work does not need to come first. Instead, service, family, and community are prioritized, and Walmart's part-time, flexible hours enable workers to retain their valued cultures.

Do workers' performances of niche specificity (their performances of differ-ence) erode their ability to mobilize for what they may need in the workplaces—such as better wages, livable working conditions? As Tsing notes, performances of niche specificity are not unambiguously empowering for workers. Following sociologist Ellen Rosen, Tsing argues that "gender discrimination *makes labor possible* in the Wal-Mart model" and that for women "the work would be untenable without coaching and shaming."[25] As Tsing puts it, one effect of this cultivation of difference at Walmart is that "[i]f work 'need not come first,' neither should wages and working conditions."[26] And Tsing points out that in a world where workers perform niche specificity, possibilities for solidarity across workers are slim; one worker's solution may be another worker's problem.[27] It's true that the chicken farmers, mushroom pickers, Walmart cashiers, and Vita workers have jobs, but what does their willingness to work in these conditions mean for others, and particularly for the rights of organized labor? Is there a slippery slope? If workers start to agree that there is a win-win to whatever work conditions they have agreed to, where do we draw the line? When eldersourcing provides meaning and flexibility (but also relatively low wages and no benefits), how do we judge whether it is exploitative or a win-win? Would we judge this differently for older adults than we would for Asian female factory workers, undocumented immigrant domestic workers, impoverished chicken farmers, Walmart cashiers, mushroom foragers, or sex workers? The Vita case challenges us to think in new ways about orthodox labor categories (retired, illegal, immoral). Rosa, Bill, Charles, Jim, and their co-workers have actually created a new stage in a worker's life, and this may well be the first look at a future to come.

POSTSCRIPT

As I wrap up this book, I count myself among the many people for whom Vita Needle evokes nostalgia. I vividly recall several watershed moments in my field-work. The first was when Fred invited me to the Vita Needle Christmas party in 2006, six months into this project. This was my initial chance to spend an extended period of time in the shop, to mingle with and interact with Vita's workers—some of whom I had already met for outside-of-work interviews. This party initiated a period of intense interview-based research, because it gave me the chance to connect to many people I had not previously met. The second was when Fred allowed me to work on the floor for the summer of 2008. This provided me with invaluable participant observation experience, and the book is replete with experiences, examples, and anecdotes from that summer. And the third, in 2010, was when Fred asked me to respond to a laudatory e-mail from a film viewer in Canada. This request indicated to me that Fred had decided he could trust my representation of the company—a level of trust established over four years of contact but probably especially when he and I had, a few months earlier, been interviewed together on PBS television for a discussion about Vita Needle.

When Fred asked me to respond to this e-mail, Vita Needle was in the midst of an especially busy production cycle—Fred did not have time to reply to an interested media consumer. The writer had seen *Pensioners Inc.* on television and was writing in to request a phone discussion with Fred so she could learn more about Vita to help her think about her own passions for responding to the needs of older adults. I was interested in hearing more about her interest in Vita Needle, so I agreed—but I strove to make sure that she and Fred understood that I was not speaking *for* Vita Needle.

In our phone call, Sue Jameson, a retirement home administrator, said that when she saw the documentary on television, she quickly saw in Vita's example an opportunity. Could she perhaps establish light work or industry within retirement-home or long-term-care settings? She wondered whether human beings had a propensity to be industrious throughout their life span, or whether the Vita story mostly told us about economic need. Sue went on to tell me a moving story about Bob, a resident of her retirement home who voluntarily took on light maintenance work (sweeping the front patio, greeting guests, shoveling light snow, and gardening). As Sue saw it, the ability to do this work improved Bob's quality of life because it gave him a sense of proprietorship. When he moved to a different setting, the new management did not allow him to take on this role. Sue tried to advocate on his behalf and predicted that "his life will be short-circuited if he is not allowed to feel purposeful." And indeed, without a job to do, Bob passed away within months of the move. Now Sue wanted to learn from his death and from the Vita story how to create appropriate programming in older-adult living settings. I was happy to share thoughts with Sue to help her move ahead with her plans.

Recently I have been asked several times by journalists to speak about Vita Needle, and although I have become more comfortable with my analysis of the company's significance, I still harbor concerns about appearing to speak *for* Vita Needle or *for* the workers—the same anxieties I had that time I was unexpectedly filmed on the shop floor. I know that every time a new media piece comes out that includes me, I am placing myself in a position of authority that some workers may wonder about. Some may even find it disturbing or upsetting, and they may wonder about my motives for engaging with the media. And yet I have chosen to share my analysis of Vita Needle with the media because I am convinced that the story is worth telling as long as I am not the only voice telling it. I remember informing the Boston PBS producer that I would be interviewed only if Fred or Frederick and at least one older worker also were participating. So this book has been about the workers' agency in the face of media attention as well as in the face of anthropological analysis—and it is also about how these categories now are intertwined as I have become part of the Vita Needle story over the years since I began this research.

In 2010 I was interviewed twice for American media coverage of Vita (on PBS television and National Public Radio), and for the NPR story it was I who had originally connected the reporter to Vita Needle. Also in 2010 I gave a keynote speech about Vita Needle to an audience in Needham that included the Vita Needle production manager, three production workers, and the wife of one worker. It was a celebratory event where I showed clips from *Pensioners Inc.* and spoke about productivity and purpose at the company. I started to wonder whether I was an observer, a participant, or an instigator. In summer 2008 Frederick expressed his concern that allowing in so much media might "affect the mystique" of Vita Needle, and he worried that workers were getting tired of the media coverage and thinking sarcastically whenever they saw a new journalist, "Great, yet another one." He also told me that the shop was so busy right then (i.e., in 2008) that they could not afford, for instance, for Pete to take a half hour break to do an interview. There was pressure on the factory floor, and the media presence was adding to it. Two years later, in 2010, he also told me that he was worried about my connecting NPR to them for the same reason—they just did not have time for more interviews.

Here I am, an anthropologist moving between worlds. I have some privileged knowledge and can help to be a translator of sorts between those worlds.[1] But my access to both sides presents me with dilemmas when I am observing the society at the same time that I am also potentially transforming it. Other anthropologists have examined what Faye Ginsburg calls a "parallax effect" when ethnographers and documentary filmmakers are producing similar representations of the same social phenomenon.[2] As the anthropologist Jeff Himpele explains in his self-reflexive study of his own efforts to study Bolivian media, anthropologists studying media producers may find that "by shifting between positions of observer and participant, feelings of obligation and duplicity can emerge as one becomes part of social hierarchies created through media institutions."[3] Himpele's description aptly captures my anxiety and ambivalence in regard both to being represented in media and to wanting to study the media.

I was complicit with the media in various ways. Sometimes it was when I helped to connect journalists or filmmakers to people—I gave contact information to the NPR reporter, I suggested whom to speak with to PBS, and I introduced the German film director Bertram Verhaag to workers whose stories I knew. While I feared being a Vita spokesperson in media coverage, I also found that media professionals were my peers who were also engaged in an interpretative and translation effort.[4] I remember my worries after a lunch meeting with Stefanie Hellge from Germany's *Brigitte* magazine. I had shared some of my analysis of issues at Vita, and suddenly I feared I was scooping myself—giving away vital information that she would publish well before my book would be completed. I wanted to speak with and engage with journalists as my subjects, but I have also been their subject or expert, and I have been drawn into their projects.

When Fred asked me to reply to that fan letter from Canada, and when he warmly responded to my representations on PBS, he was able to bring me into his world, and in so doing I became complicit with him. Himpele argues that the practice of anthropological research creates forms of affinity that reveal an often-slippery slope from rapport to complicity. In light of such a dynamic, it can transpire that for the so-called research subjects "ethnographers are subjects to be assimilated and managed as possible accomplices."[5]

In 2010 I recruited two neighbors to work at Vita Needle, and then I felt that my complicity with the managerial ranks had been sealed. I also think about the complicity between me and the workers. The workers were critical assets to me in that without their consent I would not have been able to access and understand their world. But they have also been assets in other ways, such as in their friendships, in the lessons I have learned from them, and in more practical terms, in the help they have given me in managing my professional role. I thank them all for their lives, their examples, and their friendships.

Notes

INTRODUCTION

1. To protect the privacy of the research subjects, I have changed the names and some identifying features (such as age, family details, previous occupation, and current role at Vita) of most people in this book. In some cases I have combined the stories of two or more people or changed certain cosmetic details of their stories. I use real names of politicians, professionals, and the family that owns Vita Needle. I do refer to the real names and authentic details of some people's lives if I am referring to the mass media depiction of them. Rosa Finnegan, for example, has been the main subject of media interest, and so my discussion of her motivations and experiences is based largely on what has been reported in the mass media.

2. Ages of Vita's employees are as of 2008, the year of most of my shop-floor fieldwork. The exception is the age of Rosa Finnegan, Vita's eldest, who is 99 as of the last writing in May 2011. As will become evident, Rosa's age is significant to many people inside and outside Vita.

3. Median age calculated in April 2011, as reported to me in May 2011 by Fred Hartman, Vita's president.

4. Cf. Burawoy (1991, 284), who writes, "But participant observers differ from participants precisely in their status as observers, which gives them insights into the limits of communicative action and the sources of its distortion, that is, how the system world denies freedom and autonomy in the lifeworld. As observers who also stand outside the lifeworlds they study, scientists can gain insight into the properties of the system world, which integrates the intended and unintended consequences of instrumental action into relatively autonomous institutions. Indeed, these can be understood only from the standpoint of the observer."

5. The practice of writing ethnographies in the present tense (using the "ethnographic present") has long contributed to a misrepresentation of people in the Global South, the original subjects of anthropological research, as people living in timeless and ahistorical worlds where nothing changes. (See Fabian 1983 and Clifford and Marcus 1986.) For this reason, since turning a critical eye to these concerns in the mid-1980s, anthropologists often use the past tense in their writing to make it evident that they are analyzing how their subjects understood and experienced their lives at a particular moment in time. However, I have chosen to write this book in the present tense because the people and experiences I analyze in these pages are ongoing, even as I write in mid-2011. As I type these words, at 10:15 a.m. on a Tuesday morning in May 2011, I am quite certain that Carl, Ed, and Rosa are at work less than a mile from where I am sitting (in fact it's their coffee break right now).

6. According to Massachusetts universal health-care requirements, "full-time" means thirty-five or more hours.

7. *60 Minutes* 2003; *The Economist* 1998a; Flaherty 1997; Hellge 2008; Irle 2008; Jornal Nacional 2011; Marcus 1997; *NBC Nightly News* 1998; Pratt 2007; Schepens 2003; *Today Show* 1998; Verhaag 2008; Versieux 2004; *World News Tonight* 2000; Yabe 2011, among others.

8. See SSA 2011, which states, "Under federal law, people who are receiving Social Security benefits who have not reached full retirement age are entitled to receive all of their benefits as long as their earnings are under the limits indicated below [chart appears below original text]."

9. http://www.vitaneedle.com/pages/about.htm.

10. Irle 2008, 146.

11. Ibid., 147.

12. Sheth 2003.

13. Harvey and Sherer 2005; Shea and Haasen 2006.

14. Comments appear at Shapiro 2010.

15. Sokolovsky 2009, 110.

16. From the vast literature on the concept of successful aging, Rowe and Kahn 1999 is a landmark, and there is a critical examination in Moody 2009. My contribution is to look at what people seem to seek as they age, in terms of engagement and purpose—and I ask how a factory can contribute to their sense of well-being when normally we might expect a factory to be the last possible place one could find positive engagement.

17. Terkel 1997 [1975]. A good introduction to the anthropology of work is Gamst 1995.

18. Cf. Savishinsky 2002 and Weiss 2005.

19. See Johnson 2009 for a discussion of rising senior unemployment in the late 2000s.

20. Gavin 2009; Pugh 2009.

21. Fleck 2008.

22. Abelson 2006.

23. Vita Needle may well be the most publicized case of a manufacturing facility staffed by older workers, but it is not the only one. In the early 2000s, U.S. media outfits reported on the Ohio cosmetics company Bonne Bell's policy of employing older workers (Carrie 2001; Eisenberg 2002; cf. http://www.clevelandseniors.com/for ever/bbell.htm), though a call to the company in 2010 revealed that the policy had been discontinued. Morris and Caro (1995, 33) report on a program in Michigan "that supports an automobile manufacturer who hires older people to finish wooden dashboards for luxury cars." There are numerous cases of companies targeting older workers for service jobs, such as in the case of Walmart and CVS.

24. NGA 2008. Cf. McKinsey Global Institute 2008.

25. Hamilton 2008.

26. Ekerdt 1986, 239.

27. I use this term "eldersourcing" to invoke discussions about outsourcing. I have not seen other scholarly uses of the term, and my searches find it used only by a business advisory company. See http://www.darandcompany.com/Aging_In_Place_-050809.html, which explains in a 2009 post that "[c]ompanies are also beginning to view Successful Aging as a source of labor supply (in addition to being a market). Within this demographic are millions of people who have the skills, knowledge, experience and motivation that make them an alternative pool of labor, outside the full-time employee base. Indeed, these willing and competent people are an alternative to outsourcing: eldersourcing."

28. According to 2007–9 data, the percentage of older adults in Needham is 15.8 percent compared with 13.1 percent in Massachusetts. (Needham data from United States Census Bureau 2009b; Massachusetts data from United States Census Bureau 2010.)

29. In claiming that a particular case can offer more generalizable insights, I follow sociologist Michael Burawoy's arguments in favor of the "extended case method." Burawoy argues that we can use the specificity of one case as a vehicle for comprehending larger social and economic forces (1991, 278).

30. Pew Social Trends Staff 2009.

31. Sokolovsky 2009, 107–9.
32. Oliver 2008.
33. Kaufman 1994.
34. Bateson 2010, 79–80.
35. Lamb 2009.
36. Butler 1975, 12.
37. Butler 1969, 243–44.
38. Landes 1971, 13. Cf. Landes 1959 and n.d.
39. Landes 1971, 16.
40. Landes 1971, 7.
41. Ekerdt 2008.
42. Beilenson's PowerPoint slides available at http://masshealthpolicyforum.brandeis.edu/forums/forum-pages/HealthyAging2Forum.html.
43. Press release entitled "'Rebranding Aging' Movement to Launch May 9 in Washington, D.C.," http://www.icaa.cc/media/press2011/rebranding-aging.htm.
44. Sokolovsky 2009, 110; see Moody 2009, 68 for the terms "well-derly" and "ill-derly."

PART I. UP THE STAIRS

1. According to data estimates from 2004 through 2009, the estimated median household income in Needham was $122,063, and in Massachusetts was $64,496. The estimated median house/condo value in Needham was $646,300, and in Massachusetts was $357,600. (Needham data from United States Census Bureau 2009b; Massachusetts data from United States Census Bureau 2009a.)
2. I have not done a household expense and income analysis. My understanding of economic need is based on self-reporting.
3. Irle 2008.

CHAPTER 1. MAKING MONEY FOR FRED

1. Mauss 1967 (first published in French in 1923).
2. F. Taylor 1911.
3. NetMBA n.d.
4. Personal communication, 5 January 2011. Chick and Roberts 1987 and Chick and Hood 1998.
5. Ong 2010.
6. Interview in Geirland 1996. Robert Weiss 2005, 131, 179, notes that some retirees are able to find flow in "satisfactory retirement hobbies."
7. Parker 1984, 739; see also Follett 1918, 2003 [1941].
8. On "recognition" in elder care and aging experiences, see Janelle S. Taylor 2008. More generally see Charles Taylor 1994, whose work Janelle Taylor describes as follows: "[I]n a landmark essay on 'the politics of recognition,' [Charles Taylor] contends that because a person's sense of self is grounded in his or her membership in a cultural group, when the political system in which they live fails to recognize the cultural identity of the group to which they belong this causes real harm to individuals" (325).
9. Lorber 2010.
10. Kusterer 1978; see also Devinatz 2005.
11. F. Taylor 1911, 17.
12. The practice was actually started by Fred, Mason's son.
13. Fred has explained to me that he calculates the bonuses with a formula that includes basic pay rate, managerial input, the company's annual profits, and capital expenditures.
14. Interview in Geirland 1996.

15. Csikszentmihalyi 2008, 39–40.
16. Freedman 2005, 4.
17. Csikszentmihalyi 2008, 165.
18. Ibid., 169.

CHAPTER 2. ANTIQUE MACHINERY AND ANTIQUE PEOPLE

1. Ellison 1995.
2. On the changing concept of family in the United States, see Coontz 2000, Gillis 1997, Lasch 1995, and Stacey 1997.
3. Cf. Hochschild 2001 [1997].
4. Gillis 1997.
5. Borneman 1997, 574.
6. Weston 1997; cf. Aries 1965.
7. Fred is of the fourth generation; his son Frederick is fifth-generation.
8. Their idealized Vita family is certainly not a blended postmodern family with step-children and stepparents, mixed races, or homosexual spouses, as American families are today. Cf. Coontz 2008. And certainly this is not a dysfunctional family—often in strong contrast to the workers' own biological families.
9. Even though Vita's workers are not all Protestant, they are strongly influenced by the pervasive Protestant work ethic of their New England suburban community and the era in which they were raised (see my discussion of a "Depression ethic" below). On the positive moral value Americans tend to place on the intrinsic value of hard work, see Weber 2002 and Lipset 1992. A helpful review is Roger B. Hill's "History of Work Ethic" website, http://www.coe.uga.edu/workethic/history.htm.
10. On the postwar "golden age of capitalism" see Marglin and Schor 1992.
11. Stacey 1997 and Coontz 2000.
12. Gillis 1997; cf. Lasch 1995.
13. For a discussion of the concept of the family as an ideological construct of the modern state see Collier, Rosaldo, and Yanagisako 1992.
14. American notions of ideal family dynamics are built on cultural assumptions about men's and women's abilities and inclinations, assumptions that we tend to map to nature. Therefore, we often assume that women are naturally more nurturing and men are better at material provisioning, whereas in truth these gender norms are culturally constructed.
15. If this story is true, which I could conceive, I read it as a woman jokingly express-ing a wish to be an object of desire at a stage in life when her body is far from the cultural ideal of sexualized femininity represented by the pinups.
16. O'Barr 2011.
17. I use the term "care work" after Meyer 2000 in order to flag that it is work that creates connection and belonging, as does care for children, older adults, and people with illness in an ideal scenario—a scenario such as those that Basting (2009) creates in her dementia care programming.
18. di Leonardo 1987.
19. Lamphere 1985.
20. For a similar process of creation of sameness and everyday efforts to erase dif-ference among older adults, see Keith's 1982 study of a retirement community in France.
21. Marcus 1997.
22. Hareven 1978, 1982. Cf. Hareven's comparative work on family and factory in Japan (2003).
23. Schiffman 2009.

24. Vita's workers are united by a sense of generational cohort rather than chronological age—even though I am using the term "cohort" for a span of up to forty years (I am thinking of workers in their sixties through to 99-year-old Rosa). What they share is not so much age as a point in their life course, what the anthropologist Mary Catherine Bateson 2010 has called "Adulthood II," which I discuss in chapter 5.

25. Among many sources on social capital and health, see Ferlander 2007.

26. Basso 1979.

27. English 1994.

28. Critchley 2002, 18.

29. Hellge 2008, 86.

30. According to 2007–9 data, Needham is 90.6 percent white and Massachusetts is 80.4 percent white. (Needham data from United States Census Bureau 2009b; Massachusetts data from United States Census Bureau 2010.)

31. Thanks to Mary McCuistion for these insights (personal communication, December 2010).

32. Basting 2009, 98. See also http://www.timeslips.org/.

33. For the pervasiveness of this concept of the "living dead" in reference to people with dementia, see R. Taylor 2006 and Basting 2009.

34. The concept of agency is discussed extensively in anthropology, and I take it on in chapter 5. Briefly, I note here that it refers to the human capacity to act (and not be victims of social forces around us, though social structure does influence how we are able to act).

35. Cf. Arlie Hochschild's 2001 [1997] discussion of work as a place to discuss and get solutions to home problems (163), and on assembly lines, "Work was where people learned about and judged what went on outside of work" (153).

36. Jessica Margolin e-mail to anthrodesign list, http://groups.yahoo.com/group/an throdesign, 15 December 2010, quoted with permission.

37. Ranzani 2010.

38. Lamphere 1985. See also Hareven 1978.

CHAPTER 3. NO CHAINS ON THE SEATS

1. Irle 2008, 146.

2. Boxall and Purcell 2002.

3. Christensen 2010 and also Hill et al. 2008.

4. See http://bc.edu/research/agingandwork/about/workFlexibility.html.

5. Harvey 1991; Susser and Chatterjee 1998.

6. See "Flexible Hours but Slave Labor as a Trade-off at McDonalds," http://www.aboutmyjob.com/forums/showthread.php?t=185944.

7. Risen 1989.

8. Tonelson 2002.

9. GEICO commercial, http://www.bordom.net/view/9290/Mashed_potatoes_gravy_and_cranberry_sauce_woo_.

10. Guyer 2010, 1.

11. Grazia 2005, 4.

12. Bose, Lyons, and Newfield 2010, 3, quoting Charles E. Wilson, in 1953 (Wilson was secretary of defense under Dwight Eisenhower and a former GM executive).

13. Harvey 1991, 147. Cf. Patterson 1998; Susser and Chatterjee 1998.

14. Irle 2008, 148.

15. Savishinsky 2002; Darrah, Freeman, and English-Lueck 2007.

16. On busyness see Mack 2005. See also Hochschild 2005.

17. Allen's experience of clocking out after only a few minutes would not be as easy to replicate today as it was earlier in Vita's history. Today the employer requires that workers come in for (on average) a minimum of twenty hours a week spread out over four days, though there are regular exceptions granted to this requirement.

18. In the past there were many more people at the benches working alongside Esther.

19. See, e.g., Susser and Chatterjee 1998; Freeman 1998; Patterson 1998.

20. Personal communication, e-mail, 28 April 2009 (quoted with permission).

21. Moreton 2009, 11.

22. Hellge 2008, 86.

23. Brondo et al. 2005, 202.

24. Lynch 2007.

25. Putnam 2001.

26. Hochschild 2001 [1997].

27. Ibid., 174.

28. Wertheimer 1996, 14. Cf. Sample 2003.

PART II. IN THE PRESS

1. "The Power of Experience" is no longer available on the IDEO website but is archived by the firm.

CHAPTER 4. RIDING THE GRAY WAVE

1. A short segment on Vita Needle aired on the German newsmagazine *Plus-Minus* on 15 October 2002. I use pseudonyms for the authors of this and all letters discussed in this chapter.

2. According to Nielsen, as of 2009, people 65 and over spend 210 hours and 52 minutes a month watching TV, more than any other demographic in America. That calculates to about 29 percent of total time spent watching television. Nielsen Company 2009.

3. Mazzarella 2004, 355.

4. In general I am referring to salaried workers here. Very poor laborers and small-business owners often do not often follow such a retirement model. In India, for example, "retirement" as a concept applies only to the salaried middle classes.

5. An old-age social security program was first developed in 1889 by Germany's chancellor, Otto von Bismarck, and the retirement age was set at age 70 (http://www.ssa.gov/history/ottob.html). In the United States, the retirement age was set at 65 when the program began in 1935 with the Social Security Act (http://www.ssa.gov/history/).

6. In France, the first social security law dates to 1910, when the retirement age was 65 for men and 60 for women. In 1982 President Mitterand responded to the unions and changed the age to 60 for men as well. See Sinichi 2004.

7. Laslett 1991; Oliver 2008.

8. Japanese workers stay in the labor force for a long period of time—in fact, very long by international standards. See Williamson and Higo 2007.

9. OECD 2011.

10. Ages as indicated in film captions, likely referring to ages in 2007.

11. Hellge 2008.

12. Irle 2008, 146.

13. Marcus 1997.

14. Flaherty 1997.

15. *60 Minutes* 2003.

16. I thank Michael C. Davis, an accountant with whom I consulted, for helping me understand this financial landscape. For part-time workers, the employer matches whatever

the employee pays for Social Security and Medicare. The employee is taxed 6.2 percent of gross wages for FICA (Federal Insurance Contributions Act)-SS and 1.45 percent for FICA-Med, and the employer pays these same amounts (6.2 percent and 1.45 percent), for a total of 15.3 percent that goes into state coffers. For the voluntary rates that employers pay for workers' benefits, see http://www.bls.gov/news.release/ecec.nr0.htm.

17. El Documental del Mes, January 2010, http://www.eldocumentaldelmes.com/en/documentals/47-pensioners_inc..html.

18. As Michael C. Davis notes, Rooney's supposition is not quite accurate (she muses that because the workers have Medicare and Social Security, Fred does not need to pay them benefits). If the workers were full-time, he would be legally required to pay health and retirement benefits that are over and above FICA-SS and FICA-Med (and he does this for his full-time sales staff). But for the part-time workers, although he is not required to, Fred *could* offer them those benefits, and we know that some employers do offer such benefits to part-time workers (Starbucks, for example). We can assume from Fred's media quotes that he does not feel the *need* to provide those benefits because he knows that the part-time workers are getting retirement and health benefits from the government.

19. *Greater Boston with Emily Rooney* 2010.

20. Wood et al. 1988, 254.

21. Note that even with the bonus system, the government is going to get some of Fred's money. As Michael C. Davis explained to me, it is true that Fred will not pay taxes on those profits that he uses for bonuses. "However, depending on the employee's tax bracket, the employer and/or employee would be paying the following taxes on those bonuses: (1) Social Security taxes, (2) Medicare taxes, and (3) income tax, which, in some cases, may exceed the factory's tax savings."

22. For a discussion of the relevance of Adam Smith's concepts since the beginning of the current financial crisis, see LeRoy 2010, who examines Smith in light of current debates about the proper balance between markets and government.

23. A "drawer-in," also known as a "drawer," is a person in a textile factory who "draws" warp yarn through the loom parts to arrange the warp for weaving the specified pattern.

24. Ranzani 2010.

25. The *New York Times* summarizes the reforms in "France Pension Reform," http://topics.nytimes.com/top/news/international/countriesandterritories/france/pension-reform/index.html (updated 25 October 2010).

26. See, for example, the Paris bureau chief for the *New York Times*, Steve Erlanger, interviewed on the NPR radio program *On Point with Tom Ashbrook* in an episode entitled "French Protests and Retirement Debates," 21 October 2010, http://onpoint.wbur.org/2010/10/21/france-riots-retirement.

27. Quote from Steve Erlanger in http://onpoint.wbur.org/2010/10/21/france-riots-retirement.

28. Kossowski 2008.

29. Figures on TF1 viewership are from http://www.tf1finance.fr/en/. The TV crew visited Vita on Friday, 23 May 2008; though I have a DVD of the program, I do not know its exact air date.

30. Commentators on the pension reforms and earlier reforms to lower the standard work week to thirty-five hours often raise questions about whether French people are lazy and devoid of a work ethic. In best-selling books with titles such as *The Right to Be Lazy* (Lafargue 1989 [1883]) and *Bonjour Laziness* (Maier 2005), writers have long commented on the French embracement of the concept of laziness, especially as compared with what they see as overly driven neighboring Anglo-Saxons. In a commentary on the 2010 pension reform strikes entitled "In Praise of Laziness," the historian Robert Zaretsky (2010)

argues that the French identification with a world not driven by "the soul-numbing nature of modern work" has roots documented as far back as the fourteenth century.

31. Irle 2008, 148.

32. http://www.denkmal-film.com/abstracts/Rentner_GmbH_e.html.

33. "Old, Hearty, and Efficient," CD-/DVD-Tipps, magazine column on "tips" about new DVDs (source unknown, provided by Bertram Verhaag). Translated by Michael Latham.

34. Verhaag interview in Bianco 2010. Verhaag generated this response after discussion with me.

35. Comments appear at Shapiro 2010.

CHAPTER 5. ROSA, A NATIONAL TREASURE

1. I am not naming the publication or language in order to maintain Allen's confidentiality in being interviewed by me.

2. Cf. Dornfeld 2002.

3. Wilk 2002.

4. Larkin 1997, 407 (also quoted in Ginsburg, Abu-Lughod, and Larkin 2002, 16).

5. Liechty 2002.

6. Cf. Malinowski 1920 for the concept of "fame" in the renowned anthropological case of the Kula ring exchange—where the exchange of objects also creates and spreads the fame of the owner, so the owner's name lives on separate from him or her.

7. For the Hawthorne experiments, see Gillespie 1993. A 2009 study by Steven Levitt and John List claims to debunk this study (Levitt and List 2009; cf. *Economist* 2009).

8. Cooley 1922, 152.

9. Bateson 2010a; Erikson 1995.

10. Bateson 2010a, 78.

11. Bateson 2010b.

12. Braudy 1997; Brim 2009.

13. Here I am referring to an important debate in anthropology and sociology, exemplified in the work of scholars Pierre Bourdieu (1977) and Anthony Giddens (1984), on the relationship between agency (the human capacity to act) and the social structure in which humans are embedded. From the anthropologist Saba Mahmood (2001, 2005), I think of agency as "a capacity for action that historically specific relations of subordination enable and create" (2001, 203). Thus agency and structure are not opposites but are conditions that create each other.

14. Greenblatt 2005.

15. Brim 2009, 2.

16. Shapiro 2010.

17. Braudy 1997, 607.

18. Ibid., 610.

19. Ferris 2007, 380.

20. It appears that some of Vita's workers figured this out after a few rounds with the media; hence their later reluctance to participate.

21. R. Taylor 2006.

22. Basting 2010.

23. Basting 2009.

24. Flaherty 1997; the use of pseudonyms is not noted in the publication.

25. Hellge 2008, 85.

26. Louis 1998.

27. "We've come close to mutinies over the last ten years on things like fax machines," Fred told Morley Safer from *60 Minutes*.

28. Cf. J. Taylor 2008.

29. Miller 1995, 18 (also quoted in Ginsburg, Abu-Lughod, and Larkin 2002, 10).

30. Cf. Cohen 2010, who argues that the "public" is not a given space but a zone of debate and transformability where social fields are in flux and agonistic.

31. Turner 2002, and cf. Ginsburg, Abu-Lughod, and Larkin 2002, 10.

32. Hellge 2008, 82.

33. Ibid., 86.

34. This concept of Rosa as a national treasure resonates with the post–World War II designation of Japanese older adults as "living national treasures" involved with nationally significant arts and crafts. In recent years involvement with traditional arts has become a way for Japanese older adults to experience "a counter force against the loss of social role that many retirees experience after they leave the workforce" (Moore and Campbell 2009). Similarly, Rosa's own role as a national treasure no doubt enhances her sense of self and affects those people working to preserve this treasure.

35. This is an award "to raise awareness about the contributions that older workers make in the workplace and to break down barriers associated with their employment" (http://www.experienceworks.org/site/PageServer).

CONCLUSION

1. McKinsey Global Institute 2008; NIA 2007; Piktialis 2001; Rix 2001; Ruiz 2006; Tuljapurkar, Li, and Boe 2000. A good introduction to economic and policy issues related to older workers is Johnson 2009.

2. In the late 1980s Minkler 1989 examined "business' discovery of the elderly market."

3. Burgess 1960, 20.

4. Freedman 2008; see also http://www.civicventures.org/.

5. See also Center for Health Communication 2004.

6. On Experience Corps see http://www.experiencecorps.org and http://gwbweb. wustl.edu/newsroom/PressRelease/Pages/ExperienceCorpsEvaluation.aspx.

7. Basting 2009 and http://www.timeslips.org/.

8. Butler 1975, 12.

9. Biehl 2005, 2.

10. Rodrigues 2006, 774.

11. For the example of JetBlue airlines, which famously employs an entirely home-based staff of reservation agents, see Friedman 2005, 35–38 and Keating 2005.

12. Cf. *Economist* 1998b on other reasons for the persistence of low-tech manufacturing firms in the United States (back in 1998).

13. Cf. Standing 1989; Lynch 2007.

14. Ferry 2005, 12.

15. Lynch 2007.

16. Tsing 2009, 158.

17. This quote is from Susser and Chatterjee 1998 and describes Freeman 1998. See also Freeman 2000.

18. Tsing 2009, 170.

19. Ibid., 171–72 (emphasis in original); Hamm 2007.

20. Tsing 2009, 167–68.

21. Ibid., 159.

22. Irle 2008, 148.

23. Moreton 2009, 71–72 (emphasis in original).

24. As quoted in Greenhouse and Barbaro 2005, and also available at http://walmart watch.com/issues/health_care/.

25. Tsing 2009, 161 (emphasis in original). Cf. Rosen 2006.
26. Tsing 2009, 160.
27. Ibid., 157.

POSTSCRIPT

1. Ginsburg, Abu-Lughod, and Larkin 2002, 21.
2. Ginsburg 1995.
3. Himpele 2002, 303. Cf. Dornfeld 2002.
4. Ginsburg, Abu-Lughod, and Larkin 2002, 22.
5. Himpele 2002, 304.

References

Abelson, Jenn. 2006. "Snowbirds at Work." *Boston Globe,* 1 March. http://www.boston. com/business/articles/2006/03/01/snowbirds_at_work/.

Aries, Philippe. 1965. *Centuries of Childhood: A Social History of Family Life.* New York: Vintage.

Basso, Keith H. 1979. *Portraits of "The Whiteman": Linguistic Play and Cultural Symbols among the Western Apache.* Cambridge: Cambridge University Press.

Basting, Anne Davis. 2009. *Forget Memory: Creating Better Lives for People with Dementia.* Baltimore: Johns Hopkins University Press.

——. 2010. Interlocutor comments at the business meeting of the Interest Group on Aging and the Life Course. Annual Meeting of the American Anthropological Association, New Orleans, 19 November.

Bateson, Mary Catherine. 2010a. *Composing a Further Life: The Age of Active Wisdom.* New York: Knopf.

——. 2010b. Remarks at book release for *Composing a Further Life.* Sloan Center on Aging and Work, Boston College, 22 September.

Bianco, Ana. 2010. "Cine: Entrevista a Bertram Verhaag" ["Interview with Bertram Verhaag"]. Translated by Frank Romagosa. http://www.nacionapache.com.ar/ archives/4449.

Biehl, João. 2005. *Vita: Life in a Zone of Social Abandonment.* Berkeley: University of California Press.

Borneman, John. 1997. "Caring and Being Cared For: Displacing Marriage, Kinship, Gender and Sexuality." *International Social Science Journal* 49:573–584.

Bose, Purnima, Laura E. Lyons, and Christopher Newfield. 2010. *Cultural Critique and the Global Corporation.* Bloomington: Indiana University Press.

Bourdieu, Pierre. 1977. *Outline of a Theory of Practice.* Cambridge: Cambridge University Press.

Boxall, Peter, and John Purcell. 2002. *Strategy and Human Resource Management.* New York: Palgrave Macmillan.

Braudy, Leo. 1997. *The Frenzy of Renown: Fame and Its History.* New York: Vintage.

Brim, Orville. 2009. *Look at Me! The Fame Motive from Childhood to Death.* Ann Arbor: University of Michigan Press.

Brondo, Keri, Marietta Baba, Sengun Yeniyurt, and Janell Townsend. 2005. "Fertile Ground: Homegrown Loyalty Makes For Globally Competitive Industry." *Ethnographic Praxis in Industry Conference Proceedings* 1:196–204.

Burawoy, Michael. 1991. "The Extended Case Method." In Burawoy et al., *Ethnography Unbound: Power and Resistance in the Modern Metropolis,* 271–90. Berkeley: University of California Press.

Burgess, Ernest Watson. 1960. *Aging in Western Societies.* Chicago: University of Chicago Press.

Butler, Robert N. 1969. "Age-ism: Another Form of Bigotry." *Gerontologist* 9:243–246.

——. 1975. *Why Survive? Being Old in America.* New York: Harper & Row.

Carrie, Spencer. 2001. "Cosmetics Company Tapping Growing Senior Job Pool." *Associated Press,* 27 July.

Center for Health Communication. 2004. "Reinventing Aging: Baby Boomers and Civic Engagement." Boston: Harvard School of Public Health. http://www.hsph. harvard.edu/chc/reinventingaging/Report.pdf.

Chick, Garry, and Rob D. Hood. 1998. "Do Machinists Play with Machines? Work and Outdoor Recreation among Employees in the Western Pennsylvania Machine-tool Industry." In *Play & Culture Studies*. Vol. 1, *Diversions and Divergences in Fields of Play,* edited by Margaret Carlisle Duncan, Garry Chick, and Alan Aycock, 5–17. Greenwich, Conn.: Ablex Publishing.

Chick, Garry, and John M. Roberts. 1987. "Lathe Craft: A Study in 'Part' Appreciation." *Human Organization* 46:305–317.

Christensen, Kathleen. 2010. *Workplace Flexibility: Realigning 20th-Century Jobs for a 21st-Century Workforce.* Ithaca: Cornell University Press.

Clifford, James, and George E. Marcus. 1986. *Writing Culture: The Poetics and Politics of Ethnography.* Berkeley: University of California Press.

Cohen, Lawrence. 2010. Comments on panel discussion "Circulating the Life Course: Towards an Anthropology of Care and Caregiving." Annual Meeting of the American Anthropological Association, New Orleans, 18 November.

Collier, Jane, Michelle Z. Rosaldo, and Sylvia Yanagisako. 1992. "Is There a Family? New Anthropological Views." In *Rethinking the Family: Some Feminist Questions,* edited by Barrie Thorne and Marilyn Yalom, 25–39. Boston: Northeastern Press.

Cooley, Charles Horton. 1922. *Human Nature and the Social Order.* New York: Scribner's.

Coontz, Stephanie. 2000. *The Way We Never Were: American Families and the Nostalgia Trap.* New York: Basic Books.

——. 2008. *American Families: A Multicultural Reader.* 2nd ed. New York: Routledge.

Critchley, Simon. 2002. *On Humour.* London: Routledge.

Csikszentmihalyi, Mihaly. 2008. *Flow: The Psychology of Optimal Experience.* New York: Perennial Modern Classics.

Darrah, Charles N., James M. Freeman, and June Anne English-Lueck. 2007. *Busier Than Ever! Why American Families Can't Slow Down.* Stanford: Stanford University Press.

Devinatz, Victor G. 2005. "Kusterer or Manwaring and Wood on the High-Tech Labor Process? Analyzing the Nature of Skill, Deskilling and Managerial Control of Labor in a U.S. Medical Electronics Factory." *Employee Responsibilities and Rights Journal* 17:3–17.

di Leonardo, Micaela. 1987. "The Female World of Cards and Holidays: Women, Families, and the Work of Kinship." *Signs* 12:440–453.

Dornfeld, Barry. 2002. "Putting American Television Documentary in Its Places." In *Media Worlds: Anthropology on New Terrain,* edited by Faye D. Ginsburg, Lila Abu-Lughod, and Brian Larkin, 247–263. Berkeley: University of California Press.

Economist. 1998a. "Can America's Workforce Grow Old Gainfully?" 25 July, 59. http:// www.economist.com/node/169429.

——.1998b. "Globalisation: The Strange Life of Low-Tech America." 17 October, 73. http://www.economist.com/node/172664.

——. 2009. "Light Work: Questioning the Hawthorne Effect." 4 June. http://www.eco nomist.com/node/13788427.

Eisenberg, Daniel. 2002. "Firms Brace For a Worker Shortage." *Time.* 6 May. http:// www.time.com/time/magazine/article/0,9171,1002363,00.html.

Ekerdt, David J. 1986. "The Busy Ethic: Moral Continuity between Work and Retirement." *Gerontologist* 26:239–244.

——. 2008. "The Ambiguity of Extended Work Careers." Keynote address, Ann Richards Invitational Roundtable on Gender and the Media, "Older Workers: Benefits and Obstacles for Women's and Men's Continued Employment," Brandeis University, 24 October.

Ellison, Ralph. 1995. *Invisible Man.* New York: Random House.

English, James F. 1994. "Humor as Social Practice: Rethinking Joke-Work." In *Comic Transactions: Literature, Humor, and the Politics of Community in Twentieth-Century Britain,* 5–19. Ithaca: Cornell University Press.

Erikson, Erik H. 1995. *Childhood and Society.* New York: Vintage.

Fabian, Johannes. 1983. *Time and the Other: How Anthropology Makes Its Object.* New York: Columbia University Press.

Ferlander, Sara. 2007. "The Importance of Different Forms of Social Capital for Health." *Acta Sociologica* 50 (2): 115–128.

Ferris, Kerry O. 2007. "The Sociology of Celebrity." *Sociology Compass* 1:371–384.

Ferry, Elizabeth Emma. 2005. *Not Ours Alone: Patrimony, Value, and Collectivity in Contemporary Mexico.* New York: Columbia University Press.

Flaherty, Julie. 1997. "Earning It: A Company Where Retirement Is a Dirty Word." *New York Times,* 28 December, sec. 3, p.1.

Fleck, Carole. 2008. "Shaky Economy Puts Retirement Plans on Hold." *AARP Bulletin,* 16 May.

Follett, Mary Parker. 1918. *The New State: Group Organization—The Solution of Popular Government.* London: Longmans, Green.

——. 2003 [1941]. "How Must Business Management Develop in Order to Possess the Essentials of a Profession." In *Dynamic Administration: The Collected Papers of Mary Parker Follett,* edited by Henry C. Metcalf and L. Urwick, 96–111. New York: Routledge.

Freedman, Marc. 2005. "The Boomers, Good Work and the Next Stage of Life." New Face of Work Survey, June. http://www.encore.org/find/resources/boomers-good-work-and.

——. 2008. *Encore: Finding Work That Matters in the Second Half of Life.* New York: PublicAffairs.

Freeman, Carla. 1998. "Femininity and Flexible Labor: Fashioning Class through Gender on the Global Assembly Line." *Critique of Anthropology* 18:245–262.

——. 2000. *High Tech and High Heels in the Global Economy: Women, Work, and Pink-Collar Identities in the Caribbean.* Durham, N.C.: Duke University Press.

Friedman, Thomas. 2005. *The World Is Flat: A Brief History of the Twenty-first Century.* New York: Farrar, Straus and Giroux.

Gamst, Frederick C., ed. 1995. *Meanings of Work: Considerations for the Twenty-First Century.* Albany: State University of New York Press.

Gavin, Robert. 2009. "Feeling Jobbed." *Boston Globe,* 28 February. http://www.boston.com/business/personalfinance/articles/2009/02/28/feeling_jobbed/.

Geirland, John. 1996. "Go with the Flow (Interview with Mike Csikszentmihalyi)." *Wired,* September. http://www.wired.com/wired/archive/4.09/czik.html.

Giddens, Anthony. 1984. *The Constitution of Society: Outline of the Theory of Structuration.* Berkeley: University of California Press.

Gillespie, Richard. 1993. *Manufacturing Knowledge: A History of the Hawthorne Experiments.* Cambridge: Cambridge University Press.

Gillis, John R. 1997. *A World of Their Own Making: Myth, Ritual, and the Quest for Family Values.* Cambridge, Mass.: Harvard University Press.

Ginsburg, Faye D. 1995. "The Parallax Effect: The Impact of Aboriginal Media on Ethnographic Film," *Visual Anthropology Review,* 11 (2): 64–76.

Ginsburg, Faye D., Lila Abu-Lughod, and Brian Larkin. 2002. Introduction to *Media Worlds: Anthropology on New Terrain*, edited by Faye D. Ginsburg, Lila Abu-Lughod, and Brian Larkin, 1–36. Berkeley: University of California Press.

Grazia, Victoria de. 2005. *Irresistible Empire: America's Advance through Twentieth-Century Europe*. Cambridge, Mass.: Harvard University Press.

Greater Boston with Emily Rooney. 2010. "Vita Needle's Elderly Workforce." PBS, WGBH (Boston), 10 June. http://wwf.wgbh.org/programs/Greater-Boston-11/episodes/-16493.

Greenblatt, Stephen. 2005. *Renaissance Self-Fashioning: From More to Shakespeare*. Chicago, Ill.: University of Chicago Press.

Greenhouse, Steven, and Michael Barbaro. 2005. "Wal-Mart Memo Suggests Ways to Cut Employee Benefit Costs." *New York Times*, 26 October.

Guyer, Jane. 2010. Preface to "The Life Cycle as a Rational Proposition, or 'The Arc of Intermediate Links,'" presented October 2010, for Cultures of Finance Group, Institute for Public Knowledge. Version without preface available at http://anthropology.jhu.edu/Jane_Guyer/CultureMonetarism.

Hamilton, William L. 2008. "Whatever You Do, Call It Work." *New York Times*, 21 April. http://www.nytimes.com/2008/04/21/business/retirement/21social.html.

Hamm, James H. 2007. "Pablo and Maria: A Marxian Class Analysis." *Rethinking Marxism: A Journal of Economics, Culture & Society* 19:380.

Hareven, Tamara. 1978. "The Dynamics of Kin in an Industrial Community." In "Turning Points: Historical and Sociological Studies on the Family," supplement, *American Journal of Sociology* 84:S151–S182.

——. 1982. *Family Time and Industrial Time*. Cambridge: Cambridge University Press.

——. 2003. *The Silk Weavers of Kyoto: Family and Work in a Changing Traditional Industry*. Berkeley: University of California Press.

Harvey, Carol P., and Pamela D. Sherer. 2005. "Innovative Work Models for Older Workers." In *Understanding and Managing Diversity*, edited by Carol Harvey and M. June Allard, 141–145. Upper Saddle River, N.J.: Prentice Hall.

Harvey, David. 1991. *The Condition of Postmodernity: An Enquiry into the Origins of Cultural Change*. Reprint. Oxford: Wiley-Blackwell.

Hellge, Stefanie. 2008. "Arbeiten im Alter: Die Senioren-Firma" ["Work in Old Age: The Senior Company"]. Translated by Michael Latham. *Brigitte*, November, 82–86.

Hill, E. Jeffrey, Joseph Grzywacz, Sarah Allen, Victoria L. Blanchard, Christina Matz-Costa, Sandee Shulkin, and Marcie Pitt-Catsouphes. 2008. "Defining and Conceptualizing Workplace Flexibility." *Community, Work, & Family* 11:149–163.

Himpele, Jeff D. 2002. "Arrival Scenes: Complicity and Media Ethnography in the Bolivian Public Sphere." In *Media Worlds: Anthropology on New Terrain*, edited by Faye D. Ginsburg, Lila Abu-Lughod, and Brian Larkin, 301–318. Berkeley: University of California Press.

Hochschild, Arlie Russell. 2001 [1997]. *The Time Bind: When Work Becomes Home and Home Becomes Work*. New York: Holt Paperbacks.

——. 2005. "On the Edge of the Time Bind: Time and Market Culture." *Social Research: An International Quarterly of the Social Sciences* (special issue on busyness) 72 (2): 339–354.

Irle, Mathias. 2008. "Die Treppe der Willigen" ["Stairs of the Willing"]. Translated by Michael Latham. *Brand Eins*, November, 144–153.

Johnson, Richard. W. 2009. "Rising Senior Unemployment and the Need to Work at Older Ages." The Urban Institute, Retirement Policy Program. September. http://www.urban.org/url.cfm?ID=411964

Jornal Nacional. 2011. "Cada Vez Mais Aposentados Voltam à Ativa Nos EUA" ["Retirees Increasingly Return to the Workforce in the U.S."] Globo television network, Brazil, 21 January. http://g1.globo.com/videos/jornal-nacional/v/cada-vez-mais-aposentados-voltam-a-ativa-nos-eua/1416575/#/.

Kaufman, Sharon R. 1994. *The Ageless Self: Sources of Meaning in Late Life.* Madison, Wis.: University of Wisconsin Press.

Keating, Matt. 2005. "Phone Home." *Guardian* (Manchester, U.K.). 14 October. http://www.guardian.co.uk/money/2005/oct/15/workandcareers.careers.

Keith, Jennie. 1982. *Old People, New Lives: Community Creation in a Retirement Residence.* 2nd ed. Chicago: University of Chicago Press.

Kossowski, Jacques. 2008. "Il Faut Favoriser le Travail des Seniors et le Retour à L'emploi des Retraités." ["We Should Favor the Work of Seniors and the Return to Employment by the Retired."] Translated by Eric Breitbart. *Le Figaro,* 3 May. http://www.lefigaro.fr/debats/2008/04/29/01005-20080429ARTFIG00622-il-faut-favoriser-le-travail-des-seniors.php.

Kusterer, Kenneth C. 1978. *Know-How on the Job: The Important Working Knowledge of "Unskilled" Workers.* Boulder, Colo.: Westview Press.

Lafargue, Paul. 1989 [1883]. *The Right to Be Lazy and Other Studies.* Translated by Charles Kerr. Chicago: Charles H. Kerr Publishing Co.

Lamb, Sarah. 2009. *Aging and the Indian Diaspora: Cosmopolitan Families in India and Abroad.* Bloomington: Indiana University Press.

Lamphere, Louise. 1985. "Bringing the Family to Work: Women's Culture on the Shop Floor." *Feminist Studies* 11:519–540.

Landes, Ruth. 1959. "Progress Report on Geriatric Survey, Los Angeles City Health Department." 20 August. Unpublished manuscript. National Anthropological Archives, Smithsonian Institution, series 2, box 14.

——. 1971. "Aging: Nature of Age and Culture." Unpublished manuscript. National Anthropological Archives, Smithsonian Institution, series 3, box 49.

——. N.d. "Personality of the Later-Aging in Different Societies." Unpublished manuscript. National Anthropological Archives, Smithsonian Institution, series 3, box 50.

Larkin, Brian. 1997. "Indian Films and Nigerian Lovers: Media and the Creation of Parallel Modernities." *Africa: Journal of the International African Institute* 67:406–440.

Lasch, Christopher. 1995. *Haven in a Heartless World.* New York: Norton.

Laslett, Peter. 1991. *A Fresh Map of Life: The Emergence of the Third Age.* Cambridge, Mass.: Harvard University Press.

LeRoy, Stephen. 2010. "FRBSF Economic Letter: Is the 'Invisible Hand' Still Relevant?" http://www.frbsf.org/publications/economics/letter/2010/el2010–14.html.

Levitt, Steven D, and John A. List. 2009. "Was There Really a Hawthorne Effect at the Hawthorne Plant? An Analysis of the Original Illumination Experiments." NBER Working Paper Seires, Working Paper 15016, May. http://www.nber.org/papers/w15016.

Liechty, Mark. 2002. *Suitably Modern: Making Middle-Class Culture in a New Consumer Society.* Princeton, N.J.: Princeton University Press.

Lipset, Seymour Martin. 1992. "The Work Ethic, Then and Now." *Journal of Labor Research* 13:45–54.

Lorber, Janie. 2010. "Quiet Resistance to Women on Subs." *New York Times,* 12 May. http://www.nytimes.com/2010/05/13/us/13navy.html.

Louis, Betty. 1998. "Nobody's Ever Been Fired at… America's Best Company." *National Examiner,* 10 February.

Lynch, Caitrin. 2007. *Juki Girls, Good Girls: Gender and Cultural Politics in Sri Lanka's Global Garment Industry.* Ithaca: Cornell University Press.

Mack, Arien. 2005. "Editor's Introduction." *Social Research: An International Quarterly of the Social Sciences* (special issue on busyness) 72 (2): v–vi.

Mahmood, Saba. 2001. "Feminist Theory, Embodiment, and the Docile Agent: Some Reflections on the Egyptian Islamic Revival." *Cultural Anthropology* 16:202–236.

——. 2005. *Politics of Piety: The Islamic Revival and the Feminist Subject.* Princeton, N.J.: Princeton University Press.

Maier, Corinne. 2005. *Bonjour Laziness: Jumping Off the Corporate Ladder.* New York: Pantheon.

Malinowski, Bronislaw. 1920. "Kula: The Circulating Exchange of Valuables in the Archipelagoes of Eastern New Guinea." *Man* 51:97–105.

Marcus, Jon. 1997. "Time Stands Still Here." *Boston Globe,* 29 December.

Marglin, Stephen A., and Juliet B. Schor. 1992. *The Golden Age of Capitalism: Reinterpreting the Postwar Experience.* Oxford: Oxford University Press.

Mauss, Marcel. 1967. *The Gift: Forms and Functions of Exchange in Archaic Societies.* New York: Norton.

Mazzarella, William. 2004. "Culture, Globalization, Mediation." *Annual Review of Anthropology* 33:345–367.

McKinsey Global Institute. 2008. "Talkin' 'Bout My Generation: The Economic Impact of Aging U.S. Baby Boomers." June. http://www.mckinsey.com/mgi/publications/Impact_Aging_Baby_Boomers/index.asp.

Meyer, Madonna Harrington. 2000. *Care Work: Gender, Labor, and the Welfare State.* New York: Routledge.

Miller, Daniel. 1995. "Introduction: Anthropology, Modernity, Consumption." In *Worlds Apart: Modernity through the Prism of the Local,* 1–22. New York: Routledge.

Minkler, Meredith. 1989. "Gold in Gray: Reflections on Business' Discovery of the Elderly Market." *Gerontologist* 29:17–23.

Moody, Harry. 2009. "From Successful Aging to Conscious Aging." In *The Cultural Context of Aging: Worldwide Perspectives,* 3rd ed., edited by Jay Sokolovsky, 67–76. Westport, Conn.: Praeger.

Moore, Katrina, and Ruth Campbell. 2009. "Mastery with Age: The Appeal of the Traditional Arts to Senior Citizens in Contemporary Japan." In "Aging in Japan," special issue, *Japanstudien,* 21:223–251. http://www.dijtokyo.org/publications/japanstudien_21_altern.

Moreton, Bethany. 2009. *To Serve God and Wal-Mart: The Making of Christian Free Enterprise.* Cambridge, Mass.: Harvard University Press.

Morris, Robert, and Francis G. Caro. 1995. "The Young-Old, Productive Aging, and Public Policy." *Generations* 19 (3): 32–37.

NBC Nightly News. 1998. "Living Longer: Needham, Massachusetts, Company Takes Advantage of Opportunity to Hire Older Workers." 2 January.

NetMBA. N.d. "Frederick Taylor and Scientific Management." Internet Center for Management and Business Administration, Inc. http://www.netmba.com/mgmt/scientific/.

NGA (National Governors Association). 2008. "Increasing Volunteerism among Older Adults: Benefits and Strategies for States." NGA Center for Best Practices. http://www.nga.org and O805CIVICENGBRIEF.PDF.

NIA (National Institute on Aging). 2007. *Why Population Aging Matters: A Global Perspective.* Washington, D.C.: National Institutes of Health.

Nielsen Company. 2009. "A2/M2 Three Screen Report: Television, Internet and Mobile Usage in the U.S. First Quarter." kr.en.nielsen.com/site/documents/A2M23Screens FINAL1Q09.pdf.

O'Barr, William. 2011. "Mad Men: Gender, Race, Ethnicity, Sexuality, and Class." *Advertising & Society Review* 11:4.

OECD (Organisation for Economic Co-operation and Development). 2010a. "Country Statistical Profiles, 2010." Paris. http://stats.oecd.org/Index.aspx?DatasetCode=CSP2010.

——. 2010b. "Labour Force Statistics by Sex and Age." Paris. http://stats.oecd.org/Index.aspx?DatasetCode=CSP2010.

——. 2011. "Pensions in France and Abroad: 7 Key Indicators." Paris. http://www.oecd.org/document/51/0,3746,en_2649_34757_44981747_1_1_1_1,00.html.

Oliver, Caroline. 2008. *Retirement Migration: Paradoxes of Ageing.* New York: Routledge.

Ong, Aihwa. 2010. *Spirits of Resistance and Capitalist Discipline: Factory Women in Malaysia.* Albany: State University of New York Press.

Parker, L. D. 1984. "Control in Organizational Life: The Contribution of Mary Parker Follett." *Academy of Management Review* 9:736–745.

Patterson, Thomas C. 1998. "Flexible Accumulation, Flexible Labor and their Consequences." *Critique of Anthropology* 18:317–319.

Pew Social Trends Staff. 2009. "Recession Turns a Graying Office Grayer." http://pewsocialtrends.org/2009/09/03/recession-turns-a-graying-office-grayer/.

Piktialis, Diane. 2001. "An Aging Workforce: Rethinking Human Resources Practices." *EAP Association Exchange,* September.

Pratt, Mary K. 2007. "Vita Needle: Word of Mouth Keeps Business Strong." *Boston Business Journal,* 25 May. http://www.bizjournals.com/boston/stories/2007/05/28/focus10.html.

Pugh, Tony. 2009. "Older Workers Muscling Out Teens for Summer Jobs." *McClatchy Newspapers.* http://www.mcclatchydc.com/economy/story/69461.html.

Putnam, Robert D. 2001. *Bowling Alone: The Collapse and Revival of American Community.* New York: Simon and Schuster.

Ranzani, Oscar. 2010. "Una Inyección de Vitalidad en el Trabajo." ["Injecting Life into the World of Work."] Translated by Frank Romagosa. *Pagina 12* (newspaper, Buenos Aires), 5 November. http://www.pagina12.com.ar/diario/suplementos/espectaculos/5-19804-2010-11-05.html.

Risen, James. 1989. "GM Plans to Shut Another Plant and Cut 2,100 Jobs." *Los Angeles Times,* 2 February. http://articles.latimes.com/1989-02-02/business/fi-2615_1_plant-closing.

Rix, Sarah E. 2001. "Toward Active Ageing in the 21st Century: Working Longer in the United States." Paper prepared for Japan Institute of Labour Millennium Project. http://www.jil.go.jp/jil/seika/us2.pdf.

Rodrigues, Isabel P. B. 2006. "Vita: Life in a Zone of Social Abandonment (review)." *Anthropological Quarterly* 79:773–776.

Rosen, Ellen. 2006. "How to Squeeze More Out of a Penny." In *Wal-Mart: The Face of Twenty-First-Century Capitalism,* edited by Nelson Lichtenstein, 243–260. New York: New Press.

Rowe, John Wallis, and Robert L. Kahn. 1999. *Successful Aging.* New York: Dell.

Ruiz, Gina. 2006. "Gray Eminence." *Workforce Management,* 27 March. http://www.highbeam.com/doc/1G1-143922593.html.

Sample, Ruth J. 2003. *Exploitation: What It Is and Why It's Wrong.* Lanham, Md.: Rowman and Littlefield.

Savishinsky, Joel S. 2002. *Breaking the Watch: The Meanings of Retirement in America.* Ithaca: Cornell University Press.

Schepens, Wim. 2003. *Age No Problem* (documentary film). Netherlands: VPRO Television.

Schiffman, Susan. 2009. "Effects of Aging on the Human Taste System." *Annals, the New York Academy of Science* 1170 (July): 725–729.

Shapiro, Ari Daniel. 2010. "In Their 90s, Working for More Than Just a Paycheck." *Morning Edition,* National Public Radio (NPR), 1 November. http://www.npr.org/templates/story/story.php?storyId=130566030.

Shea, Gordon F., and Adolf Haasen. 2006. "Senior Citizens Only: The World of Vita Needle Co." In *The Older Worker Advantage: Making the Most of an Aging Workforce,* 71–75. Westport, Conn.: Praeger.

Sheth, Jagdish N. 2003. "The New Model of Work: From Restructuring to Intellectual Free Agents." http://www.jagsheth.net/opinion_the_new_model.html.

Sinichi, Oka. 2004. "Pension Reform in France." *Japanese Journal of Social Security Policy* 3 (1): 1–9.

60 Minutes. 2003. "The Age Wave: Seniors Not Retiring and Staying in the Work Force." Reported by Morley Safer, CBS, 10 August.

Sokolovsky, Jay. 2009. *The Cultural Context of Aging: Worldwide Perspectives.* 3rd ed. Westport, Conn.: Praeger.

SSA (Social Security Administration). 2011. "Earnings Limits." Social Security Administration Electronic Fact Sheet, Washington, D.C.: SSA Publication No. 05–10003. January, ICN 451385. http://www.ssa.gov/pubs/10003.html.

Stacey, Judith. 1997. *In the Name of the Family: Rethinking Family Values in the Postmodern Age.* Boston: Beacon Press.

Standing, Guy. 1989. "Global Feminization through Flexible Labor." *World Development* 17:1077–1095.

Susser, Ida, and Nila Chatterjee. 1998. "Critiquing Flexible Labor." *Critique of Anthropology* 18:243–244.

Taylor, Charles. 1994. "The Politics of Recognition." In *Multiculturalism: Examining the Politics of Recognition,* edited by Amy Gutman, 25–73. Princeton, N.J.: Princeton University Press.

Taylor, Frederick Winslow. 1911. *The Principles of Scientific Management.* New York: Harper & Brothers.

Taylor, Janelle S. 2008. "On Recognition, Caring, and Dementia." *Medical Anthropology Quarterly* 22:313–335.

Taylor, Richard. 2006. *Alzheimer's from the Inside Out.* Baltimore: Health Professions Press.

Terkel, Studs. 1997 [1975]. *Working: People Talk about What They Do All Day and How They Feel about What They Do.* New York: New Press.

The Today Show. 1998. "Massachusetts Company Has Average Employee Age of 73." NBC, 19 April.

Tonelson, Alan. 2002. *The Race to the Bottom: Why a Worldwide Worker Surplus and Uncontrolled Free Trade Are Sinking American Living Standards.* New York: Basic Books.

Tsing, Anna. 2009. "Supply Chains and the Human Condition." *Rethinking Marxism: A Journal of Economics, Culture & Society* 21 (2): 148–176.

Tuljapurkar, Shripad, Nan Li, and Carl Boe. 2000. "A Universal Pattern of Mortality Decline in the G7 Countries." *Nature* 405:789–792.

Turner, Terrence. 2002. "Representation, Politics and Cultural Imagination in Indigenous Video: General Points and Kayapo Examples." In *Media Worlds: Anthropology on New Terrain,* edited by Faye D. Ginsburg, Lila Abu-Lughod, and Brian Larkin, 75–89. Berkeley: University of California Press.

United States Census Bureau. 2009a. *Fact Sheet Massachusetts, 2005–2009 American Community Survey 5-Year Estimates.* Washington, D.C.

——. 2009b. *Selected Economic Characteristics, Needham MA, 2007–2009 American Community Survey 3-Year Estimates.* Washington, D.C.

——. 2010. *Demographic Profile, Massachusetts.* Washington, D.C.

Verhaag, Bertram. 2008. *Pensioners Inc.* (documentary film). Munich: DENKmal Films, Inc.

Versieux, Nathalie. 2004. "Ces Employeurs Allemands qui Choisissent D'embaucher des Seniors" ["German Employers Who Choose to Employ Seniors"]. Translated by Lyndsey Stadtmueller. *Les Echos,* 14 September.

Weber, Max. 2002 [1905]. *The Protestant Ethic and the Spirit of Capitalism.* New York: Penguin.

Weiss, Robert S. 2005. *The Experience of Retirement.* Ithaca: Cornell University Press.

Wertheimer, Alan. 1996. *Exploitation.* Princeton: Princeton University Press.

Weston, Kath. 1997. *Families We Choose.* New York: Columbia University Press.

Wilk, Richard. 2002. "Television, Time, and the National Imaginary in Belize." In *Media Worlds: Anthropology on New Terrain,* edited by Faye D. Ginsburg, Lila Abu-Lughod, and Brian Larkin, 171–186. Berkeley: University of California Press.

Williamson, John, and Masa Higo. 2007. "Why Do Japanese Workers Remain in the Labor Force So Long?" Center for Retirement Research Working Papers, CRR WP 2007–11. May. http://escholarship.bc.edu/retirement papers/146.

Wood, John A., Justin G. Longenecker, Joseph A. McKinney, and Carlos W. Moore. 1988. "Ethical Attitudes of Students and Business Professionals: A Study of Moral Reasoning." *Journal of Business Ethics* 7:249–257.

World News Tonight. 2000. "Tighter Job Market Makes Age an Advantage, so Professionals are Coming Out of Retirement." ABC, 9 August.

Yabe, Takeshi. 2011. "Seventy-Year-Olds Can Be Greenhorns!" *Diamond Online,* 1 March. http://diamond.jp/articles/-/11306.

Zaretsky, Robert. 2010. "In Praise of Laziness." *Foreign Policy,* 24 September. http://www.foreignpolicy.com/articles/2010/09/24/in_praise_of_laziness?page=0,0.

Acknowledgments

In the course of researching and writing this book my connection to my scholarly and fieldwork community grew deeper and wider. I have many people to thank for their support. Any misunderstandings or mistakes are mine alone, and I thank the many people who helped me along the way. The first order of thanks goes to Vita Needle Company and especially to Fred Hartman, Frederick Hartman II, Mason Hartman, Rosa Finnegan, Michael La Rosa, and the many other people whom I cannot name because of privacy concerns. All those who appear in disguise in this book and the many others whose stories did not make it in: I have learned so much from you and appreciate your willingness to teach me and tolerate me.

My fantastic writing group, which grew as this project proceeded, has been an invaluable source of friendship and discussion. Sarah Lamb and I started off alone; then Elizabeth Ferry, Smitha Radhakrishnan, and Leslie Salzinger joined us successively. Even after multiple versions of many sentences, these wonderful colleagues were still willing to read more. I have worked with many research assistants since I first started this project in 2006. For their dedicated work transcribing, coding, interviewing, researching, and/or fact-checking I thank Maia Azoulay, Anne Bowlby, Nina Carey, Molly Crowther, Laura Firstenberg, Elizabeth Kneen, Christine Maloney, Elizabeth Poindexter, Sylvia Schwartz, Christina Spiegel, Emily Towers, and Carmelle Tsai. Special thanks to the sabbatical team of Danielle Good, Mary McCuistion, and Jennifer Simonovich: discussions with Mary definitely influenced my understanding of the interviews; Jenn's interview coding skills are wonderful, and her code-training skills are unmatched; and Danielle stuck with me through the entire sabbatical and beyond, copresented work with me at the Gerontological Society of America 2010 meetings, and helped me sort through, understand, and discover much that is in this book. I will miss Danielle very much but look forward to seeing her accomplishments in her own anthropology career. Thanks to Maureen Bayer from Flying Fingers and her cadre of transcribers. This project required translation from multiple languages; I thank Eric Breitbart, Julia Kirst, Michael Latham, Nicole Lee, Ryo Morimoto, David Nelson, Frank Romagosa, and Lyndsey Stadtmueller.

I thank Wellesley College's Department of Anthropology for welcoming me as a visiting scholar during my 2010 sabbatical year, and I thank Brandeis University's Department of Anthropology, where I have been a visiting research associate since 2004. Conversation with colleagues at both schools enriched my understanding, and I especially thank Anastasia Karakasidou, Philip Kohl, Jonathan Imber, David Lindauer, and Rosanna Hertz. Robert C. Hunt, Elizabeth Ferry, and others from the Economic Group at Brandeis saw pieces of this project from its very kernel of an idea through to the end.

Olin College has been a wonderful supportive workplace for me since 2004, before I had even heard about a place called Vita Needle. I thank my Olin friends and colleagues for their enthusiasm, conversation, and interdisciplinary smarts all along this journey, especially Jonathan Adler, Helen Donis-Keller, Gillian Epstein, Rob Martello, Chris Morse, Alisha Sarang-Sieminski, Lynn Andrea Stein, and Yevgeniya Zastavker. Allen Downey was a fantastic interlocutor at key points throughout the process. Support of various forms came also from Holly Bennett, Terri Dunphy, Dianna Magnoni, Richard K. Miller, Michael E. Moody, Claire O'Sullivan, Steve Schiffman, and Lydia Zeglarsky.

Others who have provided important help along the way include Arjun Appadurai, Carol A. Breckenridge, Eric Breitbart, Judy Chin, Courtney Coile, Jennifer Cole, Jason Danely, Michael C. Davis, Fritz Fleischmann, Michele Ruth Gamburd, Sarah Kuhn, Lorri Lofvers, Sonya Michel, Toby Sandler, Phyllis Segal, Jay Sokolovsky, and Robert Weiss. My gratitude extends to the many journalists with whom I met (especially Bertram Verhaag) and to the many people I interviewed who were not from Vita—many of whom never made it into the book even by pseudonym but who helped me understand the stories I did include. I am grateful to audiences, discussants, and fellow panelists where I have presented this work: Brandeis University, University of Massachusetts Boston, Boston College, the American Anthropological Association annual meetings, the Gerontological Society of America, the Northeastern Anthropological Association, and IDEO Boston. I benefited from the interdisciplinary feedback and conversation from organizers, instructors, and coparticipants at the 2007 National Institute on Aging Summer Institute on Aging Research and the 2009 RAND Summer Institute.

In the final six months I received invaluable help from Frank Romagosa, a wonderful and brilliant and always enthusiastic friend from graduate school days. I value our many e-mails and phone calls about this work and his fine editing eye. I also thank the two anonymous reviewers who sent me helpful feedback at several stages and who prodded me in important directions. It has been a great privilege and pleasure to work with Cornell University Press's Fran Benson a second time—she wanted to know more about this book even before I could call it a book. And thanks also to Katherine Liu and Ange Romeo-Hall from the press for invaluable assistance throughout the publishing process. I am grateful to Jamie Fuller for her meticulous and very smart copyediting.

The research for this book was made possible in part by financial assistance from the Ruth Landes Memorial Research Fund, a program of The Reed Foundation. I thank the fund and program administrators Mercedes Duff and David Latham. Additional funding was provided by the Research Fund of Olin College (2006–11) and by the National Endowment for the Humanities Summer Stipend Program (2009).

I dedicate this book to Vita Needle's family owners and the many workers in the Vita "family" (see chapter 2!). But I also dedicate it to my own family—Nick, Cormac, and Nicola, for whom my love is endless. They have listened to me enthuse about Vita, visited Vita with me, and even sold Girl Scout cookies there. I thank them for all the love and help, and yes, for all the meals from Nick in our family café. My parents (Frank and Kathy Lynch), in-laws (Joan and Hugh Collier), and grandparents (Esther McCann Leopold and Carl Leopold) have provided the wider supportive and loving context for this work, and I thank them all.

Too many people important to me and influential over the content of these pages have passed away while I have worked on this project. I close by remembering the lives and legacies of Julius A. Barthoff (www.juliusfilm.com), Carol A. Breckenridge, Mason Hartman, and Michael E. Moody.

Index

Page numbers followed by letters *f* and *t* refer to figures and tables, respectively.

La Rosa *(cont.)*
89, 105–6, 116; perspective on fan mail,
144; on shop floor temperature, 48; small-
town environment and, 82; training of new
workers by, 75, 94–95
Larry (Vita employee). *See* Clifford, Larry
(pseudonym)
Le Figaro (newspaper), 150, 153
legacy, media coverage and, 164–66
leisure, vs. pleasures of work, 10–11, 61
Lenti, Sophia (pseudonym), x, 30, 47
Leonard, Henry (pseudonym), 50
Lewis, Allen (pseudonym), ix, 5; agency in
media coverage, 165; on bonus check, 57;
on cultural construction of aging, 13–14; on
Depression ethic, 79, 80; on elder workers as
role models, 85–86; on flexible work schedule, 109–10; on "making money for Fred,"
38; on management, 71; on media interest,
157–58; and sense of nostalgia, 78
Liechty, Mark, 161
loyalty: elder workers and, 7; family environment and, 69; local contexts and, 115–17; at
Vita Needle, 69, 117, 119, 181

Macaulay, Ken (pseudonym), 55
machines, at Vita Needle, 2, 29; workers' concern about, 59
"making money for Fred," 11, 35–40, 44, 59, 63
management, Vita Needle: author's complicity
with, 193–94; balancing of social and economic values by, 53–56, 69–70, 74, 94; and
family environment, creation of, 69, 94–95;
fan mail and, 144; hiring policies of, 75, 89,
94–95, 105–6, 116; temperature complaints
and, 48–49; worker productivity and, 53, 59;
vs. workers' perspectives, 51, 52; workers'
relations with, 71, 170
management principles, scientific (Taylorism),
42
Marcus, Jon, 137
Margolin, Jessica, 92–93
Martin, Esther (pseudonym), ix, 36; on European tourists, 161–62; on family relationships, 67, 90; and flexible work schedule,
110; motivations for working, 66–67, 181;
and productivity policing, 54; relationships
at work, 74
Marty (Vita employee). *See* Rice, Marty
(pseudonym)
Massachusetts Healthy Aging initiative, 17
"mattering": meaning of, 165, 166; media attention and, 21, 165–66, 178; older adults and,
67, 184–85

Mauss, Marcel, 38
Mazzarella, William, 133, 149
McCain, John, 118
McDonalds, flexible work schedule at, 98–99
Mead, Margaret, 18, 165
media: contradictions inherent in, 177; forms
of engagement with, 171–76, 177; and minorities, 179; and parallel modernities, 160;
and self-understanding, 132–33, 159–66,
167, 178
media coverage of Vita Needle, 27–28, 135,
135*t*; and agency, 158, 165–68, 170–76, 179,
192; anthropological research compared to,
168; anthropologist's complicity in, 193; anxieties associated with, 123–26, 168, 169, 193;
balancing with work, 128–29; economic motives for, 180–81; and imagined possibilities,
132, 146, 161; and legacy, 164–66; letters and
e-mails in response to, 131–32, 133, 143–49,
191–92; nostalgia for time past in, 78–79;
origins of, 6, 135, 137–38; profitability theme
in, 6–7, 137, 140; vs. reality, 177; recurring
themes in, 135–37, 176; workers' response
to, 126–29, 157–58, 162–63, 169–76, 177.
See also specific media
Medicare, 71, 105; and elder employment, 5, 7,
120, 146
men's club, Vita Needle compared to, 29, 107
"men's lunch corner," at Vita Needle, 47, 49, 73
Mexico: cooperatively owned silver mine in,
187; labor costs in, 100
Mike (Vita manager). *See* La Rosa, Michael
(Mike)
Miller, Daniel, 177
minorities: media and, 179. *See also* immigrants
Mitchell, Ed (pseudonym), ix, 2–3
Mitterrand, François, 200n6
Moreton, Bethany, 115, 189
Morrow-Howell, Nancy, 184
Mortreux, Vincent, 152, 170
mother figure, at Vita Needle, 72*t*, 74
multigenerational relationships, at Vita Needle,
75–77
mushroom foragers, in California, 188

National Examiner article, 28, 135*t*, 177
National Governors Association (NGA) Policy
Academy, 10
National Public Radio, Vita Needle story on,
8, 135*t*, 192, 193; audience response to, 144,
155, 179
Needham, Massachusetts, 4; and background
of Vita Needle workers, 81–83; median